FOUNDATIONS OF SOFTWARE
A BBST WORKBOOK

CEM KANER • REBECCA L. FIEDLER

context driven press

Library of Congress Cataloging-in-Publication Data:

Kaner, Cem & Fiedler, Rebecca L.

Foundations of Software Testing

Library of Congress Control Number: 2013958183

ISBN 978-0-9898119-2-7

The Context-Driven Press logo and the Foundations of Software Testing cover design are by Susan Handman, Handman Design, New York. Interior page design is by Renato Parente.

Editor: Rebecca L. Fiedler

These materials are partially based on research that was supported by National Science Foundation research grants EIA-0113539 ITR/SY+PE: Improving the Education of Software Testers and CCLI-0717613 Adaptation & Implementation of an Activity-Based Online or Hybrid Course in Software Testing. Any opinions, findings and conclusions or recommendations expressed in this material are those of the author(s) and do not necessarily reflect the views of the National Science Foundation.

BBST is a registered trademark of Kaner, Fiedler & Associates, LLC. For more infornation, visit bbst.info.

About the Authors

Cem Kaner, J.D., Ph.D., is Professor of Software Engineering at Florida Institute of Technology, a research-focused university that was recently ranked as one of the top 200 universities in the world. Kaner is lead author of several books, including Lessons Learned in Software Testing, The Domain Testing Workbook, and Testing Computer Software. He is lead developer of the BBST (Black Box Software Testing) series of videos and online courses. Kaner holds doctorates in Psychology and in Law. He teaches courses on software testing, metrics, requirements analysis, applied statistics, and software-related law, ethics and societal issues. Kaner was honored by the Association for Computing Machinery's Special Interest Group for Computers and Society with its "Making a Difference" Award and by the Software Test Professionals with its "Software Test Luminary" Award. He was elected to the American Law Institute in recognition of his work on laws governing software quality and electronic commerce. Before coming back to university to teach (in 2000), Kaner lived in Silicon Valley for 17 years and worked as a development manager/director, programmer, tester, technical writer and development consultant.

Rebecca L. Fiedler, Ph.D., has spent decades teaching students of all ages - from Kindergarten to University. In the testing community, she works with Cem Kaner on the Black Box Software Testing (BBST) online professional development courses. She is a regular attendee and presenter at the Workshop on Teaching Software Testing and has had numerous presentations at national and international conferences in education and educational technology.

Table of Contents

Preface

This is the student workbook for the first course in the BBST® (Black Box Software Testing) series of software testing courses.

About BBST

The BBST series currently (January 2014) includes four courses: *Foundations of Software Testing, Bug Advocacy, Test Design* and *Domain Testing*.

BBST courses use a combination of exercises, lectures, quizzes, labs, group assignments, peer reviews, and an exam to help you understand key testing challenges and deal with them effectively. People learn much more by doing things and getting feedback than by watching other people do things or talk about doing things. We want you to become a skilled tester, not just a skilled testing taker, so in our courses, you have to do a lot of work.

The courses focus on these topics:

- *Foundations:* Introduction to the core concepts and challenges of software testing.

- *Bug Advocacy*: Effective investigation and reporting of program failures and design problems.

- *Test Design:* Select combinations of test techniques that, together, generate an effective suite of tests for this program, in this context. Introduces over 100 techniques, with particular attention to combinatorial, domain, risk-based, scenario-based and specification-based testing.

- *Domain Testing:* Develop practical competence with one of the fundamental techniques.

Along with the technical content of testing, we designed the series to help you develop cognitive and communication skills that we think are central to effective testing. These include:

- critical thinking and rapid learning

- working effectively with remote collaborators

- communicating your findings more effectively

- planning investments in documentation, tools and process improvement to meet your actual needs

For more on the objectives and design of BBST, see our course orientation at http://bbst.info/?page_id=9.

About Foundations

Foundations of Software Testing is our introductory course.

The learning objectives in the live (instructor-supervised) version of *Foundations* include:

- Learning about testing
  - Key challenges of testing
  - Information objectives drive the testing mission and strategy
  - Oracles are useful, but incomplete
  - Coverage is multidimensional
  - Complete testing is impossible
  - Measurement is important but difficult to do well
- Introduce you to:
  - Basic vocabulary of the field
  - Basic facts of data storage and manipulation in computing
  - Diversity of viewpoints which drive diversity of vocabulary and practice
- Improve academic skills
  - Online collaboration tools
  - Precision in reading
  - Clear, well-structured communication
  - Effective peer reviews
  - Cope calmly and effectively with assessments (such as tests designed to help you learn).

Who This Book Is For

The *Foundations* lecture videos and slides are available free on the web (http://bbst.info). In theory, anyone can work through the course material on their own. However, as the educational community keeps learning with MOOCs (Massive Open Online Courses), self-study from electronic resources is challenging. Most people give up.

We wrote this book to support students working through our course materials.

- We are particularly trying to support you if you are working through the course material on your own or with a few friends in a small, self-directed group.
- From our experience teaching BBST classes to professional and university students, we believe that many students in instructor-led courses will also find this book helpful. We expect to often assign this as required reading.

About This Book

We organize the book around the course's six Lessons. For each Lesson, we will include some of the following:

- An introduction
- Description of an orientation activity that we recommend you do before watching the lecture

- The lecture slides and a transcript of the lecture (occasionally with a correction)
- Description of an application activity that we recommend you do after watching the lecture, to apply what you've learned
- Feedback: comments on a concern or question that many students have at this point in the course
- The authors' reflection on this lesson. You might notice an oddity in the reflections. Sometimes "I" speak and sometimes "we" speak.
    - When "I" speak, the "I" is Kaner, describing some aspect of his personal history with face-to-face and online versions of BBST or his personal experience in the community.
    - When "we" speak, we are Kaner and Fiedler together, looking at the course as instructional designers and teachers who planned the online BBST (Version 1 and beyond) together.

Many of the activities significantly update or replace the activities supplied with the original release of Foundations 2010 (the third edition of BBST-Foundations).

Reflections

You probably understand what all of these are except for the reflection. In instructional-design terms, the activity of looking back over a piece of work and appraising it in terms of what has been learned since the work was completed is called *reflection*. The essay that presents the result of the activity is called *the reflection*. At the end of each Lesson, we include an article that presents our reflection on that Lesson.

Throughout the course, we encourage you to write reflections on your activities, after you read other students' reports on the same tasks. We encourage this because educators see reflections as valuable learning activities--you will learn new things as you work through the process of creating a reflection. Similarly, writing reflections on the Lessons presents us with the opportunity to gather together a diverse collection of experiences and feedback, to learn from them what we can, and to present you with an opportunity to get more out of the current course and see the early planning for the next version of the *Foundations* course.

Notes On Formatting

The lecture slides and transcript section runs the text side by side. Most slides stay within their column but some are printed double-size. The reason for this is that the text on these slides is too small to be readable in the smaller slide-size. The big slides are no more important than the small slides. They just have more (and smaller) text.

Feedback Welcome

The BBST series is an ongoing work in progress. It has been evolving since 1993 and will continue to evolve. The series has benefitted enormously from feedback from students and colleagues, and we would be glad to receive more feedback from you. We are particularly interested in your thoughts on the author reflections. We have rarely seen notes like this in other publications. We think that consideration of "what were they thinking?" can be helpful to the critical reader but we are sure there are tradeoffs that we don't yet understand.

Cem Kaner

Rebecca L. Fiedler

LESSON 1: OVERVIEW AND BASIC DEFINITIONS

Lesson Introduction

This lecture introduces you to the course. You will meet other students and discover the mechanics of how your course will operate. In terms of content, Lesson 1 is intentionally light—focusing on definitions of key terms that we will use in the course.

Testing terminology is not uniform. One reason for that is that the underlying philosophy of testing, that is reflected in the language, is not uniform. For example, some people think that a test is not a test unless there is an oracle (an expected result that will tell you whether the test passed or failed). Testing without an expected result is, to them, incompetent. For them, it is natural to include expected result as part of the definition of "test." However, other testers consider exploration of the product (which includes testing without knowledge of what will happen) to be quite useful. And others think that there are many possible oracles for the same test and that the skilled tester will focus on different potential errors (consider different oracles) at different times. To these people, the choice of oracle is a separate thing from the basic idea of a test. No definition of "test" will satisfy all three groups.

We do not attempt to satisfy everyone. Instead, we explicitly define the terms we will use in the course and expect you to understand what we mean when we use those words. Our terminology is eclectic. You will probably agree with at least some of our definitions and disagree with at least a few others.

Some students argue that a definition is wrong and demand that we correct it. They argue that the multiple-choice questions are unfair because the questions take the lecture's definitions as correct even though (in the opinion of this student) the lecture's definitions are wrong.

The course does not demand that you adopt our definitions, or our viewpoints, as your own. However, the course does demand that you make the effort needed to understand what the course is teaching.

The skill and tolerance needed to listen to someone in a way that tries to understand what they mean by the words they use, is part of a broader communication skill that we see as essential to good testing. Some testers get lost in their own opinion of what a product should do, or how it should behave, or how it should be described, and they never come to an understanding of the developers' intention or design. We think this leads to weak testing.

Readings

There are no readings for this lecture.

Slides And Notes

SLIDE 1

Hi!

Welcome to the Black Box Software Testing Courses.

_____

_____

_____

_____

_____

_____

_____

_____

BLACK BOX SOFTWARE TESTING: FOUNDATIONS

CEM KANER, J.D., PH.D.
PROFESSOR OF SOFTWARE ENGINEERING
FLORIDA INSTITUTE OF TECHNOLOGY

REBECCA L. FIEDLER, M.B.A. PH.D.
PRESIDENT: KANER, FIEDLER & ASSOCIATES

JAMES BACH
PRINCIPAL, SATISFICE INC.

This work is licensed under the Creative Commons Attribution License. To view a copy of this license, visit http://creativecommons.org/licenses/by-sa/2.0/ or send a letter to Creative Commons, 559 Nathan Abbott Way, Stanford, California 94305, USA.

These notes are partially based on research that was supported by NSF Grants EIA-0113539 ITR/SY +PE:"Improving the Education of Software Testers" and CCLI-0717613 "Adaptation & Implementation of an Activity-Based Online or Hybrid Course in Software Testing." Any opinions, findings and conclusions or recommendations expressed in this material are those of the author(s) and do not necessarily reflect the views of the National Science Foundation.

1

SLIDE 2

NOTICE

The practices recommended and discussed in this course are useful for an introduction to testing, but more experienced testers will adopt additional practices. I am writing this course with the mass-market software development industry in mind. Mission-critical and life-critical software development efforts involve specific and rigorous procedures that are not described in this course.

Some of the BBST-series courses include some legal information, but you are not my legal client. I do not provide legal advice in the notes or in the course.

If you ask a BBST instructor a question about a specific situation, the instructor might use your question as a teaching tool, and answer it in a way that s/he believes would "normally" be true but such an answer may be inappropriate for your particular situation or incorrect in your jurisdiction. Neither I nor any instructor in the BBST series can accept any responsibility for actions that you might take in response to comments about the law made in this course. If you need legal advice, please consult your own attorney.

2

_____

_____

_____

_____

SLIDE 3

My name is Cem Kaner. I have a couple of doctorates, I'm a professor of software engineering at the Florida Institute of Technology.

_____

_____

_____

_____

_____

_____

_____

SLIDE 4

I'm also the author of a few books on software testing. You can read more about me at my website, www.kaner.com.

I'm an amateur at this—taping and editing these lectures at my home, so these videos have some rough edges.

Taping at home lets me maintain ownership of the materials. Which in turn lets me license them to you under a Creative Commons license. That lets you copy them and play them for other people for free.

_____

_____

SLIDE 5

James Bach and I are the primary creators of content for this course. I think James is one of the brightest people in our field. You can see more of his work at www. satisfice.com.

_____

_____

_____

_____

_____

_____

_____

_____

SLIDE 6

Rebecca Fiedler's doctorate is in education. She's the primary designer of the online version of this course.

If your instructor read a book or took a course on how to teach this course, that book or course came from Becky.

_____

_____

_____

_____

_____

ABOUT REBECCA L. FIEDLER www.BECKYFIEDLER.COM

I've been teaching students of all ages – from Kindergarten to University – for the past 25 years. My primary interests are how people learn and how technology can make educational efforts more effective and more accessible to more people.

For a while, I served as an Assistant Professor of Education at Indiana State University and St. Mary-of-the-Woods College, but to really get to the roots of effective design of online education, especially for working professionals, it made more sense for me to go independent and focus my own time as an independent consultant.

Cem Kaner and I are co-Principal Investigators on the National Science Foundation grant that subsidizes development of these courses.

My Ph.D. (University of Central Florida) concentrations were in Instructional Technology and Curriculum. My dissertation research applied qualitative research methods to the use of electronic portfolios. I also hold an M.B.A. in Management and a Bachelor of Music (Education).

6

SLIDE 7

MANY THANKS...

The BBST lectures evolved out of courses co-authored by Kaner & Hung Quoc Nguyen and by Kaner & Doug Hoffman (now President of the Association for Software Testing), which we merged with James Bach's and Michael Bolton's Rapid Software Testing (RST) courses. The online adaptation of BBST was designed primarily by Rebecca L. Fiedler.

This is a continuing merger: we freely pilfer from RST, so much that we list Bach as a co-author even though Kaner takes ultimate responsibility for the content and structure of the BBST set.

After being developed by practitioners, the course evolved through academic teaching and research largely funded by the National Science Foundation. The Association for Software Testing served (and serves) as our learning lab for practitioner courses. We evolved the 4-week structure with AST and have offered over 30 courses to AST students. We could not have created this series without AST's collaboration.

We also thank Jon Bach, Scott Barber, Bernie Berger, Ajay Bhagwat, Rex Black, Jack Falk, Elizabeth Hendrickson, Kathy Iberle, Bob Johnson, Karen Johnson, Brian Lawrence, Brian Marick, John McConda, Melora Svoboda, dozens of participants in the Los Altos Workshops on Software Testing, the Software Test Mangers' Roundtable, the Workshops on Heuristic & Exploratory Techniques, the Workshops on Teaching Software Testing, the Austin Workshops on Test Automation and the Toronto Workshops on Software Testing and students in over 30 AST courses for critically reviewing materials from the perspective of experienced practitioners. We also thank the many students and co-instructors at Florida Tech, who helped us evolve the academic versions of this course, especially Pushpa Bhallamudi, Walter P. Bond, Tim Coulter, Sabrina Fay, Ajay Jha, Alan Jorgenson, Kishore Kattamuri, Pat McGee, Sowmya Padmanabhan, Andy Tinkham, and Giri Vijayaraghavan.

7

I'm the talking head on these videos and I'm accountable for all the mistakes. But a lot of people deserve credit for the good bits. I want to particularly thank Hung Nguyen, Doug Hoffman and Michael Bolton, who've contributed a lot of material to these slides. Many more colleagues have helped significantly over the 18 years of iterations in the development of this course, including some 32 instructors of online versions of the BBST materials. We've gotten a lot of feedback and we really appreciate it.

SLIDE 8

You can get these slides from my lab's website.

_____

_____

_____

_____

_____

_____

_____

_____

_____

_____

GETTING THESE SLIDES

Download them from ...

www.testingeducation.org/BBST

8

SLIDE 9

Throughout the series, we'll present testing as an investigation. A good investigator actively searches for information.

The point of testing is to dig up information that people need to know about the product. There are lots of ways to do this. You use the tools that are most effective under the circumstances. There's no set formula for testing, no best procedure, no best practices, no best tools. Different situations call for different approaches and different skills.

OUR APPROACH

Testing software involves investigating a product under tight constraints. Our goal is to help you become a better investigator:

• Knowledge and skills important to testing practitioners

• Context-driven
 – Diverse contexts call for diverse practices
 – We don't teach "best practices." Instead, we teach practices that are useful in the appropriate circumstances.
– http://kaner.com/?p=49

9

SLIDE 10

These lectures are used in university courses around the world because they're so closely connected to industry practice. Of course, in university courses, professors often blend our material with work of their own, so some aspects of how I describe this course will be different in a different university's course.

_____

_____

_____

_____

_____

THE ACADEMIC SERIES

Professor selects from the same:

• Videos

• Quiz questions

• Orientation exercises, labs and assignments

Blends these with her or his material, which often includes:

• More theory, or

• Glass box techniques, or

• Topics of greater interest to local industry

If you're a professor and want to talk about incorporating these materials into your courses, contact me at kaner@cs.fit.edu

10

SLIDE 11

Across the series, we have a set of learning objectives. We won't achieve all of these in this course, but we will make progress against this list.

_____

_____

_____

_____

_____

_____

_____

_____

_____

BBST LEARNING OBJECTIVES

- Understand key testing challenges that demand thoughtful tradeoffs by test designers and managers.
- Develop skills with several test techniques
- Choose effective techniques for a given objective under your constraints
- Improve the critical thinking and rapid learning skills that underlie good testing
- Communicate your findings effectively
- Work effectively online with remote collaborators
- Plan investments (in documentation, tools, and process improvement) to meet your actual needs
- Create work products that you can use in job interviews to demonstrate testing skill

11

SLIDE 12

FOUNDATIONS COURSE OBJECTIVES

Learning about testing

- Key challenges of testing
  - Information objectives drive the testing mission and strategy
  - Oracles are heuristic
  - Coverage is multidimensional
  - Complete testing is impossible
  - Measurement is important, but hard
- Introduce you to:
  - Basic vocabulary of the field
  - Basic facts of data storage and manipulation in computing
  - Diversity of viewpoints
  - Viewpoints drive vocabulary

Improving academic skills

- Online collaboration tools
  - Forums
  - Wikis
- Precision in reading
- Clear, well-structured communication
- Effective peer reviews
- Cope calmly and effectively with formative assessments (such as tests designed to help you learn).

Assessment can be helpfully hard without being risky

12

This is what we're up to in this course. This first lecture introduces basic definitions of the field. Later lectures consider the key challenges of testing. As your career evolves, you will need more education. The best educational choices available to working professionals are online. Our other goals are to help you improve your communication skills, and to work on your skills as a student in online courses.

SLIDE 13

This course is probably designed a bit differently from what you're used to.

First, these lectures contain a lot of material. We're packing a lot into a short course. The slides are very detailed, they have a lot of text. It's for your reference. I don't repeat the slides to you. I always hated that as a student. I can read the slides for myself and so can you.

So instead I talk about the ideas on the slides. Sometimes you'll want to pause the tape to synch up between what I'm saying and what's on the slide.

> **INSTRUCTIONAL APPROACH**
>
> Every aspect of the course is designed to help you learn
> - Orientation exercises (*readiness for learning*)
> - Video lectures
> - Quizzes (*no one who honestly tried to do well on the quizzes has failed the course because of low quiz scores*)
> - Labs (*one-person tasks that apply learning*)
> - Social interactions
> - Peer reviews
> - Group Assignments
> - Study-guide driven exams
>   - Exam cram forum
>   - Proctored exam
>
> 13

Second, you control the speed of the lecture. Most people learn more, and find it easier to pay attention, when information comes at them a little faster than in a standard lecture. Much of the time, you'll want to set your video player a little fast, maybe 1.2 or even 1.5 times normal speed. You can also pause the lecture. Download it to your machine, listen to 15 minutes now and the next 15 minutes later. You don't have to sit through the whole lecture at once. I wouldn't.

Third, this class is tightly scheduled. We divide every week in two—one part ends Wednesday, the other ends Saturday. Your discussions, quizzes, labs, assignments –they're are all due on a Wednesday or a Saturday. Our deadlines are firm. You must keep up. Other students depend on you to finish your tasks on time so that they can use what you've done – for example, give you a peer review. Their time is tightly scheduled too. If you're late, you make them late.

We start with orientation exercises. Do these tasks before you watch the video. The typical task requires you to stretch beyond what you know. Unless your instructor says otherwise, limit yourself to 30 minutes. It's OK if you don't successfully solve the problem. The goal is to get you thinking about it, so that when I cover it in lecture, you'll have enough experience with the difficulty of the problem to appreciate the solution, and learn from it.

There are also labs and assignments. Labs are typically homework you do on your own or with one other person. Assignments are bigger. The labs and assignments are where you apply what you've learned in lecture, in order to build your skills.

We also have quizzes. They're open book, but they're tough. Don't spend too much time on them and don't let them demoralize you. We use them to help you study and to stretch your skills in precision reading.

There's also a final exam. If you're taking this course from Florida Tech or from the Association for Software Testing, all the exam questions are drawn from a study guide that you get at the start of the course.

We expect you to develop your own answers to all of these questions. They focus your learning of the material. If you rely on someone else's answers instead of developing your own, you'll learn very little worth knowing from this course.

This course requires some work. Students who pass the standalone one-month *Foundations* course, tell us they typically spend about 12 hours per week.

It's harder to predict your time needs for university courses because these courses are organized in so many different ways. But you should expect to spend more time on this than on your average course.

SLIDE 14

OK. It's time to talk about testing.

_____

_____

_____

_____

_____

_____

_____

_____

_____

The nature of testing

14

SLIDE 15

I sometimes teach introductory programming at Florida Tech. The textbooks usually have a definition like this: A program is a set of instructions for a computer.

This definition is crazy.

_____

_____

_____

_____

_____

_____

WHAT'S A COMPUTER PROGRAM?

Textbooks often define a "computer program" like this:

```
A program is a set
    of instructions
       for a computer
```

15

SLIDE 16

It's like defining a house as a set of construction materials put together according to a house-design pattern.

We could define a house that way, but that would miss the point of a house.

A house is built for people to live in.

_____

_____

_____

_____

_____

That's like defining a house like this:

```
A house is a set of
construction materials
assembled according to
house-design patterns.
```

I'd rather define it as

```
A house is something
built for people to live
in
```

This second definition focuses on the purpose and stakeholders of the house, rather than on its materials.

16

SLIDE 17

If we don't understand who the software is for and what it's designed to do for them, we understand precious little about it.

_____

_____

_____

_____

_____

_____

_____

_____

SOMETHING BUILT FOR PEOPLE TO LIVE IN...

The focus is on

• Stakeholders
  – (for people)

• Purpose
  – (to live in)

Stakeholder:

Any person affected by:

• success or failure of a project, or

• actions or inactions of a product, or

• effects of a service.

17

SLIDE 18

I think the biggest failing of computer science education is that we overemphasize the technical aspects of our field. Certainly, students must develop many technical skills in order to develop good software.

But when we ignore the purpose of the software and the people involved with it, we teach our students bad mental habits that often stay with them through years of work experience.

_____

_____

The narrow focus on the machine prepares Computer Science students to make the worst errors in software engineering — in their first two weeks of school.

18

SLIDE 19

I want to suggest a different definition.

The program is a communication from the authors to each other, to you and to other people.

Yes, the program is written in a simplified language because the computer needs that, to run the program. But that's not the point of the program. We're not trying to make the computer happy. The computer is just a machine.

Think about fixing a program that someone else wrote. Or studying their program to figure out how your program can exchange data with it. Or using a program in order to gain information from it. All of these are communications.

A DIFFERENT DEFINITION

A computer program is

• a communication

• among several humans and computers

• who are distributed over space and time,

• that contains instructions that can be executed by a computer.

The point of the program is to provide value to the stakeholders.

19

If we focus on the machine, we don't notice this human factor, this communication between people. But we wouldn't write the code, and we couldn't improve the code, if we weren't conveying information to each other.

SLIDE 20

Our next definition is quality. In our next course, on bug advocacy, we'll consider several definitions of quality. Here, we focus on the one we find most useful.

Quality is value to some person.

The definition has two important aspects.

First, value. To say that a change would improve the quality of a product means that the change would make it worth more—or if the change is not made, the product should be worth less.

Next, value to some person. Quality is subjective. What makes a product more valuable to you might make it less valuable – lower quality – to someone else. For example, a program might be a lot easier for you to learn if we make it work very similarly to another program that you already know. That adds quality for you, but for someone who doesn't know or doesn't like your favorite program, this design might take quality away. We could create options, let people pick their own user interface, or design their own, but that adds complexity. Now people have learn about design and make choices. It might add value for some people but it probably makes the program harder, less valuable, for others.

> **WHAT ARE WE REALLY TESTING FOR?**
>
> *Quality is value to some person*
>
> *-- Jerry Weinberg*
>
> Quality is inherently subjective. Different stakeholders will perceive the same product as having different levels of quality.
>
> Testers look for different things ...
>
> ... for different stakeholders
>
> 20

SLIDE 21

That brings us to the idea of a bug.

Anything that takes away from the quality of a product is a bug.

Now, that creates an interesting problem. A bug for someone else might be a feature for you.

This might be a broader definition of the idea of a bug than you're used to. Many programmers think that only coding errors can be bugs. But that's like thinking that programs are only code for the computer. It's a narrow view.

In this course, and in the commercial world, we need to think more broadly about what makes products more valuable or less. It's not just about how the programmer intended the code to work.

> **SOFTWARE ERROR (AKA BUG)**
>
> An attribute of a software product
> - that reduces its value to a favored stakeholder
> - or increases its value to a disfavored stakeholder
> - without a sufficiently large countervailing benefit.
>
> An error:
> - May or may not be a coding error, or a functional error
>
> Design errors are bugs too.
>
> "Any threat to the value of the product to any stakeholder who matters." -- James Bach
>
> 21

SLIDE 22

We test a product to learn about its quality. Every test is an experiment that can teach us new things about the product. We run these experiments on behalf of stakeholders, people who need to understand what we find out.

_____

_____

_____

_____

_____

_____

_____

SOFTWARE TESTING
- is an empirical
- technical
- investigation
- conducted to provide stakeholders
- with information
- about the quality
- of the product or service under test

We design and run tests in order to gain useful information about the product's quality.

22

SLIDE 23

TESTING IS ALWAYS A SEARCH FOR INFORMATION

- Find important bugs
- Assess the quality of the product
- Help managers assess the progress of the project
- Help managers make release decisions
- Block premature product releases
- Help predict and control product support costs
- Check interoperability with other products
- Find safe scenarios for use of the product
- Assess conformance to specifications
- Certify the product meets a particular standard
- Ensure the testing process meets accountability standards
- Minimize the risk of safety-related lawsuits
- Help clients improve product quality & testability
- Help clients improve their processes
- Evaluate the product for a third party

Different objectives require different testing tools and strategies and will yield different tests, test documentation and test results.

23

We can't completely test a product. There are too many tests. So we have to focus our work around our information objectives. What I mean by information objective is an answer to the question, "what kind of information are we most concerned about learning from this testing?"

For example, on one project we might focus on finding as many bugs as possible. I call that bug hunting. On a different project, or at a different time in the same project, we might be less concerned with bug hunting and more concerned about how well the product matches a specification or how safe it is. We would run different tests, and focus our work in different ways, to optimize getting those different types of information.

SLIDE 24

I've now presented a few definitions, of quality, testing, and bugs. You've probably noticed that people don't always agree on what the same word means.

More about definitions

24

SLIDE 25

The underlying problem is that there are different views about what makes for good testing. People who start from strongly different theoretical positions will use the language differently.

That's how it is. I can't change that fact in this course. And I'm not going to pretend that we have the one true definitions of the technical language of testing. We have a lot of controversy in a developing field. We need to accept it and work with it.

Real dictionaries often list several definitions for the same word.

The really good dictionaries, like the *Oxford English* or *Black's Law Dictionary*, list several definitions and give you examples of how each is used, with references to an authoritative source who defined or used it that way.

THERE ARE NO "CORRECT" DEFINITIONS

- Some people don't like our definition of testing
  - They would rather call testing a hunt for bugs
  - Or a process for verifying that a program meets its specification

(Try to reconcile THOSE two definitions!)

- The different definitions reflect different visions of testing.
- Meaning is not absolute. Words mean what the people who say them intend them to mean and what the people who hear them interpret them as meaning.
- Clear communication requires people to share definitions of the terms they use. If you're not certain that you know what someone else means, **ask them**.

We would rather embrace the genuine diversity of our field than try to use standards committees to hide it or legislate it away.

25

SLIDE 26

I use a lot of technical terms in this course. If I don't give set meanings for them, you won't understand me. So I provide you with working definitions—this is what this word means in this course. That doesn't make this the right definition. It does make it the definition you need to know for tests and exams—in this course.

_____

_____

_____

_____

_____

We use "working definitions"

- We provide definitions for key concepts:
  - To limit ambiguity, and
  - to express clearly the ideas in our courses
- And we expect you to learn them.
- And we will test you on them. And give you bad test grades if you get them "wrong."
- We DON'T require you to accept our definitions as correct OR as the most desirable definitions.
- We only require you to demonstrate that you understand what we are saying.
- In the "real world", when someone uses one of these words, ask them what THEY mean instead of assuming that they mean what WE mean.

SLIDE 27

This course is about black box testing at the system level. So let's look at what that means.

_____

_____

_____

_____

_____

_____

_____

_____

_____

And now, back to the definitions

This course is primarily about "black box" "system-level" testing.

28

SLIDE 28

Let me start with the notion of black boxes. Historically, before computers and software existed, people talked about studying devices as black boxes.

The notion of a "black box" is the notion of a closed thing. You can't look inside it to see how it works. Instead, you give it inputs (like, pressing its buttons) and watch what happens.

When we do black box testing, we don't know, and don't learn, how the program was coded. We just know what it does.

What we learn from black box testing is whether the program does what it should and avoids doing what it shouldn't do.

BLACK BOX TESTING

Testing and test design without knowledge of the code (or without use of knowledge of the code).

The tester designs tests from his (research-based) knowledge of the product's user characteristics and needs, the subject area being automated (e.g. "insurance"), the product's market, risks, and environment (hardware / software).

Some authors narrow this concept to testing exclusively against an authoritative specification. (We don't.)

The black box tester becomes an expert in the relationships between the program and the world in which it runs.

29

To understand what the program should do, we have to study the needs and expectations of the people who will use it, the characteristics of the systems that will interact with it, and the regulations that will govern it.

SLIDE 29

The contrast with black box testing is glass box testing. We look into the box and design our tests based on the characteristics of the code. Many people call glass box testing, "white box".

GLASS BOX TESTING

Testing or test design using knowledge of the details of the internals of the program (code and data).

Glass box testers typically ask

- "Does this code do what the programmer expects or intends?"

in contrast to the black box question:

- "Does this do what the users (human and software) expect?"

Glass box is often called "white box" to contrast with "black box."

> The glass box tester becomes an expert in the implementation of the product under test.

30

SLIDE 30

Then there's grey box testing, or if you prefer, translucent box. The basic idea involves tests that aren't exactly black box and aren't exactly glass box. For example, you might study the values of variables that aren't visible to the end user, but that you can see using tools. This term is so broad that I'm not sure it's useful. But it shows up in a lot of blogs, so you should probably have familiarity with it.

GREY BOX?

People often ask us, "If there is black box testing and white box testing, what is grey box testing?"

We don't think there is a standard definition. "A blend of black box and white box approaches" is not very informative.

Examples of grey box:

- Studying variables that are not visible to the end user (e.g. log file analysis or performance of subsystems)
- Designing tests to stress relationships between variables that are not visible to the end user

Search the web for more examples of "grey box testing" descriptions. There are thousands.

31

SLIDE 31

"Black box" and "glass box" describe general approaches to testing. A lot of people call them techniques, but they're not.

A technique is a way of doing something. When we teach someone a technique, we teach them how to do a task. We'll look at a few techniques in the next lecture. But black and glass boxes—they're ways of thinking about test techniques. They're not techniques themselves.

ARE THESE "TECHNIQUES"?

Are "black box" or "glass box" test techniques?

We prefer to call them "approaches."

Reference.com defines "technique" as:

- "the body of specialized procedures and methods used in any specific field, esp. in an area of applied science.
- method of performance; way of accomplishing."

When someone says they'll do "black box testing," you don't know what they'll actually **do**, what tools they'll use, what bugs they'll look for, how they'll look for them, or how they'll decide whether they've found a bug.

Some techniques are more likely to be used in a black box way, so we might call these "black box techniques." But it is the technique ("usability testing") that is black box, not "black box" that is the technique.

32

SLIDE 32

Another general testing approach is called "behavioral testing." Behavioral testers test the visible behavior of the program, but they often look inside the code to gain information to guide their tests.

Behavioral testing is kind of like black box testing. Except that it misses the point of black box testing.

> ## BEHAVIORAL TESTING: A DIFFERENCE IN PERSPECTIVE
>
> **Behavioral testing is focused on the observable behavior of the product.**
>
> It is like black box testing, except that behavioral testers might also read the code and design tests on the basis of their knowledge of the code.
>
> The notion of "black box" analysis precedes software testing. "In science and engineering, a **black box** is a device, system or object which can (and sometimes can only) be viewed solely in terms of its input, output and transfer characteristics without any knowledge of its internal workings. Almost anything might be referred to as a black box: a transistor, an algorithm, or the human mind." See http://en.wikipedia.org/wiki/Black_box.
>
> Behavioral testing removes this restriction
>
> 33

_____

_____

_____

_____

SLIDE 33

If we want to use system-level testing to discover whether the program behaves as we would expect from the code, we can use behavioral testing.

As a programmer, I did a lot of behavioral testing, to see how my code actually performed. I called what I was doing glass box testing, but whatever we call it, it was certainly useful and important to do.

But when I tested other people's code, I was doing something different. My questions were less about the internal implementation and more about the value

> Several academics (and some practitioners) have attacked "black-box" testing. Boris Beizer called it "ignorance-based testing."
>
> Beizer preferred "behavioral testing" – tests of visible behavior, *informed by knowledge of the internals where possible* – as making for better test design.
>
> I think the distinction reflects an underlying difference of opinion about what testers are supposed to do.
>
> Ammann and Offutt's excellent text, *Introduction to Software Testing*, offers a sophisticated, unifying view of the field, but it focuses on verification (was something implemented correctly?). It seems blind to questions of validation (are we building the right thing?).
>
> Behavioral testing is useful when our purpose is to verify that the program does what the programmer intended.
>
> However, to the intentionally black-box tester, the focus is on what the program **should** do. For this, the tester must look **beyond** the code, to the program's relations with people and their world.
>
>
>
> 34

of the running program. Certainly, coding errors detracted from value and I wanted to find them. But to prepare for this testing, I had to learn who would use this program and why, what devices or platforms it had to interact with, what kinds of problems would make it unacceptable in its market. You can't learn these things from the code.

The idea of behavioral testing is popular among Computer Science academics. If your emphasis is on teaching novices how to program, the user needs and platform issues don't matter. The requirements for the program are whatever you tell the students. Realism doesn't matter. The exercise is academic. In that environment, black box testing might not make much sense. But when teachers of those courses describe black box testing as "ignorance-based" because their students aren't burying their noses in the code, I don't think they understand what they're writing about.

_____

_____

_____

_____

_____

SLIDE 34

Just like glass box testing is the counterpoint to black box, structural testing is the counterpoint to behavioral.

_____

_____

_____

_____

_____

_____

_____

_____

_____

> ## STRUCTURAL TESTING
>
> People who prefer "behavioral" testing to "black box" usually prefer "structural" to "glass box" or "white box."
>
> As far as we can tell, **structural testing** is the same as glass box testing.
>
> 35

SLIDE 35

Another set of distinctions that people often make are between levels of testing.

The lowest level is unit testing. I think the most common meaning of "unit testing" among working professionals is tests of small parts of a program: individual functions or methods. Over the last decade, we've seen the emergence of a new generation of unit test tools and widespread adoption of this technology among programmers.

_____

_____

> ## UNIT, INTEGRATION & SYSTEM TESTING
>
> **Unit tests** focus on individual units of the product.
> Programmers typically describe unit testing as glass box testing, focused on individual methods (functions) or individual classes.
>
>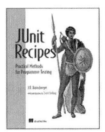
>
> 36

SLIDE 36

The concept of unit testing, however, is not necessarily tied to glass box testing of individual methods.

For example, the IEEE standard on software unit testing presents a much more general definition.

One of the black box test techniques involves running tests that focus on an individual feature. This is called function testing. Its goal is to see how well the feature itself works, without worrying about its interaction with other features. This is an example of black box unit testing.

> ## UNIT, INTEGRATION & SYSTEM TESTING
>
> IEEE standard 1008 on **software unit testing** clarifies that a unit
>
> > "may occur at any level of the design hierarchy from a single module to a complete program."
>
> If you think of it as one thing, and test it as one thing, it's a unit.
>
> > **Black box unit tests? Imagine a code library that specifies the interfaces of its functions but provides no source code. How does the programmer try out a function?**
>
> 37

_____

_____

_____

SLIDE 37

Integration testing involves testing several components together. At the lowest level, we might use unit test tools like jUnit, to pass data from one method to another and see how the units work together.

At some point, as we test more parts of the program together, we start calling it high-level integration testing.

Testing of the full, running system is just another example of integration testing.

> **UNIT, INTEGRATION & SYSTEM TESTING**
>
> **Integration tests** study how two (or more) units work together. You can have:
> - low-level integration (2 or 3 units) and
> - high-level integration (many units, all the way up to tests of the complete, running system).
>
> Integration testing might be black box or glass box. Integration testers often use knowledge of the code to predict and evaluate how data flows among the units.
>
> 38

SLIDE 38

System testing doesn't really fit on the continuum from unit tests to integration tests but it's often mentioned on that continuum. System testing is not just another name for high-level integration testing.

When we run a system test, we are trying to assess the value of the system.

> **UNIT, INTEGRATION & SYSTEM TESTING**
>
> **System testing** focuses on the value of the running system.
> "System testing is the process of attempting to demonstrate how the program does not meet its objectives"
> Glen Myers (1979), *The Art of Software Testing*, p. 110.
>
> 39

SLIDE 39

Rather than contrast system testing with unit testing, I prefer to contrast system testing with implementation-level testing.

System testing is about how valuable the program is.

Implementation-level testing is about how well the program is written.

Implementation-level is glass box testing. When we do implementation-level testing, we're asking questions like:

- How well is the code written?
- Can we optimize the code?
- Does the program work the way the programmer intended?

> **IMPLEMENTATION-LEVEL VS. SYSTEM-LEVEL**
>
> **Implementation-level testing is focused on the details of the implementation.**
> - Typically it is glass box testing.
> - Examples include unit tests, integration tests, tests of dataflows, and tests of performance of specific parts of the program. These are all implementation-level tests.
> - Typically, implementation-level tests ask whether the program works as the programmer intended or whether the program can be optimized in some way.
>
> 40

Implementation-level testing can focus on units, several units working together, or even on the flow of data between interacting systems. It's not about how much of the code we're studying. It's about how well the programmer wrote the code.

SLIDE 40

The extreme programming community prefers to use the term "programmer testing" for what I call implementation-level testing. I don't object to the term, "programmer testing", but too many of my students think this means any testing by any programmer. That persistent misinterpretation creates a concept that's just too broad to be useful. So I say implementation-level instead.

_____

_____

_____

SLIDE 41

Another contrast that people draw frequently is between functional testing and parafunctional or nonfunctional testing.

Functional testing is black box testing. But it's specifically about treating a program like a function. A function transforms input data into outputs. A functional test case specifies inputs that we will present to the program along with one or more expected outputs. This is a useful term. It gives a specific concept that we can work with.

SLIDE 42

In contrast, parafunctional testing includes everything that is not functional testing. Many people prefer to call this nonfunctional testing.

I don't find this contrast useful because the class of parafunctional tests is huge and too diverse. Testing a program for maintainability is fundamentally different from testing it for usability or for performance scalability. We have to do those kinds of testing, but lumping them together under one clumsy-sounding word doesn't help anyone think about the many types of tasks or about the need to budget time for each type. Instead, it makes a lot of different things sound the same and that encourages us to underestimate the challenge of dealing with them.

IMPLEMENTATION-LEVEL VS. PROGRAMMER TESTING

The Extreme Programming community coined the term, "Programmer Testing."
http://www.c2.com/cgi/wiki?HistoryOfProgrammerTest and http://www.manning.com/rainsberger/

- As used in that community (and by us), programmer-testing does NOT refer to *any* tests run by a programmer.
- Our impression is that Programmer Testing and Implementation-Level Testing mean the same thing
- We prefer "Implementation-Level testing" (which contrasts cleanly with System-Level testing), but you're likely to see both terms.

41

FUNCTIONAL & PARAFUNCTIONAL

Functional testing is system-level testing that looks at the program as a collection of functions. A "function" might be an individual feature or a broader capability that relies on several underlying features.

We analyze a function in terms of the inputs we can provide it and the outputs we would expect, given those inputs.

(See W.E. Howden, *Functional Program Testing & Analysis*, 1987)

42

FUNCTIONAL & PARAFUNCTIONAL

In contrast to "functional testing", people often refer to **parafunctional** or **nonfunctional** testing.

(Why *parafunctional* instead of *nonfunctional*? Calling tests "nonfunctional" forces absurd statements, like "all the nonfunctional tests are now working...")

The concept of "functional testing" is fairly well defined, but parafunctional includes anything "other than" ("para") functional. Same for non-functional.

This includes testing attributes of the software that are general to the program rather than tied to any particular function, such as usability, scalability, maintainability, security, speed, localizability, supportability, etc.

> The concept of parafunctional (or non-functional) testing is so vague as to be dysfunctional. We won't often use it in the course.

43

SLIDE 43

A lot of programming is done under contract. A customer wants a program, so they contract with a development company to write it. For many years, almost all commercial software was written this way and most of our software development standards reflect an underlying assumption of contracting-model development.

In the contract-software world, the contract usually includes a process for determining whether the customer should accept the software as fully implemented, and then pay for it.

If this process involves testing, as it usually does, we call this acceptance testing.

ACCEPTANCE TESTING #1

In early times, most software development was done under contract. A customer (e.g. the government) hired a contractor (e.g. IBM) to write a program. The customer and contractor would negotiate the contract. Eventually the contractor would say that the software is done and the customer or her agent (such as an independent test lab) would perform **acceptance testing** to determine whether the software should be accepted.

If software failed the tests, it was unacceptable and the customer would refuse to pay for it until the software was made to conform to the promises in the contract (which were what was checked by the acceptance tests).

> This is the meaning
>
> we will adopt
>
> in this course.

44

SLIDE 44

Companies also develop software for sale and they test that software, too. For example, Electronic Arts tests its games before selling them.

Other companies write software to run their own systems, and they test those before putting them into use, or as they call it, into production.

Many people call these tests acceptance testing too. I'm not a big fan of that usage, because it hides a key distinction. In traditional acceptance testing, the customer runs or supervises the testing and decides whether to accept the product.

ACCEPTANCE TESTING #2

There really is no place for acceptance testing if there are no contract-based requirements. (At least, not in the traditional sense of the word.)

But many people use the word anyway.

To them, "acceptance testing" refers to tests that might help someone decide whether a product is ready for sale, installation on a production server, or delivery to a customer.

To us, this describes a *developer's decision* (whether to deliver) rather than a *customer's decision* (whether to accept), so we won't use this term this way.

However, it is a common usage, with many local variations. Therefore, far be it from us to call it "wrong." But when you hear or read about "acceptance testing", don't assume you know what meaning is intended. Check your local definition.

Bolton, http://www.developsense.com/presentations/2007-10-PNSQC-UserAcceptanceTesting.pdf

45

In the other cases, the development group runs the tests and decides whether to release the product for sale or internal use. To me, that's a big difference.

These people seem to want to use the term acceptance testing as a synonym for system testing. I'm not going to do that.

But enough people use the term that way, or in several other ways, that you should check before assuming that you know what someone means when they tell you the software is in acceptance testing.

SLIDE 45

And finally, here's today's last definition.

Independent testing is testing that isn't done under the influence of the development team.

The classic example is testing done by an independent test lab.

For example, in the United States, makers of electronic voting machines have to get their machines and their software tested by an independent lab.

By the way, these voting machine evaluations include code inspections and unit tests as well as system tests.

Independent testing doesn't have to be black box.

… But just because testing is external doesn't mean it's independent. The voting machine maker decides which test lab will evaluate their machines and they also pay the labs. If you made these machines and you felt that the independent test lab was too critical of your products, would you contract with that lab again? Do you think the lab might design its tests to reduce its chances of losing your business? Where's the independence in that?

And independent testing doesn't have to be external. Some companies have their own independent test groups. As an example of how the company protects their independence, these testers will report to different executives from the programmers.

In practice, independence is a matter of degree. This testing is more independent than that testing.

By the way, even though some people argue that all testing should be independent, that's not necessarily what you want. Testers who work closely with the programmers can have more access to more information about the product and its implementation, and can have more influence on the testability of the product, than testers who are kept far away from the programmers. The relative benefits of collaboration versus independence are complex and depend a lot on individual corporate cultures.

INDEPENDENT TESTING

Testing done by a third party, often an external test lab. Some companies have an independent in-house test group.

The key notion is that the independent testers aren't influenced or pressured to analyze and test the software in ways preferred by the developers.

Independent labs might be retained to do any type of testing, such as functional testing, performance testing, security testing, etc.

46

SLIDE 46

I want to close this first lecture with some thoughts on your quizzes and your exam.

About that Quiz (the one you're about to take…)

47

SLIDE 47

If you're taking this course from Florida Tech or from the authors, then quizzes and exams will work a certain way. I'm going to assume throughout this course that your instructors do things my way. They'll let you know if they're doing something different.

In the *Foundations* course, there are quizzes with every lecture. The quizzes are open book. You can use these slides; you can watch the video lectures again. You can use the assigned readings and anything you want to download from the Internet.

QUIZ STANDARDS, RULES & TIPS

- BBST Quizzes are OPEN BOOK
- You are welcome to take the quiz while you watch the video or read the materials.
- You can take the quiz with a friend (sit side by side or Skype together)
- You may not copy someone else's answers. If you use someone else's answer without figuring out yourself what the answer is, or working it out with a partner (and actively engage in reasoning about it with your partner), you are cheating.
  - If you make an honest effort on the quizzes but score poorly, don't panic. The scores are for your feedback and to tell us who is *trying* to make progress in the course. No one who has honestly attempted the quizzes has ever failed the course because of low quiz grades.

48

SLIDE 48

One point of the quizzes is to help you understand the lecture and the readings. The questions emphasize details that you might have missed. They ask you to make judgments that show whether you understand how two concepts are similar and how they're different or how an idea can be applied. They sometimes make distinctions that feel new, that weren't raised exactly that way in the lecture, that you have to think about. These questions give you another opportunity to learn the course's details.

QUIZ RULES, STANDARDS & TIPS

The quizzes are designed to help you determine how well you understand the lecture or the readings and to help you gain new insights from lecture/readings.

- We will make fine distinctions. (If you're not sure of the answer, go back and read again or watch the video)
- We will demand precise reading. (The ability to read carefully, make distinctions, and recognize and evaluate inferences in what is read, is essential for analyzing specifications. All testers need to build these skills.)
- We will sometimes ask you to think about a concept and work to a conclusion.

It is common for students to learn new things while they take the quiz.

49

The other point of the quizzes is to exercise your skills in precise reading. These skills are essential for analyzing specifications, which is an important part of what testers do. It takes a long time to build those skills, so we can't wait until the "official" time for you to study spec-based testing. Instead, we start this in your first quiz.

SLIDE 49

This slide illustrates the structure of our questions. This structure is more difficult than the usual closed-book multiple-choice test. That's by design. This approach evolved over three years, in several meetings of a working group of the Association for Software Testing. The link on this slide is to the standard that we developed.

QUIZ STANDARDS, RULES & TIPS

- Typical question has 7 alternatives:
  a. (a)
  b. (b)
  c. (c)
  d. (a) and (b)
  e. (a) and (c)
  f. (b) and (c)
  g. (a) and (b) and (c)
- Score is 25% if you select one correct of two (e.g. answer (a) instead of (d).)
- Score is 0 if you include an error (e.g. answer (d) when right answer is only (a).) *People usually remember the errors they hear from you more than they notice what you omitted to say.*

For a detailed discussion of our standards, see Kaner, "Writing multiple choice test questions,"

http://kaner.com/?p=34

50

SLIDE 50

Now, here's an example of one of our questions.

Sample Quiz Question

51

SLIDE 51

WHAT IS THE SIGNIFICANCE OF THE DIFFERENCE BETWEEN BLACK BOX AND GLASS BOX TESTS?

a. Black box tests cannot be as powerful as glass box tests because the tester doesn't know what issues in the code to look for.

b. Black box tests are typically better suited to measure the software against the expectations of the user, whereas glass box tests measure the program against the expectations of the programmer who wrote it.

c. Glass box tests focus on the internals of the program whereas black box tests focus on the externally visible behavior.

d. (a) and (b)

e. (a) and (c)

f. (b) and (c)

g. (a) and (b) and (c)

52

What's the significance of the difference between black box and glass box tests?
Put your video on pause for a bit and try this question for yourself…

SLIDE 52

The answer is (b).

The most common mistake is (c). Answer (c) gives a true statement. Glass box tests do focus on the internals of the program and black box tests do focus on the externally visible behavior.

But this is like saying (in most parts of the world) that the sun rises in the morning. That's true, but it's not relevant. The question doesn't ask what the difference is between black box and glass box. The question asks what is the significance of the difference. That means, what is the importance or the impact of the difference. Answer (c) doesn't address that, (b) does.

A SAMPLE QUESTION

What is the significance of the difference between black box and glass box tests?

b. **Black box tests are typically better suited to measure the software against the expectations of the user, whereas glass box tests measure the program against the expectations of the programmer who wrote it. [CORRECT]**

c. Glass box tests focus on the internals of the program whereas black box tests focus on the externally visible behavior.

   • This is factually correct, but irrelevant. The question doesn't ask what the difference is between black box and glass box. It asks "What is the significance of the difference?"

> These might seem unfairly hard to begin with, but you'll get better at them with practice.
>
> The underlying skills have value.

53

SLIDE 53

Here's another example, with the most common error, choice (b), already highlighted.

Many people would say that (b) is correct. That independent testing IS a form of black box testing typically done by an outside test lab.

However, the question starts by saying, "According to the lecture." I just gave you the example of voting system testing, with independent test labs doing glass box testing. According to this lecture, independent testing might or might not be black box, and therefore, according to this lecture, option (b) is incorrect.

ACCORDING TO THE LECTURE, INDEPENDENT TESTING ...

a. must be done by an outside company.

b. **is a form of black box testing that is typically done by an outside test lab.**

c. is typically done by an outside company (test lab) but can be done in-house if the testers are shielded from influence by the development staff.

d. (a) and (b)

e. (a) and (c)

f. (b) and (c)

g. (a) and (b) and (c)

> Answer (b) might be correct under other definitions of independent testing but not in the definition "according to the lecture."
>
> The lecture includes any type of testing, as long it is independent.
>
> Real-life example: electronic voting systems are subject to code review and glass box testing by independent test labs.

54

There are so many conflicting definitions in our field that it's often impossible to say that X is the wrong answer, unless X is absolutely ridiculous. I don't want to insist that our definition is the "true" one. But I have to insist that you know what the lecture teaches. So, when the question says, "according to the lecture", you have to give the answer that was given in the lecture. It doesn't mean you think it's right. It means you think it's what was taught.

SLIDE 54

Our exams are a lot more flexible. These are essay-style exams, rather than multiple choice. The grading standards intentionally allow for a diversity of answers. When you answer an exam question, you should show what you learned in the course, but if you disagree with the lecture or the readings then, after demonstrating your awareness of what was taught, feel free to shred it, answering the question in a way that completely disagrees with our point of view. If you make a good argument, and write it in a clear and well-organized way, you'll get full points and our respect.

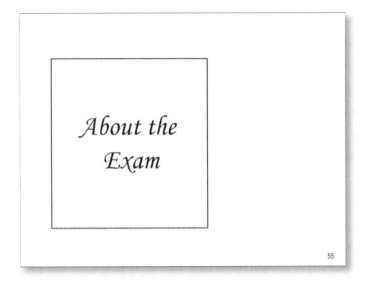

About the Exam

55

SLIDE 55

Here are a few more notes about the exams. The questions for the exams are already listed in your study guide. The exams' questions will be drawn from this list.

The exams will be closed book. You can't bring your notes. However, you will almost certainly remember your thinking and your approach when you take the exam, if you work through the questions before the exam, actually writing your own answers. It is especially valuable to review the answers with other students after you write them, and then rewrite an improved version based on their feedback.

ACADEMIC FLORIDA TECH COURSES

Our exams are closed book, essay style.

We focus students' work with essay questions in a study guide. We draw all exam questions from this guide.

We expect well-reasoned, well-presented answers. This is the tradeoff. You have lots of time before the exam to develop answers. On the exam, we expect good answers.

We encourage students to develop answers together.

Please don't try to memorize other students' answers instead of working on your own. It's usually ineffective (memorization errors lead to bad grades) and you end up learning very little from the course.

Please don't post study guide questions and suggested answers on public websites. That encourages students (in other courses) to memorize your answers instead of developing their own. Even if someone could memorize all your answers perfectly, and all your answers were perfect, this would teach them nothing about testing. It would cheat them of the educational value of the course.

We'll visit this again in a few days.

56

Memorizing other students' answers is a pretty worthless way to study. The things that you can memorize are not what is important in this course. The questions are designed to make you think through the course content in a different way. You'll learn a lot from that thinking. You won't get any of that value if you rely on someone else's answers instead of thinking them through for yourself.

Another point on this. Every year, some nice student thinks they'll do the world a favor if they post answers to these questions on the internet, so that all the later students will have answers to memorize from. Please don't do that. It's the process of developing the answer for yourself that gives you, and the future students, the educational value. Posting sample answers won't do anyone any favors.

SLIDE 56

BLACK BOX SOFTWARE TESTING:
FOUNDATIONS

END OF LECTURE 1

CEM KANER, J.D., Ph.D.
PROFESSOR OF SOFTWARE ENGINEERING
FLORIDA INSTITUTE OF TECHNOLOGY

REBECCA L. FIEDLER, M.B.A. Ph.D.
PRESIDENT: KANER, FIEDLER & ASSOCIATES

JAMES BACH
PRINCIPAL, SATISFICE INC.

This work is licensed under the Creative Commons Attribution License. To view a copy of this license, visit http://creativecommons.org/licenses/by-sa/2.0/ or send a letter to Creative Commons, 559 Nathan Abbott Way, Stanford, California 94305, USA.

These notes are partially based on research that was supported by NSF Grants EIA-0113539 ITR/SY +PE:"Improving the Education of Software Testers" and CCLI-0717613 "Adaptation & Implementation of an Activity-Based Online or Hybrid Course in Software Testing." Any opinions, findings and conclusions or recommendations expressed in this material are those of the author(s) and do not necessarily reflect the views of the National Science Foundation.

57

Feedback: On Quizzes

If you're taking *Foundations* as an instructor-led course (face-to-face or online), you are probably taking quizzes. If the instructor uses our questions, or questions based on our question-design standards, you will probably find them difficult. Some people find them infuriatingly difficult.

Please open a discussion with the instructor and the other students about some of the questions. If you are in an online version of the course, there is probably a discussion forum for that purpose. You can criticize the wording; question the answer we've marked as correct; clear up misunderstandings you have about the content; and argue with our analysis. In some classes, the quiz-discussions are quite lively. The discussion contributes substantially to the learning of the people who participate in it.

The quiz questions serve a few purposes:

- They help you check whether you understand the definitions and the key concepts.

- They highlight points, especially distinctions among concepts, that we consider important but that students often miss when they watch the lecture.

- They draw out implications of the points made in the lecture. In some cases, when you understand the ramification of one of the lecture's claims or arguments, you might conclude that you flatly disagree with it. That's OK. We aren't asking you to agree. In the discussion forum and in the essay questions, you'll have plenty of opportunity to challenge or disagree with the lecture's claims. The point of the quiz question is to help you make sure you understand what you're arguing with, before you argue with it.

- They give you practice with critical reading. Critical reading involves precision in the reading itself (figure out what the author is saying) and logical analysis (figure out whether the author's claims hang together). This is a crucially important skill for specification analysis. It underlies all of testing. It develops with practice. If your logic training is rusty, you will be uncomfortable with these questions. Don't let that bother you. You'll gradually get better at this and the underlying skills are useful.

If you're working through the course materials on your own, you won't see these quiz questions. They are not appropriate for self-study because they need the support of a discussion forum managed by someone who knows the course and the questions well.

The rest of this feedback note is for the student in the instructor-led course.

Quizzes As Assessment Tools

Many students are bothered by the difficulty of these questions. They are accustomed to getting good grades on tests and they often get much lower grades on BBST quizzes, at least at first. If you are one of those students, calm down. These questions are intended to help you improve your understanding, not to lower your grade:

- When we teach the course at university, high quiz grades can pull your course grade up, but low quiz grades will not pull your course grade down. (Exception: If you skip the quizzes, Kaner will count those zeros against your grade. But if you make an honest effort and do badly, he ignores the quiz scores when he calculates the final grade.)

- When we teach the course to professional students, students don't get a grade. They either complete the course or they don't. If you make an honest effort on the quizzes, that will count favorably toward "completion" even if the scores are low.

Some students are confused by this. They wonder why we would give quizzes if we aren't going to lower their grades to account for low scores. The answer is that there are many reasons to do assessment activities in a course. Getting a final grade is just one, and in terms of real-world value, probably the least important. Assessment activities give you opportunities to practice working with concepts or skills and they give you feedback. Most people learn more from doing things than from reading or listening. Every activity in the course, including quizzes, assignments and exams, is designed to help you learn. The feedback (or grading) is designed to help you learn too.

If you're taking this course in a university, some of these activities have to yield grades that "count" because the instructor has to give you a course grade. But even in those courses:

- The main purpose of the assessment activities in BBST is to help you learn, and you will learn more about the material even while you are writing the exam.

- The quizzes will probably not count against your final grade.

The Content Of The Quizzes

We write these questions carefully (not necessarily perfectly, but we try) and are trying to make you think carefully about what you are learning. One of our strategies is to require you to compare possible answers and evaluate them in terms of each other. We do this by structuring our questions so that we usually give you simple answers and combinations (A and B, A and C, etc.). This makes the questions harder, perhaps harder than other multiple-choice questions you have answered. When we score an answer as incorrect or partially correct, don't be dismayed by that. Instead, go back to the question and ask yourself whether this is a signal that you can learn a bit more about the topic of that question. You might learn that from the materials themselves or from participating in discussions that challenge the lesson the question is trying to point out.

It is very hard to write good multiple-choice questions, partially because we have to set the question up to mark a Right Answer in a field that allows many good answers. We will often disambiguate questions by saying, "According to the lecture, X is true." In that case, your answer has to be guided by the lecture. When you select X as the best option, that doesn't mean *you* believe X is true, it means you believe that's what we said.

You are welcome to argue about the content or wording of a question in the Quiz Discussion forum.

Additional Reading

We developed a set of guidelines for writing multiple-choice questions in a series of meetings sponsored by the Association for Software Testing. For details, see Kaner's *Writing Multiple Choice Questions* at http://kaner.com/?p=34 or an updated version in Fiedler, Kaner & Hoffman's (2011) *Black Box Software Testing Instructor's Manual* at http://testingeducation.org/BBST/instructor/BBSTInstructorsManual_Sept2012.pdf

Authors' Reflection On Lesson 1

Lesson 1 is about facts and definitions. The lesson has no activities (beyond figuring out how to navigate the course, which is complex enough) and so we have no activity-updates.

Updating The Facts

Some of the facts presented in Lesson 1 are outdated.

- The AST dictionary project closed. AST has many projects that compete for volunteer time. The dictionary was a complex project that never achieved critical mass.

- The Certificate program in Software Testing at Florida Tech never got off the ground. We had an agreement in principle at the time we published the slides. However, we hadn't yet finalized the details. Standards and processes for accrediting American universities have tightened and gotten more complex and more paperwork-intensive in recent years. The process of creating and supervising a university-based certificate program became much more complex soon after we published the slides. As we came to understand the challenges of the new rules, we and Florida Tech agreed that instead of creating a university-based certificate, we should form a separate corporation (Kaner, Fiedler & Associates, LLC) to manage BBST and give certificates as appropriate.

- The co-authorship of *Foundations'* slides with James Bach is largely obsolete. As we noted on Slide 7, the co-authorship was largely based on our incorporation of slides and activities from James' *Rapid Software Testing* course. We liked the graphic design of several of his slides and we liked several of his exercises and distinctions. Many of the changes in *Foundations* have been significant adaptations or replacements of those materials. The slides are the same, and will stay the same until we publish the next edition of *Foundations*. But many of the activities are very different. At this point, we have no reason to believe that James would agree with the points made in several of our activities. In some cases, we believe he would disagree vigorously.

About The Definitions

- *The definition of quality:* On slides 21-22, we present Jerry Weinberg's definition of quality: "Quality is value to some person." We agree with this definition, but sometimes it is restated as "Quality is value to some person who matters." We reflect that view on slide 22, quoting James Bach's definition of a bug: "Any threat to the value of the product to any stakeholder who matters."

  We don't agree with that reframing of the definition. We have never agreed with it. We think that everyone matters. One of us even wrote a book, *Bad Software*, that was focused on helping consumers who "don't matter" get compensation from companies who dismissed them as powerless.

  Consider an example, based on several real situations. Imagine a contracting firm (SoftCo) that writes billing software for a big company (BigCo) that then uses the software to create bills for its customers. Imagine a bug that occasionally overcharges the customers, but in a way that is hard for the small customer to prove incorrect. Suppose that BigCo realizes there is probably a bug but is completely unmotivated to fix it. BigCo's customers might not like it, and some of them might complain that they think they might be paying too much, but until and unless they bring a lawsuit, the BigCo of this example will treat these people as if they don't matter and following BigCo's lead, so will SoftCo.

  It is true that no stakeholder who has influence over the development budget is arguing that this is a bug that needs to be investigated and fixed. However, that doesn't make the bug go away. The code is still wrong and the customers are still being cheated. To the customers, this is a bug. Even if they have no power to get it fixed, it is a bug and the software has negative value for them. We see no ethical justification for deciding, *as a matter of definition*, that when someone who has no power is being cheated by a software defect, that defect is not a bug.

Weinberg's definition of quality is subjective: value to some person. Under his definition, a program can have high value to one person, no value to another, and negative value to a third. In our view, consideration of whether one of those people has power is totally different from considering the value of the software to that person.

■ *The distinction between black box and behavioral testing*. This is an important distinction to some people, especially some academics. Some of these people are important members of our community and their views deserve recognition. However, we don't think this is a valuable distinction. We think it is confusing and that it reflects a lack of understanding of the nature of black box testing. This disagreement provides a wonderful setup for a debate about the nature of testing. Unfortunately, to understand and appreciate the disagreement requires deeper insight than we can expect from students of an introductory course like Foundations. For some students, this distinction and our comments on it are quite interesting, but for many (we suspect, most) students, the presentation is simply confusing. In retrospect, it doesn't belong in this course.

■ *The distinction between glass box and programmer testing*. Kaner teaches a course on programmer testing. This is an important distinction to him. However, as with the presentation of behavioral testing, the concepts underlying programmer testing are far enough afield of this course that the definition adds no value for many (we think most) of our students.

2

LESSON 2: STRATEGY

Lesson Introduction

This lecture introduces you to *context-driven testing:*

- The goal underlying the preparatory exercise and the required reading is to open your mind to the great variety of testers' roles. If you have no preconception about testers and their roles, you will learn something new that will help when you interview for your first testing job. If you come to the course with a narrow view of the roles of testers and test groups, this lesson will challenge you to unlearn your narrow view.

- The lecture defines testing as a service to stakeholders. In particular, it is an empirical search for quality-related information about the product, on behalf of those stakeholders. The key stakeholders often have different informational needs. To meet those needs, testers have to adjust how they test (what they do, what tools they use, how they prioritize their time).

- Testers must also adjust to the practical realities of the project, such as the budget, the schedule, the skills of the staff, and the availability of suitable tools.

At its core, context-driven testing reflects this dual adjustment: to the needs of the key stakeholders and to the practical realities of the project.

Readings

The following reading is required:

- Kaner, C., Hendrickson, E., & Smith Brock, J. (2001). Managing the proportion of testers to (other) developers. Pacific Northwest Software Quality Conference. Portland, OR. Retrieved from http://www.kaner.com/pdfs/pnsqc_ratio_of_testers.pdf

The following readings are recommended:

- Bach, J. (2006). Heuristic test strategy model, Version 4.8. Retrieved from http://testingeducation.org/BBST/foundations/Bach_satisfice-tsm-4p-1.pdf

- Kaner, C. (1999). Recruiting software testers. Quality Assurance Institute Annual International Quality Conference. Orlando, FL. Retrieved from http://www.kaner.com/pdfs/qaijobs.pdf

- Kohl, J. (2010, August 6). How Do I Create Value with my Testing? Jonathan Kohl's Blog. Retrieved from http://testingeducation.org/BBST/foundations/Kohl_Blog_CreateValue.pdf

Orientation: Role Of The Testing Group

Please try this task before reading the lecture notes or watching the lecture. Spend about 20 minutes on it, not more than an hour. Give yourself enough time to consider your organizational context and briefly but understandably describe it to the other students. After you've written yours, read a few other students' posts. In many classes, we see a *lot* of diversity.

Please describe the role of the test group in your organization. (If you are not working for a company that has a test group, please describe the situation of the test group in some other company that you know.)

- What services does your group provide?

- Try to describe, in one relatively short sentence, the most important value that your group is designed or expected to provide to your company.

- Who does the manager of your group report to? (What is the role of that person? Are they primarily focused on customer support? Product development? Marketing? Corporate quality assurance? Some other function?)

- How large is your group and how does its size compare to the size of the development group(s) whose work you test? Is the balance of work, between you and them, reasonable?

- What are the key organizational challenges for your group? (When we say "organizational challenges," we're thinking about your roles, responsibilities, budget, ability to get training, ability to influence decision-making, etc.)

- How do you think this compares to the "typical" test group?

- How would you change this?

Slides And Notes

SLIDE 58

Welcome to this second lecture on the *Foundations of Software Testing*.

BLACK BOX SOFTWARE TESTING: FOUNDATIONS: LECTURE 2. STRATEGY

CEM KANER, J.D., PH.D.
PROFESSOR OF SOFTWARE ENGINEERING
FLORIDA INSTITUTE OF TECHNOLOGY

REBECCA L. FIEDLER, M.B.A. PH.D.
PRESIDENT: KANER, FIEDLER & ASSOCIATES

JAMES BACH
PRINCIPAL, SATISFICE INC.

This work is licensed under the Creative Commons Attribution License. To view a copy of this license, visit http://creativecommons.org/licenses/by-sa/2.0/ or send a letter to Creative Commons, 559 Nathan Abbott Way, Stanford, California 94305, USA.

These notes are partially based on research that was supported by NSF Grants EIA-0113539 ITR/SY +PE: "Improving the Education of Software Testers" and CCLI-0717613 "Adaptation & Implementation of an Activity-Based Online or Hybrid Course in Software Testing." Any opinions, findings and conclusions or recommendations expressed in this material are those of the author(s) and do not necessarily reflect the views of the National Science Foundation.

58

SLIDE 59

Today we look at how test groups are organized and how they organize their work.

One of today's important lessons is how diverse our field is. We can't point to one main objective or one best strategy for testing or one standard way that test groups are organized. We'll look at several possibilities.

OVERVIEW: FUNDAMENTAL TOPICS

- Why are we testing? What are we trying to learn? How should we organize our work to achieve this? *Information objectives drive the testing mission and strategy*
- How can we know whether a program has passed or failed a test? *Oracles are heuristic*
- How can we determine how much testing has been done? What core knowledge about program internals do testers need to consider this question? *Coverage is a multidimensional problem*
- Are we done yet? *Complete testing is impossible*
- How much testing have we completed and how well have we done it? *Measurement is important, but hard*

59

SLIDE 60

TODAY'S READINGS

Required:

- Cem Kaner, Elisabeth Hendrickson & Jennifer Smith-Brock (2001) , "Managing the proportion of testers to (other) developers."
http://kaner.com/pdfs/pnsqc_ratio_of_testers.pdf

Useful to skim:

- James Bach, "The Heuristic Test Strategy Model"
http://www.satisfice.com/tools/satisfice-tsm-4p.pdf

- Cem Kaner (2000), "Recruiting software testers."
http://kaner.com/pdfs/JobsRev6.pdf

- Jonathan Kohl (2010), "How do I create value with my testing?", http://www.kohl.ca/blog/archives/000217.html

- Karl Popper (2002, 3rd Ed.) , *Conjectures and Refutations: The Growth of Scientific Knowledge (Routledge Classics).*

Your class may use other readings, but we had these in mind when creating this lecture.

60

We have several recommended readings.

The required paper highlights the extent to which testers do different things in different companies.

This is one aspect of understanding how test efforts are organized. My paper on recruiting software testers and Jonathan's paper on value, consider other aspects.

SLIDE 61

Now let's start by considering the definition of testing.

I think Glen Myers' definition is the most popular among testers—we often see ourselves as bug-hunters.

I prefer James Bach's definition because it drives home an important point. Every test is a question. If you already know the answer, it might be a demonstration, but it's not a test.

WHAT IS SOFTWARE TESTING?

Some definitions are simple and straightforward.

Testing is:

- "the process of executing a program with the intent of finding errors."
Glen Myers (1979, p. 5), Art of Software Testing

- "questioning a product in order to evaluate it."
James Bach.

61

SLIDE 62

Many textbook definitions of testing are pretty long because they're trying to describe a complex concept.

_____

_____

_____

_____

_____

_____

_____

_____

WHAT IS SOFTWARE TESTING?

"The process of operating a system or component under specified conditions, observing or recording the results, and making an evaluation of some aspect of the system or component." (IEEE standard 610.12-1990)

"Any activity aimed at evaluating an attribute or capability of a program or system and determining that it meets its required results.... Testing is the measurement of software quality." Bill Hetzel (1988, 2nd ed., p. 6), Complete Guide to Software Testing.

Others are a little more complex

62

SLIDE 63

Here's my working definition. Let's go through it one bit at a time.

_____

_____

_____

_____

_____

_____

_____

_____

_____

SOFTWARE TESTING

- is an empirical
- technical
- investigation
- conducted to provide stakeholders
- with information
- about the quality
- of the product or service under test

63

SLIDE 64

Tests are experiments. We're looking for data. Along with running experiments, testers gather data from other sources, such as technical support records and competing products. These help us understand what the product should do, so that we can design our experiments more effectively and make better sense of our results.

_____

_____

_____

_____

DEFINING TESTING

An empirical
- We gain knowledge from the world, not from theory. (We call our experiments, "tests.")
- We gain knowledge from many sources, including qualitative data from technical support, user experiences, etc.

technical
- We use technical means, including experimentation, logic, mathematics, models, tools (testing-support programs), and tools (measuring instruments, event generators, etc.)

64

SLIDE 65

We test software on behalf of someone else. Those people are our stakeholders.

Most of the time, we test as part of a product development effort, to help the project run better and to improve the product. In these cases, our stakeholders are the product's stakeholders, the people who have a stake—something to gain or to lose—in the success of the project.

Sometimes, though, the success of the testing project is not at all connected to the success of the underlying product.

For example, I worked for a software company that sometimes bought other companies. Part of our process was to evaluate the products of the company we were thinking of buying. If that company's software was buggy or hard for the programmers to maintain, we offered a lot less money or we walked away from the negotiations. Who wants to buy a company that makes second-rate products?

My stakeholders had an interest in the success of my testing project, but my success was in getting them the information they needed, not about making the product I was testing better.

> ### DEFINING TESTING
>
> An empirical, technical ...
>
> **... investigation**
> - An organized and thorough search for information.
> - This is an active process of inquiry. We ask hard questions (aka run hard test cases) and look carefully at the results.
>
> **conducted to provide stakeholders**
> - Someone who has a vested interest in the success of the testing effort
> - Someone who has a vested interest in the success of the product
>
> > A law firm suing a company for having shipped defective software has no interest in the success of the product development effort but a big interest in the success of its own testing project (researching the product's defects).
>
> 65

SLIDE 66

When I say information, I mean that we're learning things that we don't already know. Karl Popper was one of the most influential philosophers of science. His writing is required reading for doctoral students in many fields because of the clarity and importance of his ideas. Popper savaged experiments that were really dressed-up demonstrations. You don't design an experiment to confirm something you already know. Design it to challenge what you believe. Design experiments that are much more likely to fail if you're wrong. This, Popper says, is the essence of research.

> ### DEFINING TESTING
>
> An empirical, technical investigation conducted to provide stakeholders ...
>
> **... with information**
> - The information of interest is **often** about the presence (or absence) of bugs, but other types of information are sometimes more vital to your particular stakeholders
> - In information theory, "information" refers to reduction of uncertainty. A test that will almost certainly give an expected result is not expected to (and not designed to) yield much information.
>
> > Karl Popper argued that experiments designed to confirm an expected result are of far less scientific value than experiments designed to disprove (refute) the hypothesis that predicts the expectation.
> > See his enormously influential book, Conjectures & Refutations.
>
> 66

Many testers run the same set of tests over and over. Every time the programmers change the program, they rerun the old tests and the program passes all or almost all of them, over and over. This isn't testing. Or it's incompetent testing. We learn nothing when the program passes these tests.

People dress up these tests by saying their goal is to confirm that every feature that used to work still works. They call this a best practice. They give it a fancy name, regression testing.

If we followed Popper, we could still test the old features, but we'd use new tests. We want to test each feature more harshly each time, maybe by testing it with more complex data or by testing on different platforms, or it in combination with other features. Whether the program passes or fails the test, we learn something new. This is information.

SLIDE 67

Information – what we learn from our tests – is not necessarily bugs. We want to learn anything about the quality of the software that is useful to our stakeholders.

_____
_____
_____
_____
_____
_____
_____
_____

DEFINING TESTING

An empirical, technical investigation conducted to provide stakeholders with information …

… about the quality
• Value to some person

of the product or service under test
• The product includes the data, documentation, hardware, whatever the customer gets. If it doesn't all work together, it doesn't work.
• A service (such as custom programming) often includes sub services (such as support).
• Most software combines product & service

67

SLIDE 68

Stakeholders don't all have the same information needs. They differ across projects, and across people within the same project.

For example, the sales people might ask you to develop a pre-release demo script for a product. This isn't about looking for bugs. Everyone knows the product doesn't fully work yet, but salespeople need safe scenarios, scenarios that let them avoid the bugs while showing what this product will be able to do when it's done.

The testing you're going to do will depend on your information objectives – the types of information that your stakeholders need.

THERE ARE MANY DIFFERENT INFORMATION OBJECTIVES

• Find important bugs
• Assess the quality of the product
• Help managers assess the progress of the project
• Help managers make release decisions
• Block premature product releases
• Help predict and control product support costs
• Check interoperability with other products
• Find safe scenarios for use of the product
• Assess conformance to specifications
• Certify the product meets a particular standard
• Ensure the testing process meets accountability standards
• Minimize the risk of safety-related lawsuits
• Help clients improve product quality & testability
• Help clients improve their processes
• Evaluate the product for a third party

Different objectives require different testing tools and strategies and will yield different tests, test documentation and test results.

68

_____
_____
_____
_____
_____
_____
_____
_____
_____
_____
_____
_____
_____
_____

SLIDE 69

Different situations will lead to different information objectives. Here's an example of a contrast:

In the first case, the question is whether the product is ready for sale. This is not the test group's decision. But testers can influence it. If you believe the product's in bad shape, you can hunt for bugs that demonstrate just how serious the problems are. If you find a serious enough bug, one of the key stakeholders will decide to hold the release until that bug is fixed. We call that a show-stopper bug.

> ### DIFFERENT CONTEXTS → DIFFERENT INFORMATION OBJECTIVES
>
> | | |
> |---|---|
> | Mass-market software, close to release date. The test group believes the product is too buggy and that better-informed stakeholders wouldn't ship it. | Software fails in use and causes serious losses. A law firm hires testers to determine what caused the failures and when the seller found these bugs. |
> | *These testers are likely to do bug-hunting, looking for important bugs that will cause key stakeholders to reconsider whether they are willing to release the product* | *These testers won't do general bug-hunting. They'll try to determine how (and in how many ways) they can replicate specific failures and they'll study corporate quality records.* |
>
> 69

In the second case, the software has already been released. It failed badly in the field and the test group is working for a lawyer. This group isn't looking for show-stoppers. The show has already happened The group is looking for information that will help the lawyer understand the software's problems and explain them to the judge and jury.

_____

_____

_____

SLIDE 70

On every project, it's useful for the test team to explicitly define its mission. A mission statement is a brief, focused description of a group's or project's core objectives.

On a specific project, your mission is typically to achieve your primary information objective. For example, if your group is tasked with investigating compatibility of a program with a new operating system, your mission is to get that information.

> ### YOUR TESTING MISSION
>
> Your "mission" is your answer to the question, "Why are you testing?"
>
> - Typically, your mission is to achieve your primary information objective(s).
>   - If there are too many objectives, you have a fragmented, and probably unachievable, mission.
>   - Awareness of your mission helps you focus your work. Tasks that help you achieve your mission are obviously of higher priority (or should be) than tasks that don't help you achieve your mission.
>
> 70

Being clear about your mission is important because you don't have enough time to do every test-related task. Tasks that are otherwise worthwhile, but are not relevant to your mission for a given project are probably tasks that you are not going to do for this project.

_____

_____

_____

_____

_____

SLIDE 71

As the project evolves, your mission will probably change. Early in the project, you might do bug hunting. Later, you might help the project manager understand the quality of the software well enough to decide whether or not to release the product. You would test differently for these objectives. The bug-hunter spends most of her time in areas of high risk or unknown risk, not low risk areas that are either almost bug free or that no one cares enough about to fix bugs if bugs are found. In contrast, the status assessor might take a more detailed look at each part of the product, spending much more time than the bug-hunter on low risk areas.

> **YOUR TESTING MISSION(S)**
>
> - The test group's mission probably changes over the course of the project. For example, imagine a 6-month development project, with first code delivery to test in month 2.
> - Month 2 / 3/ 4/ 5 may be bug-hunting
>   - Harsh tests in areas of highest risk.
>   - Exploratory scans for unanticipated areas of risk.
> - Month 6 may be helping the project manager determine whether the product is ready to ship.
>   - Status and quality assessments. Less testing.
>   - Tests include coverage-oriented surveys.
>
> Make your mission explicit. Be wary of trying to achieve several missions at the same time.
>
> 71

SLIDE 72

Once you understand what your mission is, you have to decide how to achieve it. The broad plan for achieving your mission is your strategy.

> **TESTING STRATEGY**
>
> *Given a testing mission, how will you achieve it?*
>
> - We define
>   - *strategy* as the set of ideas that guide your test design
>   - *logistics* as the set of ideas that guide your application of resources, and
>   - *Plan* as the combination of your strategy, your logistics and your project risk management.
>
> See Bach's "Heuristic Test Planning: Context Model" http://www.satisfice.com/tools/satisfice-cm.pdf
>
> 72

SLIDE 73

In particular, the strategy you develop will be your basis for deciding what types of test tools and techniques to use.

> **TESTING STRATEGY**
>
> *Given a testing mission, how will you achieve it?*
>
> - The test strategy takes into account:
>   - Your resources (time, money, tools, etc.)
>   - Your staff's knowledge and skills
>   - What is hard / easy / cheap (etc.) in your project environment
>   - What risks apply to this project
> - To choose the best combination of resources and techniques
>   - that you can realistically bring to bear
>   - to achieve the your mission
>   - as well as you can under the circumstances
>
> See Bach's "Heuristic Test Strategy Model" http://www.satisfice.com/tools/satisfice-cm.pdf
>
> 73

SLIDE 74

The set of possible tests of any nontrivial program is infinite. The designer's task is to create a relatively small set of tests that will expose most of the most significant bugs that you could find if you tested completely.

Testing strategy blends into test design. The overall decisions about which techniques to use or not use are strategic. The decisions about how to use the techniques to create the right set of tests are design decisions.

This slide lists some questions that can guide the strategic and design choices. For example, if your staff are all non-programmers, a strategy that relies on heavily automated tests is likely to fail. We'll look at these in more detail in our course on test design.

> **STRATEGY AND DESIGN**
> Think of the design task as applying the strategy to the choosing of specific test techniques and generating test ideas and supporting data, code or procedures:
> - Who's going to run these tests? (What are their skills / knowledge?)
> - What kinds of potential problems are they looking for?
> - How will they recognize suspicious behavior or "clear" failure? (Oracles?)
> - What aspects of the software are they testing? (What are they ignoring?)
> - How will they recognize that they have done enough of this type of testing?
> - How are they going to test? (What are they actually going to do?)
> - What tools will they use to create or run or assess these tests? (Do they have to create any of these tools?)
> - What is their source of test data? (Why is this a good source? What makes these data suitable?)
> - Will they create documentation or data archives to help organize their work or to guide the work of future testers?
> - What are the outputs of these activities? (Reports? Logs? Archives? Code?)
> - What aspects of the project context will make it hard to do this work?
>
> 74

SLIDE 75

Your choice of techniques matters because you find different things with different techniques. Here are two of the most widely used techniques.

People who understand their own business and wonder how well your program meets their needs will often test with scenarios. A scenario is a story about how people will use software in a real-life situation. The test is designed for realism, not power. Failure indicates that something important is wrong with the software.

In contrast, domain testing is the professional tester's most widely used technique. You might have heard this called equivalence class analysis or boundary testing. Same thing. Imagine testing setting page margins in a word processor—we're testing how much blank space the program leaves between the edge of the printing on the page and the edge of the page. Domain testing checks the extreme cases—the narrowest possible margins and the widest possible margins. Along with mistakes, margins that are a little too narrow or a little too wide. If the program has margin bugs, the extreme value tests will probably expose them quickly. Unlike scenarios, we don't worry about a test's realism. Our question isn't whether people would actually intentionally set margins to these values. It's whether the program can handle them.

Working with different techniques helps you think about the program in different ways, design different tests and find different bugs.

> **TWO EXAMPLES OF TEST TECHNIQUES**
>
> | Scenario testing | Domain testing |
> |---|---|
> | Tests are complex stories that capture how the program will be used in real-life situations. | For every variable or combination of variables, consider the set of possible values. |
> | These are combination tests, whose combinations are credible reflections of real use. | Reduce the set by partitioning into subsets. Pick a few high-risk representatives (e.g. boundary values) of each subset. |
> | These tests are highly credible (stakeholders will believe users will do these things) and so failures are likely to be fixed. | These tests are very powerful. They are more likely to trigger failures, but their reliance on extreme values makes some tests less credible. |
>
> 75

SLIDE 76

James Bach finds it useful to talk about test techniques as if they were recipes. Just as a recipe describes different ingredients and how to combine them, a technique describes several aspects of a type of test.

_____

_____

_____

_____

_____

_____

_____

TEST TECHNIQUES (BACH)

A test technique is like a recipe. It tells you how it puts together some ingredients. Then you vary it to suit your needs.

A technique typically tells you how to do several (rarely all) of these:

- Analyze the situation
- Model the test space
- Select what to cover
- Determine test oracles
- Configure the test system
- Operate the test system
- Observe the test system
- Evaluate the test results

It takes several different recipes to create a complete meal.

76

SLIDE 77

Bach's list considers more issues than any particular technique will address.

For example, domain testing teaches us how to analyze a program. It gives a model that guides design of individual tests. It also suggests where to look to see whether the program passed a test.

But domain testing doesn't specify what equipment to test on or how to set up the lab, who should run the tests, or whether or how to automate the tests. It suggests data to collect, but not how to capture or store that data or whether we could use a tool to interpret test results. Other techniques might focus more on these aspects of testing and less on the others.

DOMAIN TESTING (ILLUSTRATES THE COMPONENTS OF THE RECIPE)

Analyze the situation	We want to imagine the program as a collection of input and output variables. What are their possible values?
Model the test space	Follow a stratified sampling model, biased for higher probability of failure: For each variable, split possible values into groups that are treated equivalently. Consider valid & invalid values. Test at least one from each group, preferably the one most likely to show a failure. Next, test groups of a few variables together, applying a similar analysis.
Select what to cover	Which variables and combinations will we test?
Determine test oracles	Do we look only for input-rejection or output overflow?
Configure the test system	What equipment do we test on? Are we using tools to create tests? Execute them? Set everything up.
Operate the test system	Execute the tests (e.g. run the automation)
Observe the test system	Watch the execution of the tests. Is the system working correctly? (e.g. if human testers follow scripts, what actually happens while they test this way?)
Evaluate the test results	Did the program pass the tests?

77

We'll come back to this list in the course on test design. If you don't see a lot of value in these lists today, don't worry about it. As you gain experience in the field, there will probably be a point at which these lists will help you gain insight into the meaning of test techniques and test strategies, and how to pick techniques that balance each other's weaknesses and blind spots. Later still, you'll probably outgrow these lists and develop your own way to characterize and compare strategies and techniques.

But for now, as you learn more about test techniques, you might get to a point where you feel as though you're drowning in unrelated details. When you get there, think of these lists as stepping stones for a river of confusion. They're not perfect, and they're a little slippery, but if you need the help, they're what we've got.

_____

_____

_____

_____

SLIDE 78

So far today, we've hit six major concepts.

We test in order to find quality-related information for our stakeholders

We focus our testing to make sure we achieve our information objectives. On a given project, our mission is to achieve those objectives, to get the specific types of information that our stakeholders need.

To achieve our mission, we develop a strategy. For our purposes today, the main component of the testing strategy is the guidance it gives us on what test techniques we should use, and when, and how much we should rely on each.

For the rest of today, we'll consider how testing efforts are organized.

> **REVIEW**
>
> So far today:
> - Testing
> - Stakeholders
> - Information objectives
> - Mission
> - Strategy
> - Test techniques
>
> Next:
> - How is the testing effort organized?
>
> 78

SLIDE 79

There is no one way to organize a testing effort.

But let me start with an example that is fairly typical.

SoftCo creates software that it sells to other people, in this case tax preparation software. Their customers buy the finished product and an update service. They can probably cancel at any time.

SoftCo writes and tests its own code. Programmers, managers, testers, technical support staff and executives all work in the same building. Testers have the opportunity to meet other influential people in the company and to build up social relationships with them.

> **A "TYPICAL" CONTEXT**
>
> SoftCo creates tax preparation software.
> - Sell 100,000 copies per year
> - Two planned updates (incorporating changes in the tax code twice per year.)
> - Used by consumers and some paid preparers of tax returns
> - Programming and testing are done within the company, at the same corporate headquarters.
> - Test group (4 or more testers) reports to its own manager.
>
> *How will this project work?*
>
> This is like the projects we had in mind in *Testing Computer Software*.
>
> 79

The company even has informal meetings and celebrations to encourage its staff to get to know each other. People, including testers, take each other out for dinner or for friendly conversations at the local pub or café and when the need arises for discussions about troubled projects that go around the formal chain of command in the company. Those discussions are made possible through the informal network.

This informal communication network is a common feature of American companies, especially companies that produce intellectual property, like software.

SLIDE 80

Across companies, test groups differ enormously. Some companies call their staff testers, business analysts, or quality engineers, or software development engineers in test. The name doesn't matter. What does matter is how diverse the group is. Some companies try to hire people with similar backgrounds, similar education, skills, attitudes—and with that, come similar weaknesses and blind spots. I don't think this works very well.

If I was hiring for SoftCo's test group, I'd look for a very diverse set of skills. SoftCo makes tax preparation software, so they do a lot of database access and a lot of calculation. I'd like testers who understand how to break databases and how to confuse programs that work with numbers.

I'd go to law schools and recruit recent graduates who specialize in tax law. These would be my group's subject matter experts. If I was writing factory automation software, I'd find someone who understands factories.

As a test manager, I develop an understanding of the types of information that my group will often be asked to provide, and I recruit people who are really good with each of those types of information.

The result is a group in which every person is special, every person can cross-train every other person, every person offers value, and every person has their own opportunity to gain the respect of many different stakeholders.

> **A "TYPICAL" CONTEXT: TYPICAL GROUP**
>
> SoftCo's test group includes:
> - Tester skilled with databases and calculations
> - Bug-hunter
> - Tool smith
> - Tax lawyer (subject matter expert)
> - Tester interested in network issues (including security & performance)
> - Configuration tester
> - Writer (writes test docs well)
> - Test group manager
>
> See Kaner (2000), "Recruiting Software Testers", http://www.kaner.com/pdfs/JobsRev6.pdf
>
> The details of this list are less important than the diversity of this group. Everyone is particularly good at something. Collectively, they will be expert at testing this class of application.
>
> 80

SLIDE 81

Test groups do many tasks. The ones I describe here are commonplace among software publishers.

Testers become experts in the product, including its market, its potential users and uses, the ways it can fail and their possible consequences. The testers analyze specifications, hunt for bugs, and develop tools – their tools might be code or specially designed data sets or procedures – these tools will help them be more efficient in the future.

When testers find bugs, including design bugs, they research them well enough to write reports that make clear what the problem is and why it's important.

Testers also make good use of the the company's informal communication networks to find out more of what's going on and to help other people understand the status of the project.

> **A "TYPICAL" CONTEXT: TYPICAL TASKS**
>
> - Research ways this product can fail or be unsatisfactory (essentially a requirements analysis from a tester's point of view)
> - Hunt bugs (exploratory risk-based testing)
> - Analyze the specification and create tests that trace to spec items of interest
> - Create sets of test data with well-understood attributes (to be used in several tests and archived)
> - Create reusable tests (manual or automated)
> - Create checklists for manual testing or to guide automation
> - Research failures and write well-researched, persuasive bug reports
>
> **Most in-house test groups do most of these tasks.**
>
> 81

SLIDE 82

This slide describes these tasks in something of a time line.

There are variations across companies, but as a rule developed over the past 27 years, when I visit a software company or a company that makes hardware products that have customer-visible embedded software, like cell phones, I have come to expect these activities to be seen as normal things for testers to do.

Note how many of these tasks are not strictly about hunting for bugs, writing bug reports, or designing and automating tests.

A "TYPICAL" CONTEXT: TASKS OVER TIME

- Testers get notes on what changes are coming, perhaps on a product-development group wiki. The notes are informal, incomplete, and have conflicting information. Testers ask questions, request testability features, and may add suggestions based on technical support data, etc.
- Throughout the project, testers play with competitors' products and/or read books/magazines about what products like this **should** do.
- Programmers deliver some working features (mods to current shipping release) to testers. New delivery every week (delivery every day toward the end of the project).
- Testers start testing (learn the new stuff, hunt for bugs) and writing tests and test data for reuse.
- Once the program stabilizes enough, design/run tests for security, performance, longevity, huge databases with interacting features' data, etc.
- Testers hang out with programmers to learn more about this product's risks.
- Later in the project, some testers refocus, to write status reports or run general regression tests, create final release test.
- Help close project's details in preparation for release.

Along with "testing", these testers are involved in a diverse set of quality-related activities and release-support activities. These groups' scope varies over time and across test managers' and execs' attitudes.

82

SLIDE 83

The diversity of tasks in typical test groups becomes even more apparent when you consider the activities in this list. I'm never surprised to see a test group that does some of these tasks. Most test groups do some of these tasks, but they differ a lot as to which of these tasks.

_____

_____

_____

_____

_____

_____

A "TYPICAL" CONTEXT: LESS COMMON TASKS

- Write requirements
- Participate in inspections and walkthroughs
- Compile the software
- Conduct glass box tests
- Write installers
- Configure and maintain programming-related tools, such as the source control system
- Archive the software
- Investigate bugs, analyzing the source code to discover the underlying errors
- Evaluate the reliability of components that the company is thinking of using in its software
- Provide technical support
- Demonstrate the product at trade shows or internal company meetings

Few test groups provide all these services, but many in-house test groups provide several. The more of these your staff provides, the more testers and the more skill-set diversity you need. See Kaner, Hendrickson & Smith-Brock for discussion

83

SLIDE 84

It's rare for a company's testers to do all of these things. For example, a company that treats its testers as part of the programming team is less likely to build a close collaboration between the testers and sales or marketing or customer support.

_____

_____

_____

_____

_____

_____

_____

_____

A "TYPICAL" CONTEXT: LESS COMMON TASKS

- Train new users (or tech support or training staff) in the use of the product
- Provide risk assessments
- Collect and report statistical data (software metrics) about the project
- Build and maintain internal test-related tools such as the bug tracking system
- Benchmark competing products
- Evaluate market significance of various hardware/software configurations (to inform their choices of configuration tests)
- Conduct usability tests
- Lead or audit efforts to comply with regulatory or industry standards (such as those published by SEI, ISO, IEEE, FDA, etc.)
- Provide project management services.

These illustrate tradeoffs between "independence" and "collaboration." Groups that see themselves as fundamentally independent provide a narrower range of services and have a narrower range of influence.

84

SLIDE 85

Let me distinguish between the mission for a specific testing project and the mission of the group as a whole.

For the project, your mission is dictated by the needs of your stakeholders. But for the group, the mission reflects the group's self-image or its reason for existing.

If we think in terms of the services test groups provide, some see themselves purely as bug-hunters. Many others see themselves as quality advocates or even as quality enforcers. Others see themselves as fully integrated into the development group and provide several types of services intended to make the overall group more effective and more efficient.

MISSIONS (IN-HOUSE)

- The typical missions that I've encountered when working with in-house test groups at mass-market software publishers have been much broader than bug-hunting.
- I would summarize some of the most common ones as follows (Note: a single testing project operates under one mission at a time):
  - Bug hunters
  - Quality advocacy
  - Development support
  - Release management
  - Support cost reduction

Many group's missions include their core goal for their own staff. For example, a group might see the services it provides as vehicles to support the education or career growth of its staff.

85

SLIDE 86

The tester's world changes a bit in IT organizations.

Software publishers sell the products that their development groups create.

In contrast, companies don't sell what their information technology groups create. The IT organization is part of the company's infrastructure, not part of its product or service development.

Many American companies treat their development, production and sales organizations much more generously and with more respect than their infrastructure. They distinguish between profit centers and cost centers. They work aggressively to squeeze the costs out of their cost centers. Many of these companies see IT as a cost center.

CHANGE OF CONTEXT: IN-HOUSE IT?

- Several in-house IT organizations are reorganizing testing to try to get comparable benefits.
- I have no sense of industry statistics because the people who contact me have a serious problem and are willing to entertain my ideas on how to fix it.
- These managers complain about:
  - Ineffectiveness of their testers
  - Attention to process instead of quality
  - Lack of product / service knowledge
  - Lack of collaboration

An executive at a huge company explained to me why they were outsourcing testing.

"We can't get good testing from our own staff. If I have to get bad testing, I want it cheap."

86

I have seen effective test groups in IT organizations, with skilled, career-satisfied testers. But I've also seen fundamental incompetence in many IT test groups, and I've seen it tolerated for longer than I would ever expect in a publisher. Worse, I've met too many consultants and conference speakers who cater to incompetence in IT testing by spreading tolerance for whining, excuse-making and obstructionist attitudes.

If it's not absolutely clear what your value is to your company: how your services contribute to the effectiveness and success of IT and how IT contributes to the success of the company—and especially if the tasks you do are routine, essentially mindless tasks, your salary is probably going nowhere and your days in this job are probably numbered.

SLIDE 87

Another type of test group is fully independent. When we talk about outsourcing, we're talking about retaining a separate test organization to do the testing, usually because the outsourcer's services are perceived as cheaper.

_____

_____

_____

_____

_____

_____

_____

> **CHANGE OF CONTEXT: EXTERNAL LAB**
>
> People send their products for testing by an external lab for many reasons:
> - The lab might offer specific skills that the original development company lacks.
> - The customer (such as a government agency) might require a vendor to have the software tested by an independent lab because it doesn't trust the vendor
> - The company developing the software might perceive the outsourcer's services as cheaper
>
> 87

SLIDE 88

Testing by an external lab is fundamentally different from testing in-house. They might have better tools. They might have better skills. Or they might not, too.

But what they lack is expertise in their client's business. The external test group is rarely an expert in its client company's products or their market. And their links to the client's informal communications network are probably pretty weak.

The external lab probably looks mainly for obvious bugs or mismatches between the product's behavior and what is laid out in a set of documents.

> **CHANGE OF CONTEXT: EXTERNAL LAB**
>
> | DIFFERENCE | CONSEQUENCES |
> |---|---|
> | They might be more skilled with some testing technology or at some specific testing tasks | • They might be more effective in some types of tests, e.g. producing better scripts (automated) faster for routine (e.g. domain) techniques |
> | They don't understand our market (expectations, risks, needed benefits, competitors) or the idiosyncratic priorities of our key stakeholders. | • They probably won't be as good at benefit-driven testing (e.g. scenario)
• Their exploratory tests will be less well informed by knowledge of this class of product
• Their design critiques in bug reports will be less credible and less welcome |
> | They don't have collaborative opportunities with local developers and stakeholders | • They will need more supporting documentation
• They will generate more documentation and need it reviewed
• They will be unavailable or ineffective for collaborative bug-fixing, release mgmt. etc. |
>
> When I talk of "bug advocacy", friends whose experience is entirely "independent lab" think I am talking about pure "theory." Context constrains what tester roles are possible, and that shapes the possible missions.
>
> 88

Remember, the difference between verification and validation. Verification is about asking whether a product was built correctly. Test labs usually do verification.

In contrast, validation is about asking whether the right product was built. When a tester argues that the product won't serve the needs of its users, her perspective is validation.

Most companies don't expect external labs to do validation. Some react with hostility to external labs' critiques of the product's design or its value for its intended market.

That doesn't mean that external labs can't do validation. But if you're a tester or test manager in a lab and that's a service you want to provide, you need to work this explicitly out with your client.

So how do we deal with all this organizational variation in this course? I think we have to make some assumptions. For the rest of this course, I'll assume that you are either working for a software publisher or for a competent test group within an IT organization. Most of what I'll present will be appropriate for external labs doing verification, but you need to supply your own relevance filter.

SLIDE 89

BLACK BOX SOFTWARE TESTING: FOUNDATIONS

END OF LECTURE 2

CEM KANER, J.D., PH.D.
PROFESSOR OF SOFTWARE ENGINEERING
FLORIDA INSTITUTE OF TECHNOLOGY

REBECCA L. FIEDLER, M.B.A. PH.D.
PRESIDENT: KANER, FIEDLER & ASSOCIATES

JAMES BACH
PRINCIPAL, SATISFICE INC.

These notes are partially based on research that was supported by NSF Grants EIA-0113539 ITR/SY +PE "Improving the Education of Software Testers" and CCLI-0717613 "Adaptation & Implementation of an Activity-Based Online or Hybrid Course in Software Testing." Any opinions, findings and conclusions or recommendations expressed in this material are those of the author(s) and do not necessarily reflect the views of the National Science Foundation.

89

Application: Mission Of Testing

The goal of this activity is to apply what you've just learned about the mission of testing.

Imagine testing a program that includes spreadsheet features. Your work will be focused on testing those features. Please consider doing that work in each of the five contexts that follow.

- Your goal is to gain insight into how the differences in these contexts will drive differences in the testing mission and strategy.

- To answer the discussion questions for each of the five contexts, you will need to keep your answers short. Don't write more than a page per context. (Half a page is probably enough.)

- You should not spend more than 90 minutes on this task. If you reach 90 minutes and you have answered these questions for at least two contexts, stop and submit your work.

The Contexts

- Context 1: Early development in a somewhat-agile environment

  You are working as a tester, not as a programmer. The project manager assigns you to the development team early in the project. She wants you to test along with the programmers as they write code. Her primary goal is to reduce implementation-related risk in the project. She wants you to help the programmers deliver clean code and she wants you to help her and her staff identify, understand and control the implementation-risks.

- Context 2: Late in development

  You have joined the project close to the project's release date. Your company will release the product to the general public (a consumer product) or to another organization in your company or another company. Whoever you are releasing the product to, they expect it to work and they need it to work well. The project manager expects you to test the product in ways that will help her understand whether the product is ready to release, and if not, how close to releasable quality it is.

- Context 3: Custom software

  Your company is doing custom software development, writing this program for someone else, to a specification that was negotiated and incorporated into the development contract. Your objective is to test the program in a way that lets you determine whether it will be acceptable to the customer (as indicated by conformity with the specification).

- Context 4: Medical software

  You have joined the development team for a spreadsheet component of a product that will be used in medical services, to track treatment history, prescriptions, etc. Doctors and nurses will rely on the information stored here when medicating or otherwise treating their patients. Your objective is to test in whatever way will most help the company get approval of the US Food & Drug Administration. (If you are not in the United States, think of approval by the main regulatory organization in your country's government that is responsible for the safety and reliability of medical technology.

- Context 5: Computer game

  You have joined the development team for a role-playing computer game. The spreadsheet features will keep track of character attributes, for example the character's experience points, health, age, and equipment or spells it is carrying.

For each of these contexts, write a report that answers the following discussion questions:

1. What is your primary information objective?

2. What is the mission of your testing?

3. What do you think a good strategy would be for your testing? Please give a *short* answer to this that considers the following questions:

   - How aggressively should you hunt for bugs? Why?

   - Which bugs (or types of bugs) are more important than most others? Why?

   - Which bugs (or types of bugs) are less important than most others? Why?

   - If you know some testing techniques, are there any you would consider particularly important for this context? Why are they so important for this context? Are there any techniques that are significantly less important for this context? Which one(s) and why?

   - Suppose that you are testing a numeric input field. The specification says that the field must accept single digits but it does not say how the program should respond to letters. Should you test with letters? Why or why not? Would you change your answer (and if you would, how would you change it) if you are pressed for time and you have to not test something else in order to have time to test for error-handling (like letter-handling) here.

   - How extensively will you document your work, and why?

A Few Suggestions

If you generate answers that are pretty much the same for each of the five contexts, you aren't considering the differences among the contexts carefully enough. Even if we were testing the same spreadsheet features in each case, we would approach the testing of them very differently in each of these contexts. You should, too.

Don't try to write a test plan. Don't tell us how you will test each feature. Don't give script-like instructions. Don't describe the details of individual test cases unless you need a small number of specific examples to help you explain your much more general ideas about the testing strategy as a whole.

Working With A Study Group

If you're working through this book on your own, try to find some other people who want to work through the book too. If you work with a few other people, you can read and critique each other's answers. If you can't create a study group, try to find someone who is willing to be your coach while you work through the book. You want someone who has testing experience, who is willing to read your answers and give you feedback. The ideal reviewer will have taken this course and become familiar with this task already.

Once you complete your work, share it with others in your group. Read answers from two other students and comment on those answers.

Here are some questions to consider as you review other students' work:

- What were the three most significant similarities between the other student's work and yours?

- What were the three most significant differences?

- What did you learn from the other student's answers?

- What guidance do classmates offer to the student whose work you are reviewing, to help the author write a better second draft?

After you have done this for two students, reflect on your own answers:

- What was particularly good about your work?

- What changes would you make to achieve a better second draft? (Don't actually write a second draft. The notes you create as you do your reflection will be sufficient for you to get the learning benefit.)

When you review someone else's work, it is easy to say that they did a great job, without saying much beyond that. Don't do that. Give specific positive and negative feedback. The vague, general flattery doesn't take any time, but it doesn't teach you anything and it doesn't help the person who gets it.

Feedback: On Reflections

When you do a task, set your finished work aside for a few days. Read new information (such as answers from other students) about the task and how to do it. Then go back and reread what you wrote. Read it as if you were reading someone else's work. What are its strengths and weaknesses? How can it be improved?

This activity is called a *reflection*. (We use the same name for the document you create that presents your reflection-activity's questions and answers).

Reflections are not easy. It can be hard to step back from your own work and critique it. It can be hard to tell other people the ways in which a piece of your work is weak. It can be hard to admit to yourself (or to others) that someone else did a better job than you. It can be hard to imagine and describe possible improvements.

Yes, reflections are hard work, but they make you ask questions that will build your insight into your own work and the work of others. They encourage you to describe your concerns and your ideas with specificity. This is much more instructionally effective than simply reading someone else's answers. You will learn more from it and you will be able to describe what you learned more easily.

Authors' Reflection On Lesson 2

Distinguishing between testing mission, testing strategy, and test design is very challenging for students who are just learning about testing. We teach the distinctions again in the *Test Design* course, after the students have learned about many test techniques and ways to compare and contrast the techniques. Even with this second exposure, keeping these concepts distinct and clear is difficult for many students. People generally develop a sense of these concepts as they gain experience. Until they have enough experience, we think they will find these distinctions hard.

The difficulties keep motivating us to try new versions of the orientation activity and the application activity. Both of these have strong roots in what we've tried before, but the versions presented in this workbook are substantially different from the 2010 release of *Foundations*..

The most significant difference lies in the Application activity, in which students compare testing strategies across contexts. This is a big task. It can be very time consuming. To limit the task, we used to assign one context per student. You might be tempted to take that kind of "divide and conquer" approach with your study group. This didn't work well. The students thought mainly about their own context. When they saw a different analysis for a different context, they often interpreted the differences as driven by individuals (one person does things one way, a different person does things differently) rather than as arising from a difference in contexts. Those individual differences created a distraction.

This book's version of that activity will take you longer to complete but we think it will teach you more.

3

LESSON 3: ORACLES

Lesson Introduction

This lesson introduces you to *oracles*.

The classical view of oracles is that they are mechanisms for determining whether a program has passed or failed a test. For example, see Miller & Howden (1978) and Wikipedia: *Oracle_(software_testing)*. Along with this idea of the oracle, there is a classical idea that testers will (or even *must*) have an oracle for every test. Thus, for example, Glen Myers (1979) tells us that we must have an expected result for every test.

This lesson presents a different view. Ideally, you will take three things away:

1. *No test has one true oracle. The best we can achieve are useful approximations.* We think that Elaine Weyuker (1980) was the first author to point this out. Douglas Hoffman (1998) published a pair of diagrams that illustrate the core problem. We expect you to understand and remember these diagrams and their implications. When you specify a test, you decide some things that you will intentionally do and some behaviors of the software under test that you will intentionally look at as results of the test. But your specification is necessarily incomplete.

It does not describe all aspects of the hardware and software state, before or after the test. For example, how often do you specify how fragmented the computer's memory will be before and after a test? Because of this, oracles are usually useful but they *can* be wrong: The program can appear to pass a test while failing in ways that you do not notice, or it can appear to fail even though it is actually responding appropriately. A decision rule that is fallible but useful is called a *heuristic*. All oracles are heuristics.

2. *We can describe the process of deciding that a program probably passed or failed a test as the outcome of a comparison and identify several widely-used comparators.* For example, you might decide that the program under test is probably broken because its behavior is inconsistent with what it did before, or inconsistent with the behavior of an important behavior, or inconsistent with the behavior described in a specification. We expect students to learn the *consistency heuristics* presented in Bolton's (2005) *Testing without a map*.

3. *It is useful to have a collection of many very specific oracle heuristics to support test automation.* If a program is supposed to calculate the square root of 4 and it gives 3 instead of 2, that's a bug. When testing a function that takes square roots, you might check whether the program's outputs match the outputs of another square-root calculator that you trust. You might square a square root to see if you get back the original number. You might check whether repeatedly taking square roots uses up memory. None of these tests is comprehensive—the program can fail in ways that these tests will not notice—but each of these tests describes a specific comparison that is useful and that can be automated. You could test a billion square roots in any or all of these ways. The lecture slides provide a long table of examples of these types of oracles.

The most serious weakness of this lesson is that it overemphasizes (1) and (2) relative to (3). The consistency heuristics are intellectually satisfying because they capture and classify most (maybe all) types of oracles. But they are a generalization. They don't present the design details that we find useful to automate our testing. We draw your attention back to the specific oracles in the quizzes and study guide questions (and later, in the *BBST Test Design* course).

Readings

The following reading is required:

- Bolton, M. (2005, January). Testing wtihout a map. Better Software, 25–28. http://testingeducation. org/BBST/foundations/Bolton_2005-01-TestingWithoutAMap.pdf

The following readings are recommended:

- Kelly, M. (2006, April 28). Using Heuristic Test Oracles. informIT. Retrieved from http://www. testingeducation.org/BBST/foundations/Kelly_UsingTestOracles.pdf

- Koen, B. (2011, September 1). The Engineering Method and the Heuristic: A Personal History. Retrieved from http://testingeducation.org/BBST/foundations/Koen_EngineeringMethod.pdf

- Weyuker, E. (1982). On Testing Non-Testable Programs. *The Computer Journal*, 25(4), 463–470. http://testingeducation.org/BBST/foundations/Weyuker_ontestingnontestable.pdf

Orientation: Testing A Word Processor

Please try this task before reading the lecture notes or watching the lecture. Spend at least 15 minutes on it, preferably 30 minutes. Give yourself enough time to appreciate the difficulty of this task but don't spend more than 45 minutes.

The overall goal of this activity is to get you thinking about the question: *How can you tell whether the program is operating correctly?* The setting for the activity is something you have probably worked with many times—a text editor that can display characters on the screen in many different fonts.

Your task is to determine whether text on the screen is displayed in the correct font.

Please answer these questions:

1. How could you determine whether the editor is displaying text in the correct typeface?

2. How could you determine whether the editor is displaying text in the right size?

3. How would you test whether the editor displays text correctly (in any font that the user specifies)?

Please describe your thinking about this problem in general and describe any specific strategies that you are considering.

Terminology Notes

A font is a set of characters of a single size of a typeface. For example,

- the font of this paragraph is Palatino, size 10 points

- the font of this paragraph is Palatino, size 12 points.

- ### the font of this paragraph is Palatino, size 14 points.

- the font of this paragraph is Gill Sans, size 10 points.

- the font of this paragraph is Gill Sans, size 12 points.

- ### the font of this paragraph is Gill Sans, size 14 points.

In these examples, *Palatino* and *Gill Sans* are the names of two *typefaces*. A program could display text in the correct typeface but the wrong size or the right size but the wrong typeface.

People normally talk about type sizes in terms of *points*. A point is approximately $1/_{72}$ of an inch. However, as you can see in the examples above, point sizes are not precisely mapped to sizes of letters. The letters in one 12-point font (such as Palatino) can be larger or smaller than the letters in a different 12-point font (such as Gill Sans).

For more on typefaces, fonts and point sizes, see

- https://en.wikipedia.org/wiki/Font

- https://en.wikipedia.org/wiki/Point_%28typography%29

- https://en.wikipedia.org/wiki/Computer_font

Some Things to Consider In Your Answer

If you are thinking of a strategy that would require an infinite amount of time, you can't do that. Try to think of a way to do this testing that you can actually finish.

You cannot test every possible font. There are tens of thousands of different fonts. If someone uses a font that you did not specifically test, how will you know from your testing whether the program will display that one correctly?

Computer fonts are supplied to the computer in files. Sometimes, the content of a font file contains errors. If the program appears to misbehave when it displays a set of characters in that font, how will you know whether the program is in the program or in the font file?

Slides And Notes

SLIDE 90

Welcome to this third lecture of the *Foundations of Software Testing*.

BLACK BOX SOFTWARE TESTING: FOUNDATIONS:

LECTURE 3. ORACLES

CEM KANER, J.D., PH.D.
PROFESSOR OF SOFTWARE ENGINEERING
FLORIDA INSTITUTE OF TECHNOLOGY

REBECCA L. FIEDLER, M.B.A. PH.D.
PRESIDENT: KANER FIEDLER & ASSOCIATES

JAMES BACH
PRINCIPAL, SATISFICE INC.

This work is licensed under the Creative Commons Attribution License. To view a copy of this license, visit http://creativecommons.org/licenses/by-sa/2.0/ or send a letter to Creative Commons, 559 Nathan Abbott Way, Stanford, California 94305, USA.

These notes are partially based on research that was supported by NSF Grants EIA-0113539 ITR/SY +PE: "Improving the Education of Software Testers" and CCLI-0717613 "Adaptation & Implementation of an Activity-Based Online or Hybrid Course in Software Testing." Any opinions, findings and conclusions or recommendations expressed in this material are those of the author(s) and do not necessarily reflect the views of the National Science Foundation.

90

SLIDE 91

The question I want to consider today is how to tell whether a program passed or failed one of our tests.

OVERVIEW: FUNDAMENTAL TOPICS

- Why are we testing? What are we trying to learn? How should we organize our work to achieve this? *Information objectives drive the testing mission and strategy*
- How can we know whether a program has passed or failed a test? *Oracles are heuristic* ⇐
- How can we determine how much testing has been done? What core knowledge about program internals do testers need to consider this question? *Coverage is a multidimensional problem*
- Are we done yet? *Complete testing is impossible*
- How much testing have we completed and how well have we done it? *Measurement is important, but hard*

91

SLIDE 92

TODAY'S READINGS

Required:

- Michael Bolton (2005), "Testing without a map," http://www.developsense.com/articles/2005-01-TestingWithoutAMap.pdf

Useful to skim:

- James Bach (2010), "The essence of heuristics", http://www.satisfice.com/blog/archives/462
- Michael Kelly (2006), "Using Heuristic Test Oracles", http://www.informit.com/articles/article.aspx?p=463947
- Billy V. Koen (1985), *Definition of the Engineering Method*, American Society for Engineering Education (ASEE). (A later version that is more thorough but maybe less approachable is *Discussion of the Method*, Oxford University Press, 2003).
- Billy V. Koen (2002), "The Engineering Method and the Heuristic: A Personal History", http://www.me.utexas.edu/~koen/OUP/HeuristicHistory.html
- Elaine Weyuker (1980), "On testing nontestable programs", http://ia311202.us.archive.org/1/items/ontestingnontest00weyu/ontestingnontest00weyu.pdf

Your class may use other readings, but we had these in mind when creating this lecture.

92

Today's main reading is Michael Bolton's *"Testing without a map,"* which explains his and James Bach's list of oracle heuristics.

SLIDE 93

In testing, an oracle is usually described as tool that helps the tester decide whether a program passed or failed a test. The general form of the definition includes any kind of mechanism used by the tester, even a specification. The narrower form is a reference program. For example, we can tell if one spreadsheet calculates correctly by comparing its results to another spreadsheet.

ONCE UPON A TIME...

There used to be two common descriptions of "oracles:

1. An oracle is a mechanism for determining whether the program passed or failed a test.
2. An oracle is a reference program. If you give the same inputs to the software under test and the oracle, you can tell whether the software under test passed by comparing its results to the oracle's.

93

SLIDE 94

Here are a few other oracle-related terms that I'll use freely throughout these lectures.

_____

_____

_____

_____

_____

_____

_____

_____

_____

_____

A LITTLE MORE TERMINOLOGY

SUT: Software (or system) under test. Similarly for the application under test (AUT) and the program under test (PUT).

Reference program: If we evaluate the behavior of the SUT by comparing it to another program's behavior, the second program is the reference program or the **reference oracle**.

Comparator: the software or human that compares the behavior of the SUT to the oracle.

94

SLIDE 95

Testing would be a lot easier if we had real oracles. But we don't.

Consider the reference oracle, for example. When we compare calculations in two spreadsheets, both will match but be wrong, whenever the two programs have the same error. Nancy Leveson's work on safety-critical systems demonstrated that this happens more often than you might think. Different implementations can depend on the same wrong algorithm or the same common misunderstanding of the algorithm.

> *Unfortunately, the ideas underlying the common oracle definitions are wrong.*

95

In addition, the spreadsheet under test might be right, but mismatch the reference spreadsheet because the reference oracle has a bug.

So, sometimes a reference program lets us miss a bug and other times, it points out something that isn't a bug at all.

SLIDE 96

Elayne Weyuker published a brilliant paper in 1980 that demonstrated that in most cases, the traditional oracles simply don't exist. She then laid out ideas for what we'll call heuristic oracles in today's lectures.

_____

_____

_____

_____

ORACLE

"The **oracle assumption** ... states that the tester is able to determine whether or not the output produced on the test data is correct. The mechanism which checks this correctness is known as an oracle.

"Intuitively, it does not seem unreasonable to require that the tester be able to determine the correct answer in some 'reasonable' amount of time while expending some 'reasonable' amount of effort. **Therefore, if either of the following two conditions occur, a program should be considered nontestable.**

"1) There does not exist an oracle.

"2) It is theoretically possible, but practically too difficult to determine the correct output." (Pages 1-2)

"Many, if not most programs are by our definition nontestable." (Page 6)

Weyuker, "On testing nontestable programs", 1980. http://ia311202.us.archive.org/1/items/ontestingnontest00weyu/ontestingnontest00weyu.pdf

96

SLIDE 97

The problem is that there are few or no guaranteed-to-be-correct mechanisms for checking the correctness of a test result. Instead, when we compare a test result to an expected result, we have to make a judgment.

And our judgment is fallible. And so is our data.

_____

_____

_____

_____

THE NEED FOR JUDGMENT
- When we describe **testing** as a
  - **process of comparing empirical results to expected results**
- We must consider that even the basic process of **comparison**
  - **requires human judgment, based on an understanding of the problem domain**

97

SLIDE 98

If you look at software engineering standards documents, like IEEE Standard 829, they expect every test case to be fully specified. This includes all of the input conditions, including the test environment, along with the expected result.

_____

_____

_____

_____

_____

Let's start by considering how we specify a test

98

SLIDE 99

But how _do_ you specify your test environment?

Here's a snapshot of the task manager window on my computer. All of these programs are memory resident. Most start up when I boot my computer. I have no idea how to tell what version of these programs I'm running.

Programs running in parallel with the program under test can affect the behavior of the program under test. They can interfere with its access to system resources, they can slow it down, and sometimes they can access the same parts of memory.

CAN YOU SPECIFY _YOUR_ TEST CONFIGURATION?

Comparison to a reference function is fallible. We only control some inputs and observe some results (outputs).

For example, do you know whether test & reference systems are equivalently configured?

- Does your test documentation specify ALL the processes running on your computer?
- Does it specify what version of each one?
- **Do you even know how to tell:**
  - What version of each of these you are running?
  - When you (or your system) last updated each one?
  - Whether there is a later update?

99

I've run into enough failures over the years that were eventually traced to interaction with a memory-resident program that I see these as obviously relevant to every test.

I've only rarely seen a test that specifies all of the versions of all the memory-resident programs. And that specification would be pointless because any of these can be updated without you realizing it.

SLIDE 100

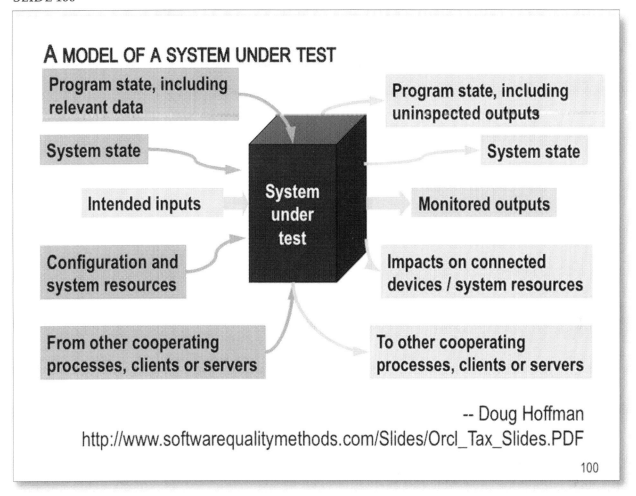

Weyuker's work was profoundly ignored by the academic software engineering community. It took 18 years before Doug Hoffman thought through the same problems and brought the same problem to a conference of testing practitioners. Their jaws dropped when they saw this chart.

When we run a test, we specify inputs and we look at outputs. For our inputs, we can specify as much we choose, including details about our system configuration as well as the specific data that we feed to the program.

But we always leave some things unspecified. When was the last time you saw a test that specified all the memory-resident programs? Or how much free memory and free hard disk space the system had? Or what time of day, or which day of the month, the test should be run? Usually, these are irrelevant. But not always. That's one of the key causes of hard-to-reproduce bugs. The bug depends on something that we're not aware of, and not intentionally manipulating.

In addition, we don't look at all the outputs. Imagine giving a program that adds numbers 2 and 3. The program gives back 5, like it should. Did it pass the test? Maybe. But what if it took 6 hours of calculations to give you that result? Wouldn't that be unacceptable? How often do you measure the time it takes to get the result as part of your test? Many automated tests are written to be completely blind to this. As long as they eventually get 5 as the answer to 2+3, they report a pass.

SLIDE 101

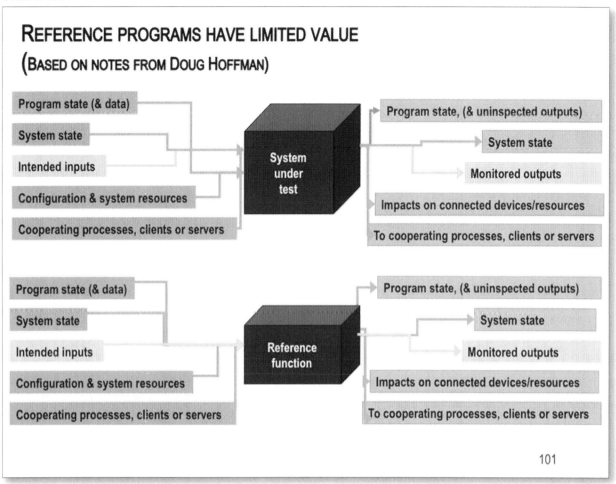

Hoffman continued by discussing the reference oracle. Now we have two programs with inputs. We say we give the same input to each and monitor the same outputs, but comparisons are even harder. Do we check whether the first program uses the same amount of memory as the second? Or takes the same time?

All that we can say is that they behave similarly in the ways that we think they should behave similarly, to the extent that we are noticing how they behave.

SLIDE 102

Suppose you decide to measure response time for every test. Now if the program takes an hour to add 2 plus 3, you'll notice it. But what about memory use? Or the extent to which memory is fragmented? Or what's on the disk? Or whether your program contains malware that triggers an explosion of emails whenever you use a feature that should have nothing to do with email.

Hoffman concluded that we can't monitor every potentially relevant aspect of our input or of our output. All we can do is hope that, most of the time, the variables we are not monitoring are not relevant when we decide whether the program passed or failed a test.

> **OUR OBSERVATIONS CAN FAIL IN MANY WAYS**
>
> Selective attention and inattentional blindness
> - Humans (often) don't see what they don't pay attention to.
> - Programs don't see what they haven't been told to pay attention to.
>
> This is often the cause of irreproducible failures. We pay attention to the wrong conditions.
> - But we can't attend to all the conditions
>
> 102

SLIDE 103

The same problems come up when you automate testing. Hoffman and I consulted to a company that built 1100 different diagnostics into their machines' firmware. After any test, we could run any of these diagnostics.

But every time we ran one of the diagnostics, running it changed the state of the computer. If we ran two diagnostics, the first one told us about the results of the test. The second told us about the state of the system after our test and then after our first diagnostic. The more diagnostics we ran after a test, the more our results reflected the side effects of our diagnostic series rather than the results of the test.

We cannot observe every aspect of the outcome of our tests.

> **A PROGRAM CAN FAIL IN MANY WAYS**
>
> 1100 embedded diagnostics
> - Even if we coded checks for each of these diagnostics
>   - the side effects (data, resources, and timing)
>   - would provide us a new context for Heisenberg uncertainty.
>
> **Our tests cannot practically address all of the possibilities**
>
> 103

SLIDE 104

Therefore we cannot be certain that the program passed a test that it appeared to pass.

"IT WORKS"

really means

"IT APPEARS
TO MEET
SOME REQUIREMENT
TO SOME DEGREE."

104

SLIDE 105

Any decision-support tool that is sometimes wrong, but still useful, is a heuristic. All oracles are heuristics. They're fallible, but still useful.

An oracle is a
heuristic principle
or mechanism by
which you
recognize a
potential problem.

105

SLIDE 106

Reliance on heuristics is a basic fact of engineering. Billy Koen presented this eloquently in a classic introductory engineering text, along with explaining the essential characteristics of heuristics.

Heuristics can contradict each other, or lead you to incorrect conclusions. They are fallible but useful and they allow us to make progress on problems that have no authoritative solutions.

MAINSTREAM ENGINEERING RELIES
FUNDAMENTALLY ON HEURISTICS

- "A heuristic is anything that provides a plausible aid or direction in the solution of a problem but is in the final analysis unjustified, incapable of justification, and fallible. It is used to guide, to discover, and to reveal.

- "Heuristics do not guarantee a solution.

- "Two heuristics may contradict or give different answers to the same question and still be useful.

- "Heuristics permit the solving of unsolvable problems or reduce the search time to a satisfactory solution.

- "The heuristic depends on the immediate context instead of absolute truth as a standard of validity."

"The engineering method is the use of heuristics to cause the best change in a poorly understood situation within the available resources"
Billy V. Koen (1985, p. 70), Definition of the Engineering Method, American Society for Engineering Education.

106

SLIDE 107

The mistake that many testers make is to treat a heuristic as if it were a rule, instead of a guideline.

_____

_____

_____

_____

_____

_____

_____

_____

TESTING IS ABOUT IDEAS. HEURISTICS GIVE YOU IDEAS.

- A heuristic is a fallible idea or method that may you help simplify and solve a problem.
- Heuristics can hurt you when used as if they were authoritative rules.
- Heuristics may suggest wise behavior, but only in context. They do not contain wisdom.
- Your relationship to a heuristic is the key to applying it wisely.

"Heuristic reasoning is not regarded as final and strict but as provisional and plausible only, whose purpose is to discover the solution to the present problem."
- George Polya, How to Solve It

107

SLIDE 108

When evaluating tests, we can make two types of errors. I've diagrammed these in a signal detection chart, a chart that we'll see a lot more of in the _Bug Advocacy_ class.

The first error is the Miss. The program appeared to pass the test, but actually it failed.

The second error is the False Alarm. The program appeared to fail the test, but under the specific circumstances, its behavior was appropriate.

When we rely on a heuristic oracle, we can make either mistake.

FALLIBLE DECISION RULES

	How the tester interprets the test	
	Bug	Feature
The actual state of the program		
Bug	Hit	Miss
Feature	False alarm	Correct acceptance

Decisions based on oracles can be erroneous in two ways:

- **Miss**: We incorrectly conclude that the program passes because we miss the incorrect behavior (or the software and the oracle are both wrong)
- **False Alarm**: We incorrectly conclude that the program failed because we interpret correct behavior as incorrect.

A fallible decision rule can be subject to either type of error (or to both).

108

SLIDE 109

There's an important consequence to this decision-rule problem. It constrains our ability to automate tests. We'll see in later classes that there are ways to work with or around this constraint, but it's a significant problem. And it's a problem that many of the people who promote test automation most vehemently just don't understand.

_____

_____

_____

_____

ORACLES & TEST AUTOMATION

We often hear that most (or all) testing should be automated.

- Automated testing depends on our ability to programmatically detect when the software under test fails a test.
- Automate or not, you must still exercise judgment in picking risks to test against and interpreting the results.
- Automated comparison-based testing is subject to false alarms and misses.

Our ability to automate testing is fundamentally constrained by our ability to create and use oracles.

109

SLIDE 110

Let's consider an example. Here's a screen shot from Open Office's word processing program. Open Office is free software but it is a direct competitor to Microsoft Office. People use both for the same purposes. Open Office was designed to be fully compatible with Microsoft so that people in the same company could work equally conveniently with either product, passing files back and forth, sometimes editing in Word, sometimes in Open Office.

This test shows how Open Office displays text in different font sizes.

If you look closely, you can see that the program displays different fonts as the same. For example, letters that are 7.5 points and 8.5 points are displayed as the same size. Same for 13.5 points and 15, and for 16 and 18.

People will use this Open Office for serious work, including laying out complex documents. If it can't display font sizes correctly, this is a serious problem.

SLIDE 111

In contrast, consider WordPad. WordPad comes free with the Microsoft operating systems but people use it to do very simple editing.

From this picture, there's no obvious problem.

SLIDE 112

To look more closely, we can set WordPad side by side with Word. They look similar.

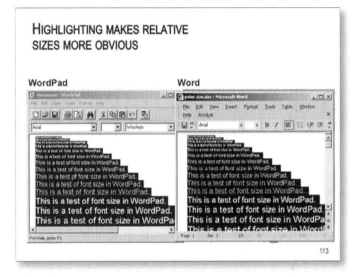

SLIDE 113

But we can make our test more precise in an easy way. By highlighting the text in Word and in WordPad, we can see how long and how tall each line is and we can compare the visual patterns of WordPad and Word.

This is one of the important tactics of test design. When results require human inspection, find a way to make a more thorough inspection easy. Side-by-side comparisons with a reference program go a long way toward that goal.

In this case, we see that, just like Open Office, WordPad doesn't handle differences in sizes consistently. Look at the top 6 lines in the WordPad display. The third and the fourth lines shouldn't be almost the same size.

SLIDE 114

So we see some differences. Word sizes the fonts correctly. WordPad and OpenOffice do not.

Should we care about these differences? There's no mechanical system that can answer that for you. You have to make your own, human, judgment.

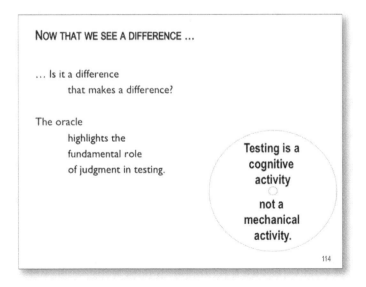

SLIDE 115

To evaluate a test result, it's useful to think about risk, or consequence.

In the case of WordPad, getting the font sizes a little wrong poses almost no risk. No one would do serious word processing with this program, or expect it to be useful for precise page layout.

_____

_____

_____

_____

_____

RISK AS A SIMPLIFYING FACTOR

- For Wordpad, we don't care if font size meets precise standards of typography!
- In general it can vastly simplify testing if we focus on whether the product has a problem that matters, rather than whether the product merely satisfies all relevant standards.
- Effective testing requires that we understand standards as they relate to how our clients value the product.

> Instead of thinking about pass vs. fail, Consider thinking problem vs. no problem.
> Michael Kelly (2006), "Using Heuristic Test Oracles" http://www.informit.com/articles/article.aspx?p=463947

115

SLIDE 116

In contrast, for Word or InDesign, a professional desktop publishing program, or for Open Office, this would be a big problem. All three programs are designed to encourage users to expect professional quality formatting of text.

_____

_____

_____

_____

_____

RISK AS A SIMPLIFYING FACTOR

What if we applied the same evaluation approach
- that we applied to WordPad
- to Open Office or MS Word or Adobe InDesign?

In risk-based testing,
- we choose the tests that we think are
  - the most likely to expose a serious problem,
- and skip the tests that we think are
  - unlikely to expose a problem, or
  - likely to expose problems that no one would care about.

> The same evaluation criteria lead to different conclusions in different contexts

116

SLIDE 117

If you're one of my students, you probably worked an exercise before watching this video. The exercise asks how you would decide whether Open Office displays fonts correctly.

If we wanted to test this thoroughly, here are some of the things we'd have to check:

We'd have to test with every font, because the program might handle some fonts perfectly but fail with others. Yes, I've seen this happen. We can blame this on nonstandard encoding of some fonts, but if Word displays the font correctly and Open Office doesn't, it's a problem.

We'd have to test with every character

And we'd have to test interactions with a lot of other variables that might be relevant.

WHAT WOULD WE EXAMINE IF WE WERE COMPARING FONT HANDLING IN PROFESSIONAL WORD PROCESSORS?

Some examples:
- Every font size (to a tenth of a point).
- Every character in every font.
- Every method of changing font size.
- Every user interface element associated with font size.
- Interactions between font size and other contents of a document.
- Interactions between font size and every other feature.
- Interactions between font sizes and graphics cards & modes.
- Print vs. screen display.

117

SLIDE 118

Working through the puzzle, students often say that they can tell if a character's size is correct by measuring it.

Things aren't that simple. The measure of the height of a character is called a point. There are 72 points to the inch. Unless there aren't. And some characters that are 10 points tall are much shorter than their counterparts in other typefaces.

So instead of attempting exact measurements, which can be very hard, we rely on simpler heuristics, such as comparing how big characters are relative to each other, or relative to the display in a more trusted program.

> **WHAT EVALUATION CRITERION?**
> - What do you know about typography?
>   - Definition of "point" varies. There are at least six different definitions
>   http://www.oberonplace.com/dtp/fonts/point.htm
>   - Absolute size of characters can be measured, but not easily
>   http://www.oberonplace.com/dtp/fonts/fontsize.htm
> - How closely must size match to the chosen standard?
> - **Heuristic approaches**, such as:
>   - relative size of characters
>   - comparison to MS Word
>   - expectations of different kinds of users for different uses.
>
> Testing is about ideas.
>
> Heuristics give you ideas.
>
> 118

SLIDE 119

Let's come back to the original idea, that in testing we compare a test result to an expected result.

There are four problems with this:

First, our expectations can be wrong. If a program doesn't work the way its specification says, that's often because the specification is wrong, or outdated. If a program doesn't work the same way as a reference program, that's often because the reference program has a bug.

Second, even if the program and the oracle match, there might still be a bug. That's what the 2+3 takes 5 hours example

> **REVIEW...**
> We started with the traditional views:
> - Testing is a process of comparing empirical results to expected results
> - An oracle is a mechanism for determining whether the program passed or failed a test.
>
> Four problems:
> - Our expectations are not necessarily correct
> - Our expectations are not complete
> - A mismatch between result and expectation might not be serious enough to report
> - Our expectations are not necessarily credible.
>
> The traditional perspective doesn't work, but we still need, have, and use, test oracles.
>
> 119

was about. No reference program covers all possible comparisons. No specification is complete. There are always aspects of the program – in most cases there are very significant aspects of the program – for which the tester has to figure out what is right or wrong for herself.

Open Office and WordPad had essentially the same bug with fonts, but I argued that it was a serious bug for Open Office and a trivial one for WordPad. When James teaches this, he says that he probably wouldn't report this bug formally, he would only mention it to the programmers informally. My practice is a little different. I want all failures on the record, so I report every mismatch between test results and expectations. But if I think it's minor, I say so. I don't spend much time on it and I never press anyone to fix it. To decide how seriously to take a bug, we have to rely on human judgment. The oracle rarely helps.

Finally, there is the credibility problem. When you say that the program is not working correctly, why should anyone believe you? Maybe no one will challenge you if your oracle is a specification or a respected reference program. But what should you do when a program misbehaves in a way that isn't covered by an oracle that someone else told you to use? Ignore it? Report it anyway and hope you don't have to defend it? We report it, but we want to make sure the reader clearly understands why we think it's a problem.

SLIDE 120

CONSISTENCY ORACLES

Consistent within product: Function behavior consistent with behavior of comparable functions or functional patterns within the product.

Consistent with comparable products: Function behavior consistent with that of similar functions in comparable products.

Consistent with history: Present behavior consistent with past behavior.

Consistent with our image: Behavior consistent with an image the organization wants to project.

Consistent with claims: Behavior consistent with documentation, specifications, or ads.

Consistent with standards or regulations: Behavior consistent with externally-imposed requirements.

Consistent with user's expectations: Behavior consistent with what we think users want.

Consistent with purpose: Behavior consistent with product or function's apparent purpose.

All of these are heuristics. They are useful, but they are not always correct and they are not always consistent with each other.

120

Bach and Bolton approached this a different way. If the program does something that doesn't look right, what is the basis for that feeling? How do testers argue that the program isn't working correctly?

Bach and Bolton developed a list of consistency heuristics that describe most people's expectations.

For example, when you compare the program to a specification, or an advertisement, or a user manual, you're looking for inconsistencies with the company's claims about the product.

When you compare results with a reference program, you're looking for inconsistency with a comparable product. There are limits to comparability. As we've seen, two products might be comparable in some ways--they might both add numbers, but incomparable in other ways—such as managing memory differently.

SLIDE 121

Other comparisons aren't as easy because the reference points aren't laid out as clearly for you. For example, if the program makes it hard to do something, does that matter or not?

You might have to decide why people would use this product. If the reason they buy the product is to be able to do this task, and it's too hard, that's an inconsistency with their expectations, and that will make them grumpy. It's probably also an inconsistency with what our company thinks is the purpose of the product—what we intend people to want to do with it.

USE CONSISTENCY ORACLES FOR TEST REPORTING

Something seems inappropriate.

How can you explain to the programmers (or other stakeholders) that this is bad?

Consider: Consistency with purpose

- What's the point of this product? Why do we think people should use it? What should they do with it?
- Does this error make it harder for them to achieve the benefits that they use this product to achieve?
- Research the product's benefits (books, interview experts, course examples, specifications, marketing materials, etc.)
- Use these materials to decide what people want to gain from this product.
- Test to see if users can achieve these benefits. If not, write bug reports. Explain what benefit you expect, why (cite the reference) you expect this, and then show the test that makes it unachievable or difficult.

Tie the reports to the facts and data you collected in your research

121

SLIDE 122

The consistency heuristics rely on your knowledge. If you don't get that knowledge from an easy-to-use source, like a well-written specification, you have to go get it for yourself.

CONSISTENCY ORACLES OFTEN REQUIRE RESEARCH

Example:

Consistency with purpose

- How do you know what the purpose of the product is?
- Even if you know (or think you know) the purpose, is your knowledge credible? Will other people agree that your perception of the purpose is correct?

Junior testers are like children, waiting for this type of information to be handed to them, and whining when they don't get it.

Competent testers ask for the information, but if they don't get it, they do their own research.

122

SLIDE 123

Let's consider one of the hardest issues to argue from—consistency with purpose. Sometimes it will be obvious to everyone that a program is supposed to make a certain task easy, but its design makes that task hard. If it's obvious enough, all you have to say is, "I'm trying to do this, and look at all the work it takes to do it."

But other times, the programmers don't understand the purpose of the program or the benefits the program should give to the customer. This is especially a problem in companies that think of programmers as technicians who merely write code to implement whatever is given to them in a specification. You'll see that attitude in a lot of textbooks and it has infested too many companies.

In these cases, when you report a problem, the programmers will say, "but we did what we were supposed to." They can be right, but the program can still be defective. Your argument is with whoever is telling the programmers what to do, not with the programmers themselves.

> **CONSISTENCY ORACLES OFTEN REQUIRE RESEARCH**
>
> **Consistency with purpose**
> What questions should you ask in order to guide your research?
> Here's an example of at least one aspect of the purpose of the product:
>> ***What should people want to achieve from this type of product?***
>> – What is the nature of this task?
>> – How do people do it in the world?
>> – What do people consider "success" or "completion" in this type of task?
>
> 123

SLIDE 124

To make your argument, or to learn that your perception is incorrect, you have to do your own research. You have to find sources of information that justify – or refute – your impression that the point of a program like this is to make tasks like this easy.

Some of my colleagues tell me that, at their company, testers aren't welcome to spend their time on this.

That's true at many companies, but the company only pays for 40 hours of your time. What you do with the rest of your time is up to you. To a large degree, in my experience in American and Canadian companies, many of the things people do to advance their career they do in their own time.

> **CONSISTENCY ORACLES OFTEN REQUIRE RESEARCH**
>
> **Consistency with purpose**
> What sources can you consult to answer these questions? Here are a few examples…
>
> • Internal documents: such as specifications, marketing documents
> • Competing products: what they do and how they work (work with them, read their docs and marketing statements) and published reviews of them
> • Training materials, books, courses: for example, if you're testing a spreadsheet, where do people learn how to use them? Where do people learn about the things (e.g. balance sheets) that spreadsheets to help us create?
> • Users: Read your company's technical support (help desk) records. Or talk with real people who have been using your product (or comparable ones) to do real tasks.
>
> Credibility doesn't come automatically to you as a tester.
> You have to earn it by getting to know what you are talking about.
>
> 124

Other testers make the point even more firmly. At their company, management doesn't want testers to evaluate the design of the product, just the implementation. This is probably the right attitude if you're working at an independent test lab, on a class of product that you will test only once. Your career advancement will probably come from doing what the development company contracts with your lab to do, and learning the skills to do it more efficiently.

But I see this attitude among some managers, and many testers, at companies who are testing their own software, especially in IT organizations.

Look, in that situation, you have to be careful. You have to pick your arguments. You have to make sure that you're right before you speak. And you have to make sure that your sources of information will be so good that people will want to pay attention to them. But if you have that, it will usually benefit your company to hear what you have to say, and it will usually benefit you.

The more you understand about your company's business and how your products serve your company's business needs, the more respect you can gain and the faster you can rise in the company. It's up to you.

SLIDE 125

Let me sum up on the consistency oracles.

We use these in three common ways.

When we find a bug, we try to figure out why we think it's a bug. If the answer isn't obvious, it's often useful to ask, "what type of inconsistency am I reacting to?" And then do some research to see if our hunch that something is wrong is something we should act on.

When we report a bug, sometimes we need to explain why we think it's a bug. These heuristics often guide our thinking about how to structure that explanation—I

> ### USE CONSISTENCY ORACLES
> * To guide bug evaluation
>   - Why do I think something is wrong with this behavior?
>   - Is this a bug or not?
> * To guide reporting
>   - How can I credibly argue that this is a problem?
>   - How can I explain why I think this is serious?
> * To guide test design
>   - If I know something the product *should be* consistent with, I can predict things the product should or should not do and I can design tests to check those predictions.
>
> 125

think this is a bug because I think people will expect it to do something else. And I think that because…

And finally, we use these oracles to guide design. Any time I know what the product is supposed to do, I can design tests to check whether the product does it.

SLIDE 126

ANOTHER LOOK AT ORACLES (BASED ON NOTES FROM DOUG HOFFMAN)

	Description	Advantages	Disadvantages
No Oracle (automated test or incompetent human)	• Doesn't explicitly check results for correctness ("Run till crash")	• Can run any amount of data (limited by the time the SUT takes) • Useful early in testing. We generate tests randomly or from an model and see what happens	• Notices only spectacular failures • Replication of sequence leading to failure may be difficult
No oracle (competent human testing)	• Humans often come to programs without knowing what to expect from a particular test. They figure out how to evaluate the test while they run the test.	• See Bolton (2010), "Inputs and expected results", http://www.developsense.com/blog/2010/05/a-transpection-session-inputs-and-expected-results/ • People don't test with "no oracles". They use general expectations and product-specific information that they gather while testing.	• Testers who are too inexperienced, too insecure, or too dogmatic to rely on their wits need more structure.
Complete Oracle	• Authoritative mechanism for determining whether the program passed or failed	• Detects all types of errors • If we have a complete oracle, we can run automated tests and check the results against it	• This is a mythological creature: software equivalent of a unicorn

126

Bach and Bolton's list of consistency heuristics is one structure that many people find useful. Another structure that's been in the works for about 14 years comes from Doug Hoffman, who publishes ideas about how to compare and evaluate oracles in a set of tables.

SLIDE 127

MORE TYPES OF ORACLES (BASED ON NOTES FROM DOUG HOFFMAN)

	Description	Advantages	Disadvantages
Heuristic Consistency Oracles	Consistent with • within product • comparable products • history • our image • claims • specifications or regulations • user expectations • purpose	• We can probably force-fit most or all other types of oracles into this structure (classification system for oracles) • James Bach thinks it is really cool • The structure illustrates ideas for test design and persuasive test result reporting	• The structure seems too general for some students (including some experienced practitioners). • Therefore, the next slides illustrate more narrowly-defined examples, inspired by notes from Doug Hoffman
Partial	• Verifies only some aspects of the test output. • All oracles are partial oracles.	• More likely to exist than a Complete Oracle • Much less expensive to create and use	• Can miss systematic errors • Can miss obvious errors

127

I can't walk through all the details in these tables in a lecture. There's too much here. This is something you have to read through on your own. But I can make some comments as we go.

Doug's fundamental insight was that all oracles are heuristic. Testing provides partial answers that might be useful, rather than evaluations that are always complete and correct.

SLIDE 128

MORE TYPES OF ORACLES (BASED ON NOTES FROM DOUG HOFFMAN & MICHAEL BOLTON)

	Description	Advantages	Disadvantages
Constraints	Checks for • impossible values or • Impossible relationships Examples: • ZIP codes must be 5 or 9 digits • Page size (output format) must not exceed physical page size (printer) • Event 1 must happen before Event 2 • In an order entry system, date/time correlates with order number	• The errors exposed are probably straightforward coding errors that must be fixed • This is useful even though it is insufficient	• Catches some obvious errors but if a value (or relationship between two variables' values) is incorrect but doesn't obviously conflict with the constraint, the error is not detected.
Familiar failure patterns	• The application behaves in a way that reminds us of failures in other programs. • This is probably not sufficient in itself to warrant a bug report, but it is enough to motivate further research.	• Normally we think of oracles describing how the program should behave. (It should be consistent with X.) This works from a different mindset ("this looks like a problem," instead of "this looks like a match.")	• False analogies can be distracting or embarrassing if the tester files a report without adequate troubleshooting.

128

Constraint testing illustrates the idea of the partial oracle. It might be too hard to tell whether an answer is right or wrong, but easy to tell whether it is plausible or impossible. If the program tells us that an American postal code has 6 digits, or a Canadian postal code has only numbers, no letters, it doesn't matter what the exact code is, it's wrong. These types of tests don't ever confirm that the program works. They only make some types of errors obvious.

SLIDE 129

MORE TYPES OF ORACLES (BASED ON NOTES FROM DOUG HOFFMAN)

	Description	Advantages	Disadvantages
Regression Test Oracle	• Compare results of tests of this build with results from a previous build. The prior results are the oracle.	• Verification is often a straightforward comparison • Can generate and verify large amounts of data • Excellent selection of tools to support this approach to testing	• Verification fails if the program's design changes (many false alarms). (Some tools reduce false alarms) • Misses bugs that were in previous build or are not exposed by the comparison
Self-Verifying Data	• Embeds correct answer in the test data (such as embedding the correct response in a message comment field or the correct result of a calculation or sort in a database record) • CRC, checksum or digital signature	• Allows extensive post-test analysis • Does not require external oracles • Verification is based on contents of the message or record, not on user interface • Answers are often derived logically and vary little with changes to the user interface • Can generate and verify large amounts of complex data	• Must define answers and generate messages or records to contain them • In protocol testing (testing the creation and sending of messages and how the recipient responds), if the protocol changes we might have to change all the tests • Misses bugs that don't cause mismatching result fields.

129

A regression test is a repeat. We ran the test in a previous build of the program. Now we're running it again. If the program passed the test last time, we can capture its output and compare the old output with the new output. If the output is different this time, then perhaps the new output is wrong. Or perhaps the old output is outdated.

Regression test oracles are very common. Some people use these as the basis for all of their test automation. But I keep meeting people who tell me about their projects, and how 90% or more of the mismatches they found between the current version's output and the regression test output were not bugs at all. Some tell me that most of their test time is spent updating the old tests, over and over as the program changes. I've personally seen this at some large companies. Yes, the execution of these tests has been automated. But the manual labor associated with updating these tests over and over is huge, mindless, and unproductive. It finds almost no bugs and gives little assurance that new bugs aren't there.

SLIDE 130

The next several oracles are based on models.

A model is a simplified representation of a system, usually one that makes a representation or a process easier to notice.

> ## MODELS
>
> The next several oracles are based on models.
>
> - A model is a simplified, formal representation of a relationship, process or system. The simplification makes some aspects of the thing modeled clearer, more visible, and easier to work with.
> - All tests are based on models, but many of those models are implicit. When the behavior of the program "feels wrong" it is clashing with your internal model of the program and how it should behave.
>
> 130

SLIDE 131

We can build models of almost anything. Think of someone selling an insurance policy, and using a program to help him understand the customer's needs and the price for the policy. That program implements a model of the sales process. The program makes features available—the features that the software designers believed would be important at this point in the sales discussion. The program asks questions to get information the designers thought would be relevant and it does not ask questions about information the designers considered irrelevant.

> ## WHAT MIGHT WE MODEL IN AN ORACLE?
>
> - The physical process being emulated, controlled or analyzed by the software under test
> - The business process being emulated, controlled or analyzed by the software under test
> - The software being emulated, controlled, communicated with or analyzed by the software under test
> - The device(s) this program will interact with
> - The reactions or expectations of the stakeholder community
> - The uses / usage patterns of the product
> - The transactions that this product participates in
> - The user interface of the product
> - The objects created by this product
>
> 131

To the extent that the software helps the salesperson get the right information quickly and sell the right policy, this is a good model.

To the extent that the salesperson has to work around the software, or feels that he's being asked the wrong questions or in the wrong order, or in a confusing way, the software's model is wrong.

SLIDE 132

The oracle can implement a different model and check whether the program is consistent or inconsistent with the viewpoint built into the oracle.

In designing an oracle, the tester can use whatever information she considers relevant.

_____

_____

_____

_____

_____

WHAT ASPECTS OF THE THINGS WE MODEL MIGHT GUIDE OUR CREATION OF A MODEL?

- Capabilities
- Preferences
  - Competitive analysis
  - Support records
- Focused chronology
  - Achievement of a task or life history of an object or action
- Sequences of actions
  - Such as state diagrams or other sequence diagrams
  - Flow of control
- Flow of information
  - Such as data flow diagrams or protocol diagrams or maps
- Interactions / dependencies
  - Such as combination charts or decision trees
  - Charts of data dependencies
  - Charts of connections of parts of a system
- Collections
  - Such as taxonomies or parallel lists
- Motives
  - Interest analysis: Who is affected how, by what?

132

SLIDE 133

The goal of this modeling is not necessarily to prove the software right or wrong. The goal is often to develop a better understanding of the software and a set of launching points for further investigation, sometimes resulting in bug reports and sometimes resulting in refinement of the oracle's models.

_____

_____

_____

_____

_____

_____

WHAT MAKES THESE MODELS, MODELS?

- The representation (the model) is simpler than what is modeled: It emphasizes some aspects of what is modeled while hiding other aspects
- You can work with the representation to make descriptions or predictions about the underlying subject of the model
- Using the model is easier or more convenient to work with, or more likely to lead to new insights than working with the original.

133

_____

_____

_____

_____

_____

_____

_____

_____

_____

_____

_____

_____

_____

_____

_____

_____

_____

_____

SLIDE 134

MORE TYPES OF ORACLES (BASED ON NOTES FROM DOUG HOFFMAN)

	Description	Advantages	Disadvantages
State Model	• We can represent programs as state machines. At any time, the program is in one state and (given the right inputs) can transition to another state. The test provides input and checks whether the program switched to the correct state	• Good software exists to help test designer build the state model • Excellent software exists to help test designer select a set of tests that drive the program through every state transition	• Maintenance of the state machine (the model) can be very expensive (e.g. the model changes when the program's UI changes.) • Does not (usually) try to drive the program through state transitions considered impossible • Errors that show up in some other way than bad state transition can be invisible to the comparator
Interaction Model	• We know that if the SUT does X, some other part of the system (or other system) should do Y and if the other system does Z, the SUT should do A.	• To the extent that we can automate this, we can test for interactions much more thoroughly than manual tests	• We are looking at a slice of the behavior of the SUT so we will be vulnerable to misses and false alarms • Building the model can take a lot of time. Priority decisions are important.

134

The next three slides look at widely used models that we can test against. For example, with the state model, if we know what state the program is in, we know what it can do next—and what it can't. In a presentation to the Workshop on Model Based Testing, James Tierney and Harry Robinson described Microsoft's use of state models. In many cases, the most valuable information came while they were exploring the program to build the model. They found many inconsistencies that not only made the model much harder to understand. They obviously made the program harder for users to understand. When the program is much more complex than the simplified representation in the model, sometimes the fix is to make the program simpler instead of making the model more complex.

SLIDE 135

MORE TYPES OF ORACLES (BASED ON NOTES FROM DOUG HOFFMAN)

	Description	Advantages	Disadvantages
Business Model	• We understand what is reasonable in this type of business. For example, • We might know how to calculate a tax (or at least that a tax of $1 is implausible if the taxed event or income is $1 million). • We might know inventory relationships. It might be absurd to have 1 box top and 1 million bottoms.	• These oracles are probably expressed as equations or as plausibility-inequalities ("it is ridiculous for A to be more than 1000 times B") that come from subject-matter experts. Software errors that violate these are probably important (perhaps central to the intended benefit of the application) and likely to be seen as important	• There is no completeness criterion for these models. • The subject matter expert might be wrong in the scope of the model (under some conditions, the oracle should not apply and we get a false alarm) • Some models might be only temporarily true
Theoretical (e.g. Physics or Chemical) Model	• We have theoretical knowledge of the proper functioning of some parts of the SUT. For example, we might test the program's calculation of a trajectory against physical laws.	• Theoretically sound evaluation • Comparison failures are likely to be seen as important	• Theoretical models (e.g. physics models) are sometimes only approximately correct for real-world situations

135

Some models that we build into an oracle might have nothing to do with the software, except that the software is wrong if it doesn't conform to their predictions. For example, if the software gives a calculated result that would violate the laws of gravity, the software has a bug.

SLIDE 136

MORE TYPES OF ORACLES (BASED ON NOTES FROM DOUG HOFFMAN)

	Description	Advantages	Disadvantages

Mathematical Model	• The predicted value can be calculated by virtue of mathematical attributes of the SUT or the test itself. For example:
	  - The test does a calculation and then inverts it. (The square of the square root of X should be X, plus or minus rounding error)
	  - The test inverts and then inverts a matrix
	  - We have a known function, e.g. sine, and can predict points along its path
		Good for
		• mathematical functions
		• straightforward transformations
		• invertible operations of any kind
			• Available only for invertible operations or computationally predictable results.
			• To obtain the predictable results, we might have to create a difficult-to-implement reference program.

Statistical	• Checks against probabilistic predictions, such as:
	  - 80% of online customers have historically been from these ZIP codes; what is today's distribution?
	  - X is usually greater than Y
	  - X is positively correlated with Y
		• Allows checking of very large data sets
		• Allows checking of live systems' data
		• Allows checking after the fact
			• False alarms and misses are both likely (Type 1 and Type 2 errors)
			• Can miss obvious errors

136

Statistical models are interesting because they let us work with output that could be correct, but it is so improbable as to be suspicious.

SLIDE 137

MORE TYPES OF ORACLES (BASED ON NOTES FROM DOUG HOFFMAN)

	Description	Advantages	Disadvantages
Data Set with Known Characteristics	• Rather than testing with live data, create a data set with characteristics that you know thoroughly. Oracles may or may not be explicitly built in (they might be) but you gain predictive power from your knowledge	• The test data exercise the program in the ways you choose (e.g. limits, interdependencies, etc.) and you (if you are the data designer) expect to see outcomes associated with these built-in challenges • The characteristics can be documented for other testers • The data continue to produce interesting results despite many types of program changes	• Known data sets do not themselves provide oracles • Known data sets are often not studied or not understood by subsequent testers (especially if the creator leaves) creating Cargo Cult level testing.
Hand Crafted	• Result is carefully selected by test designer	• Useful for some very complex SUTs • Expected result can be well understood	• Slow, expensive test generation • High maintenance cost • Maybe high test creation cost
Human	• A human decides whether the program is behaving acceptably	• Sometimes this is the only way. "Do you like how this looks?" "Is anything confusing?"	• Slow • Subjective • Credibility varies with the credibility of the human.

137

Finally, we have the human. You are an oracle. Your intuition about whether the program's behavior is appropriate is imperfect but you can detect oddities that no one ever considered programming into the automated oracles. And you have insight into what is confusing, what is insulting, and what is unhelpful. Recognition of these as problems is too complex for a test machine.

SLIDE 138

Summing up ...

- Test oracles can only sometimes provide us with authoritative failures.

- Test oracles cannot tell us whether the program has passed the test, they can only tell us it has not obviously failed.

- Oracles subject us to two possible classes of errors:

  - Miss: The program fails but the oracle doesn't expose it

  - False Alarm: The program did not fail but the oracle signaled a failure

Tests do not provide complete information.

They provide partial information that might be useful.

138

So let's sum up on the oracles and then get to a quick note on the exam.

Sometimes, a program behaves in a way that is obviously wrong. In these cases, if we can notice the behavior and recognize the error, we can report it without having to spend much time thinking about it.

But other times, the failure is harder to spot, harder to recognize, or harder to explain. If we think of oracles as hard and fast rules, if we think of all testing as evaluation of the program against hard and fast rules, then we'll miss a lot of these harder problems.

Treating oracles as heuristics gives us more freedom to think about partial answers, about results that are suspicious or unlikely rather than necessarily wrong, and about design choices that might be problematic even if they were put into the code intentionally.

SLIDE 139

Now, about that exam.

_____
_____
_____
_____
_____
_____
_____
_____
_____
_____

> *About the*
> *Exam*
>
> 139

SLIDE 140

These videos are used in a lot of different courses. I can only talk about the ones I know about at Florida Tech and at the Association for Software Testing. In those courses, we publish a study guide that contains every question that you can be asked on the exam. We also include links to a paper that offers heuristics for answering essay-exam questions well and two videos that explain how we do our grading.

If your course uses a study-guide based exam structure, it probably also includes a discussion forum where students can post draft answers and critique each other's

> **LECTURE WRAPUP**
>
> It's time to start working through the study guide questions. You'll learn more by working through a few questions each week than by cramming just before the exam.
>
> Note: most courses based on these videos provide a study guide with 30-100 essay questions. The typical exam is closed book, and takes most or all of its questions from this set. The goal is to help you focus your studying and to think carefully through your answers:
>
> • Early work helps you identify confusion or ambiguity
> • Early drafting makes peer review possible
>
> The course website should include links to at least two videos that illustrate our approach to grading essay questions and at least one paper on "Answering Essay Questions".
>
> 140

drafts. I strongly suggest that you draft your own answer first, then compare notes with the other answers.

Students who wait until a few days before the exam to start working through these questions lose most of the educational benefit of the study-guide based exam structure. The essay questions provide a good review of the material. They get you thinking about the lecture in a different way. And unlike the multiple choice tests, in the essay questions, you can tell us that you disagree with the lectures and offer your own point of view as an alternative.

_____
_____
_____
_____
_____
_____
_____
_____
_____
_____

SLIDE 141

BLACK BOX SOFTWARE TESTING:
FOUNDATIONS
END OF LECTURE 3

CEM KANER, J.D., PH.D.
PROFESSOR OF SOFTWARE ENGINEERING
FLORIDA INSTITUTE OF TECHNOLOGY

REBECCA L. FIEDLER, M.B.A. PH.D.
PRESIDENT: KANER, FIEDLER & ASSOCIATES

JAMES BACH
PRINCIPAL, SATISFICE INC.

These notes are partially based on research that was supported by NSF Grants EIA-0113539 ITR/SY +PE: "Improving the Education of Software Testers" and CCLI-0717613 "Adaptation & Implementation of an Activity-Based Online or Hybrid Course in Software Testing." Any opinions, findings and conclusions or recommendations expressed in this material are those of the author(s) and do not necessarily reflect the views of the National Science Foundation.

141

Application: Using The Consistency Heuristics

The point of an oracle is to help you decide whether a product's behavior is inappropriate—and if so, to help you explain persuasively to someone else why they should consider it inappropriate.

The lecture describes several oracle heuristics defined in terms of user expectations about consistency, based on work by James Bach and Michael Bolton (See Bolton's (2005) *"Testing Without a Map"*.[1])

In our experience, students need to try to apply these to testing situations before they understand them well enough to use them at work. This assignment gives you an opportunity to apply them in practice.

1   http://testingeducation.org/BBST/foundations/Bolton_2005-01-TestingWithoutAMap.pdf

Review of the Concept

The descriptive quotes below are from Bolton (2005), with minor editorial clarifications in [brackets].

- *Consistent with the vendor's image (reputation):* "The product's look and behavior should be consistent with an image that the development organization wants to project to its customers or to its internal users. A product that looks shoddy often is shoddy."

- *Consistent with its purpose:* "The behavior of a feature, function, or product should be consistent with its apparent purpose. [For example, help messages should be helpful.]"

- *Consistent with user's expectations:* "A feature or function should behave in a way that is consistent with our understanding of what users want, as well as with their reasonable expectations."

- *Consistent with the product's history:* "The feature's or function's current behavior should be consistent with its past behavior, assuming that there is no good reason for it to change. This heuristic is especially useful when testing a new version of an existing program."

- *Consistent within product:* "The behavior of a given function should be consistent with the behavior of comparable functions or functional patterns within the same product unless there is a specific reason for it not to be consistent."

- *Consistent with comparable products:* "We may be able to use other products as a rough, de facto standard against which our own can be compared."

- *Consistent with claims:* "The product should behave the way some document, artifact, or person [who has the authority to make promises about the product, such as a salesperson] says it should. The claim might be made in a specification, [a demonstration of the product], a Help file, an advertisement, an email message, [a sales pitch] or a hallway conversation."

- *Consistent with statutes, regulations, or binding specifications:* "The product [must comply] with legal requirements [and restrictions]." [The key difference between this oracle and consistency with claims is that the claims are statements made by the developer while statutes, regulations, and some types of specifications are imposed on the developer by outside organizations.]

Each oracle gives you a different type of inconsistency to consider.

If the program operates inconsistently with one of the heuristics, the structure of your argument is, "This [aspect of the program] appears to be unacceptable because it is inconsistent with the way we believe it should work. The basis for our belief is <history of the product><specification><etc.>"

Applying the Concept: Four Scenarios

In the scenarios below, we're going to describe a product and an aspect of the product that some people might not like. We'll present the four products first. Then, we'll suggest some consistency heuristics. Your challenge is to:

- Apply the consistency heuristic to the product in a way that builds a case that the product should be revised ("fixed")

- —OR—Explain why this particular heuristic won't be very helpful for advocating for change to this product.

The Scenarios

1. *Computer Game:* A software company, GameCo, is about to release a computer game that includes violence, explicit graphics (blood, gore, immodestly dressed people), drugs, and strong language. Some people who shop for computer games (or supervise what their children buy) would probably be offended by these aspects of this game. You suspect that some aspects of the game are so striking that they might be featured (unfavorably) in cable TV news shows. *Can you use arguments based on these heuristics to convince GameCo to tone down its game?*

2. *Government-Contract Software*: Early in my career, I met someone who claimed to be working for a large government contractor (call them Xco). Xco had a contract to "independently test" the software being created for by another large government contractor (call them Yco). The software was "fully specified" in the contract between Yco and a large government agency. The tester had run a simple test. She entered a letter into a data entry field that was supposed to accept numbers. She knew users weren't supposed to enter a letter there but she considered it inappropriate that the software crashed (gave a brief and unfriendly error message, then halted, losing whatever other good data had already been entered.) When she reported this, her management at Xco rejected the bug report. The specification that Yco was working from said that the program *should* accept numbers (and it *did*) but it did not say what the program should do if it got a non-number. Therefore, Yco determined they could do whatever they thought was appropriate when the user did something that was outside of the scope of the specification. In this case, Yco thought that a crash would be a good way to teach the user to stop doing things like that. Therefore, given this specification, Yco would argue that this is not a bug and say that if the government does not like it, they can file a modification to the specification and pay for the new code. *Can you use arguments based on these heuristics to convince Xco and Yco that this is a bug?*

3. *Desktop Publishing Software:* BookCo publishes software that lets you create and format documents as books that will be published in print or online. One of the features that BookCo's program offers is cross-referencing. At any point in the text, you can insert a link to a paragraph in any other point in the text. When BookCo's program prints or displays your book, the link will read "see <first few words in the paragraph> on page <the page number>." Most commonly, people will link to paragraphs that are headings, so a typical link might read "see Chapter 5 on page 63". BookCo also lets you create a book index. You can insert another link at any place in the book and that link will show up in the index at end of the book as some text and a page number. However, the two types of links don't work well together. If you cross-reference to a heading and then to mark the heading for the index, BookCo's program gives an error message. The workaround is to delete the index link and link to the start of the first paragraph after the heading instead. However, when you delete the index link, sometimes BookCo's program doesn't

completely delete it. Instead, it leaves part of the link code in the document, which later causes other corruption or crashes. This is an intermittent problem. It is hard to troubleshoot. BookCo has been given files with this problem and customers have said grumpy things about it but BookCo has not allocated enough time or resource to troubleshoot the problem and get it fixed. *Can you use arguments based on these heuristics to convince BookCo to raise the priority of this bug*?

4. *Stock-Trading Software:* TraderCo sells software that analyzes trends in stock prices and tells you when to buy and sell specific stocks. No software makes perfect predictions, but TraderCo has a customer base that is reasonably satisfied that TraderCo's statistical methods are sound. TraderCo also records the prices that you buy and sell the stock at, and the commissions and fees you pay, giving you information that maps to the reporting requirements of the tax authority in the United States (the IRS). Note, though, that when you buy stock through an American broker or on an American exchange, your broker will give you year-end paperwork that includes detailed information and meets the tax authority's requirements. TraderCo's report is merely for your information, not for filing your taxes. TraderCo sometimes makes errors when it records purchases or sales, so its records are usually correct but far from always. *Can you use arguments based on these heuristics to convince TraderCo to raise the priority of this bug?*

The Analysis: An Example

Consider Scenario 1, the Computer Game. Imagine trying to argue that the offensive-to-some nature of some game interactions are inappropriate on the basis of:

- The company's image (this will damage your reputation)
- The user's expectations (the user will be shocked by this, SHOCKED!)
- Bad reactions from regulators. For example, the Entertainment Software Rating Board (ESRB) might rate the game as unsuitable for many users and that might cause some schools to bar the game from their campus.

Imagine that GameCo is a company like Apple, or Disney. Arguments like these might be very powerful.

- *(Reputation.)* If I was going to build a set of arguments like this, I would look for pronouncements by GameCo that their products are family-friendly. I would look for other evidence that GameCo tries to market to young children and are seen as a trustworthy source of content and games.

- *(Reputation, expectations, comparable products.)* I would look for cases in which GameCo (or a competitor) had published something a little bit more violent or more sexually explicit than their norm. How did customers respond? How did GameCo respond? For example, if customers complained and GameCo apologized and modified the product, people will expect GameCo to stick with family-friendly products.

On the other hand, imagine that GameCo is Rockstar Games, whose motto appears to be "Uniting Conservatives and Liberals in Hatred since 1968").[2] This is the company that publishes Grand Theft Auto. GTA 5 was described by ESRB as having "Blood and Gore, Intense Violence, Mature Humor, Nudity, Strong Language, Strong Sexual Content, Use of Drugs and Alcohol".[3]

---

2   http://www.rockstargames.com/
3   http://www.esrb.org/ratings/search.jsp

If GameCo was like Rockstar Games, you would probably find it difficult to argue that this new game was inconsistent with GameCo's reputation, the expectations of their customers, or that this game would give them an unanticipated level of trouble with regulators.

Why Is This Example Important?

Bach and Bolton called these their "consistency heuristics". The structure of the argument is that some aspect of a program is bad because it is inconsistent with something that we, as testers, think is reasonable to expect about the program. We expect it to be consistent with the company's reputation (or at least not to damage it), to live up to published claims, to not get the publisher in trouble (or more trouble than the publisher anticipates), to work like products that are similar to it, and so on.

If the product that you are testing is not actually inconsistent with one of these types of expectations, then there is no point using that expectation as a basis for arguing that the program needs to change. It is a waste of everyone's time. If you do it, it suggests to the person reading your reports that you don't understand their company's business.

Pick your consistency heuristics wisely. Make your strongest arguments and skip the rest.

Your Assignment: Phase 1

a. *For the Government-Contracted Software example*, assume that there is a document labelled "Specification" that was attached to the contract. Assume that it in fact does not mention specifically what the program should do with letters entered into number fields. *What research would you do (what information would you gather and how would you gather it) to build a case that this behavior should be considered inconsistent with claims or with regulations or with the purpose of the product.*

b. *For the Desktop Publishing Software example*, assume that BookCo is aware of customer complaints, that it has (and knows it has) customer files that were corrupted by index-related bugs in ways that customers cannot recover from, that it does not know the root cause of the corruption and anticipates that it would take a lot of work to debug this. *Which two consistency heuristics look the most promising for persuading this publisher to budget additional time and money to troubleshoot this bug? What research would you do? Be specific—give reasonable examples of information that you would search for and how you would search for it. Be realistic—give examples of things that you could reasonably expect to find from your research that could be persuasive. Finally, which two consistency heuristics look the LEAST promising for this bug, and why?*

c. *For the Stock-Trading Software example,* assume that users can get essentially the same tax-related information from their broker as from this software. Why do they need absolutely accurate information from TraderCo's product? They aren't buying stocks through TraderCo. They aren't banking through TraderCo. They aren't filing tax returns using TraderCo's forms. *Which heuristics would help you demonstrate that TraderCo's bugs are still important and they need to be fixed? Why?*

Your Assignment: Phase 2

After you have completed Phase 1, read other students' answers and post comments on two students' work.

- Do you understand from their description what information they are actually looking for?

- Do you think they are looking for the right information?

- Do you think they have a realistic chance of finding that information?

- Is there something else they should be looking for?

- Do you understand what argument they are trying to make?

- Will their information support their argument?

- Does their answer demonstrate an ability to plan for contingencies? Have they considered what argument they will make (or whether they should make no argument) if they get other information that does not support the argument they initially wanted to make?

Authors' Reflection On Lesson 3

Lesson 3 is about Oracles. We see the oracle problem as one of the defining problems of software testing. It is one of the reasons that skilled testing is a complex cognitive activity rather than a routine activity.

Hard problems are often hard to teach. We think our handling of oracles is the weakest part of the current version of *Foundations*. The lectures are what they are—we will replace them when we find the 1000-2000 hours needed to create Version 4. What we can do now is clarify some of the content and replace activities and readings.

The Oracle Problem

When I first studied testing, I learned that a test involved comparison of the test result to an expected result. The expected result was the *oracle*: the thing that would tell you whether the program passed or failed the test. For automated testing, we would look to a *reference program* as our oracle. The reference program generates the expected results. Run the test, compare its results to the results from the reference program.

The emphasis on expected results comes because it is so easy to design tests that are so hard or so time-consuming to evaluate that testers might not recognize it when a program fails a test. In practice, not noticing failures has been a serious problem. Glen Myers' classic book on testing (*The Art of Software Testing*, 1979) cited IBM data showing that testers often missed bugs when they ran tests but didn't compare the results against an expected result. Myers' recommendation was to always include the expected result in the description of every test. A test without an expected result was not a test.

The expected result is often called the *oracle*.

Oracle is an interesting choice of terminology, because the oracles of Greece (the original "oracles") were mythological.[4] Greek tragedies are full of stories of people who misinterpreted what an oracle told them and behaved (on the basis of their understanding) in ways that brought disaster on them.

If we define a software testing oracle as a tool that tells you whether the program passed your test, we are describing a myth—something that doesn't exist. Relying on the oracle, you might make either of the classic mistakes of decision theory:

- The *miss*: you believe the program has passed even though it did something wrong.

- The *false alarm*: you believe the program has failed even though it has behaved appropriately.

---

4   http://en.wikipedia.org/wiki/Oracle

So we soften the definition: *a software testing oracle is a tool that helps you decide whether the program passed your test.*

Seen this way, oracles are heuristic devices: they are useful tools that help us make decisions, but sometimes they point us to the wrong decision.[5]

The *Oracle Problem* is this:

> We need authoritative oracles ("authoritative" = an oracle that is always correct), but we can't have them.

Without authoritative oracles (also known as complete oracles or perfect oracles), how can you tell whether the program passed or failed a test? And how can you specify a test in a way that a junior tester or a computer can run the test and correctly tell you whether the program passed it?

The answer that the lecture presents is that we can't have authoritative oracles, so we have to make do with heuristics.

---

5 http://www.testingeducation.org/BBST/foundations/Koen_EngineeringMethod.pdf

A Common Misunderstanding

We think the most common misunderstanding of the lecture is confusion between "oracles" and "heuristics." For many students, both words are new. They mix them up.

A heuristic is a rule of thumb, an imperfect guide. It might imperfectly guide you about what to do or imperfectly guide you about what decision to make. For example, these are heuristics:

- When the United States Federal Reserve announces a monetary policy designed to make the economy expand (such as by reducing interest rates), many investors will buy stocks that do well in an expanding economy and will avoid investments that do best in a contracting economy. The underlying heuristic (investor folk wisdom) is *Don't fight the Fed*.

- When a chess player plans a series of moves that are designed to establish control of the squares in the center of the board, the player might not know how that will lead to eventual victory. What she knows is the heuristic, *Take control of the center*, which usually (but not always) leads to victory if you achieve that control.

- When police use racial profiling, deciding on the basis of race (and dress and demeanor) that a person should be searched for drugs or a weapon, the decision rule is imperfect. The argument is that it reflects a statistical reality, that some people are more likely to be dangerous than others. That argument might or might not be statistically sound and the impact of a rule like this might be to alienate some members of society (when people realize they will be treated as criminals and outcasts no matter how they behave, this might impact the probability that they will act violently in the future). But the rule itself is based on the patrolman's calculus: *imperfect-but-useful-enough-to-maybe-save-my-life*.

All of these are heuristics. None are oracles. None involve software testing.

The relationship between oracles and heuristics is this: It is useful to analyze oracles as heuristics—as imperfect decision *guides* rather than as perfect decision *rules*.

Alternative Views Of Oracles

This lesson tries to weave a compromise between two visions of oracles, which we associate with Hoffman (and Weyuker) on one side and to Bach and Bolton on the other.

In some ways, the difference between their views is very sharp. However, we see the same essential underlying insight in both views— oracles are heuristic devices. We decided to write the lecture to emphasize this idea and downplay the differences. In retrospect, that was maybe a good idea, but it didn't work.

The lecture provided two lists of oracle heuristics:

- *The Expectation-Consistency Heuristics* (or consistency heuristics), based on Bach's and Bolton's work.

- *The Partial Oracles*, based on Hoffman's work.

Expectation-Consistency Heuristics

This group of slides focuses on Bach and Bolton's consistency heuristics. The lectures follow an explanatory approach that we learned from an early version of Bach's *Rapid Software Testing* (RST) Course.[6]

We think that Bach's reaction to the insight that oracles are heuristics has been to emphasize the fundamental importance of the human evaluator in testing. The details of his view have evolved over time. Perhaps the best current statement is in a recent blog post.[7]

In general, we feel that *Foundations* presents this material well:

- Students understand the consistencies and (generally) find them compelling. The list *feels* complete—any specific oracle you can think of can be classified as an example of one of their consistencies.

- The orientation exercise (testing fonts), taken from RST, was designed to show the difficulty of coming up with automatable oracles.

- The application activity requires students to apply the consistency heuristics.

The main revision that this part of the course needed was the shift of emphasis, from using the expectation-consistencies as a framework for designing tests (something they were not initially designed for and that they don't help much with) to using them as a framework for assessing and communicating problems the tester finds with the product. The revision to the application activity accomplishes that.

---

6   http://www.satisfice.com
7   http://www.satisfice.com/blog/archives/856

Partial Oracles

This group of slides was originally intended to focus on Hoffman's collection of partial oracles that support test automation. We organized them around a table that listed oracles and gave some additional information about each.

Unfortunately, we (and the table) lost focus. We listened to too many reviewers who had too many incompatible suggestions. We mixed together too many ideas about the specific oracles, about how to generate these types of oracles, and about other test-evaluation ideas, yielding a final result that no one understands.

The next few pages offer a replacement for that material.

Partial Oracles and Automation

We think Hoffman's primary question has always been how to create useful oracle mechanisms to support automated testing.

The Nature Of Test Automation

All software tests are automated to some degree and all are manual to some degree. The interesting questions are not about whether we are automating our testing but *how much* and *in what ways*.

- *Traditional "automated" testing relies on the regression oracle.* The program compares the result of the current test to the result from last time. If they match (and if a human pronounced that result correct last time) then the automation tool declares that the program has passed the test. As tests go, this is not very powerful. If the program passed the test before, it will probably pass it again. A regression suite of 10,000 tests is a collection of 10,000 tests that the program has already shown it can pass. Maybe we would find more problems if we tried tests that the program had *not* already shown it can pass.

- *The alternative is to run new tests every time*. It is easy enough to write programs that can create and run new tests, but how can you tell whether the program passed them? As Hoffman and I see it, the most important constraint on our ability to automate tests lies in our ability the create automatable oracles. If you can program the computer to assess the results of a family of tests, you can develop high value, high volume automated testing that covers all (or any subset portion) of that family.[8] The more ways you can assess test results, the broader your collection of families, the more of your testing you can usefully automate. The challenge that Weyuker and Hoffman established is that no mechanism will perfectly assess test results. Sometimes the program will fail a test in a way that the automaton doesn't notice; sometimes the program will behave correctly but the automaton will incorrectly call it a failure. *Can you usefully automate testing in the face of these types of errors?*

---

8   http://kaner.com/?p=278

The Opportunity For Automation

Hoffman often describes oracles as *partial* rather than as heuristic. A *partial oracle* pays attention only to part of the result. For example, if you are testing a program that adds two numbers, you could check whether the sum is correct.

The risk (what makes this oracle partial) is that even if the program gets the right sum, it might be behaving incorrectly. For example, it might have a memory leak or it might run too slowly or it might also corrupt some other area of memory. Checking the sum won't tell you about those other problems.

However, checking the sum will tell you whether the sums are correct and that is useful to know (useful-but-sometimes-incorrect = heuristic).

What is special about the partial oracles is that they are programmable. You can create automated tests that will check the behavior of the program against the result predicted by (or predicted against by) any of these oracles or by any (well, probably, almost any) combination of these oracles.

Given a programmable oracle you can do high volume automated testing.[9] You can detect whatever failures that oracle can expose. For example, you might test with several oracles:

- One oracle predicts how long an operation should take (or a range of possibility). If the program takes substantially more or less time, that's a problem.

- Another oracle can predict the calculation result of the operation (or the functional result if you're doing something else, like sorting, that isn't exactly a calculation)

- Another oracle might predict the amount of free memory, or at least might tell you whether a large data set (or memory-intensive calculation) should fit in memory. If so, you can detect memory leaks this way.

No matter what combination of oracles you use, you will miss some types of errors. You cannot test *all* the dimensions of the result of a test with any oracle or any combination of oracles.

We believe you can use this imperfect approach to make testing more thorough and more efficient. Imagine testing a feature by machine using *some* oracles. Then continue testing with a human who painstakingly designs and runs each test individually. That person will know that she doesn't have to waste time checking whether certain types of bugs are there or not, because if they were there, the automaton would already have exposed them. Thus she can focus her time more valuably on the risks that remain.

---

9   http://kaner.com/?p=278

A List Of Partial Oracles

Replace the table with this list:

- *Constraint oracle:* We use the constraint oracle to check for impossible values or impossible relationships. For example an American ZIP code must be 5 or 9 digits. If you see something that is non-numeric or some other number of digits, it cannot be a ZIP code. A program that produces such a thing as a ZIP code has a bug.

- *Regression oracle:* We use the regression oracle to check results of the current test against results of execution of the same test on a previous version of the product.

- *Self-verifying data:* We use self-verifying data as an oracle. In this case, we embed the correct answer in the test data. For example, if a protocol specifies that when a program sends a message to another program, the other one will return a specific response (or one of a few possible responses), the test could include the acceptable responses. An automated test would generate the message, then check whether the response was in the list or was the specific one in the list that is expected for this message under this circumstance.

- *Physical model:* We use a physical model as an oracle when we test a software simulation of a physical process. For example, does the movement of a character or object in a game violate the laws of gravity?

- *Business model:* We use a business model the same way we use a physical model. If we have a model of a system, we can make predictions about what will happen when event X takes place.

The model makes predictions. If the software emulates the business process as we intend, it should give us behavior that is consistent with those predictions. Of course, as with all heuristics, if the program "fails" the test, it might be the model that is wrong.

■ *Statistical model:* We use a statistical model to tell us that a certain behavior or sequence of behaviors is very unlikely, or very unlikely in response to a specific action. The behavior is not impossible, but it is suspicious. We can test whether the actual behavior in the test is within the tolerance limits predicted by the model. This is often useful for looking for patterns in larger sets of data (longer sequences of tests). For example, suppose we expect an eCommerce website to get 80% of its customers from the local area, but in beta trials of its customer-analysis software, the software reports that 70% of the transactions that day were from far away. Maybe this was a special day, but probably this software has a bug. If we can predict a statistical pattern (correlations among variables, for example), we can check for it.

■ *Statistical oracle:* Another type of statistical oracle starts with an input stream that has known statistical characteristics and then check the output stream to see if it has the same characteristics. For example, send a stream of random packets, compute statistics of the set, and then have the target system send back the statistics of the data it received. If this is a large data set, this can save a lot of transmission time. Testing transmission using checksums is an example of this approach. (Of course, if a message has a checksum built into the message, that is self-verifying data.)

■ *State model:* We use a state model to specify what the program does in response to an input that happens when it is in a known state. A full state model specifies, for every state the program can be in, how the program will respond (what state it will transition to) for every input.

■ *Interaction model:* We can build an interaction model to help us test the interaction between this program and another one. The model specifies how that program will behave in response to events in (actions of) this program and how this program will behave in response to actions of the other program. The automaton triggers the action, then checks the expected behavior.

■ *Calculation oracle:* We use calculation oracles to check the calculations of a program. For example, if the program adds 5 numbers, we can use some other program to add the 5 numbers and see what we get. Or we can add the numbers and then successively subtract one at a time to see if we get a zero.

■ *Inverse oracle:* The inverse oracle is often a special case of a calculation oracle (the square of the square root of 2 should be 2) but not always. For example, imagine taking a list that is sorted low to high, sorting it high to low and then sorting it low to high. Do we get back the same list?

■ *Reference program:* The reference program generates the same responses to a set of inputs as the software under test. Of course, the behavior of the reference program will differ from the software under test in some ways (they would be identical in all ways only if they were the same program). For example, the time it takes to add 1000 numbers might be different in the reference program versus the software under test, but if they ultimately yield the same sum, we can say that the software under test passed the test.

This list is incomplete. As you imagine additional oracles that are specific enough to support automation, add them to your list.

The Instructional Problem

In retrospect, we think there were three problems with our treatment of Bach and Bolton's consistencies:

- The expectation consistencies provide a useful way to think about a bug after you find it, when you try to report it. The list of consistencies can structure your thinking as you try to figure out how to explain to someone else why a particular program behavior feels wrong. (What feels wrong about it?). However, even though *we do find them helpful for evaluating test results, we don't find them helpful for designing tests.*

- We think they are particularly *worthless for designing automated tests*. Automated testing depends on oracles—the automated-testing-program that runs a zillion tests has to decide whether the software under test passed each test or not. The consistencies help a human think about individual test results. They are good for that. But they don't guide testers (not us, not the testers we know, not the students we teach) toward oracle ideas that are specific enough to be programmed into an automaton that will then apply them to thousands of tests, classing their results as passing or failing.

- We emphasized the expectation consistencies so much in *Foundations* that *we captured our students' imagination and interfered with their thinking* about how to use oracles to design tests, especially automated tests.

An Exam Question That Illustrates The Problem

Here's an example of an exam question that our students have handled poorly year after year:

> Suppose you have written a test tool that allows you to feed commands and data to Microsoft Excel and to Open Office Calc and to see the results. The test tool is complete, and it works correctly. You have been asked to test a new version of Calc and told to automate all of your testing. What oracles would you use to help you find bugs? What types of information would you expect to get with each oracle?
>
> **Note: Don't just echo back a consistency heuristic. Be specific in your description of a relevant oracle and of the types of information or bugs that you expect.**

In exam after exam, when we gave students a specific scenario like this (often with this "Note", emphasized in bold italics). The question clearly involved automated testing. We asked them to suggest what oracles they would use to support their automated testing and how they would use those oracles to support their automated testing, they typically gave back a list of expectation-consistency heuristics. They typically had no suggestions about how to use these to support the automation.

- We tried to correct this problem by raising the problem in supplementary lectures. It didn't work.

- We went even further, telling students that this was a classic problem in this course and they needed to answer questions about oracles in test design with specific oracles. It didn't work.

- We went even further, telling students as *part of the exam question itself* that this question called for specific ideas about the oracles they would design into specific tests and they shouldn't rely on general descriptions of consistencies. It didn't work.

- Even when we gave a set of exam questions to students in advance, and they would draft an answer in advance with full benefit of time, course notes, lecture notes and videos, discussions with each other, and anything they could find on the web—even when these questions had cautionary notes about this being a question about test automation and they shouldn't just present a consistency oracle—it still didn't work.

The underlying problem is not that these students lack technical skill. Advanced university students in software engineering take this course and flunk this question too. They know how to code and they often have lots of ideas about test automation. They just don't know, in this course, how to integrate the material they learned about oracles with the idea of test automation.

Discussions with these students were what convinced us that the course's attention to the consistency-expectation heuristics overwhelmed its coverage of the more specific partial oracles. The students simply didn't think of the automatable oracles.

An Important Instructional Heuristic

When *a few* students give bad answers on an exam, *the problem is in the students*. They don't understand the material well enough.

When *a lot of* students give bad answers on the exam, *the problem is in the instruction*. It's the responsibility of the teacher to troubleshoot and fix this.

When a lot of students give bad answers that are weak in a consistent way, something specific in the instruction leads them down that path. In our experience, that something is often something the instructor is particularly attached to.

We like the consistencies a lot. But we think that in the *Foundations* course, they are an attractive nuisance (an almost-irresistible invitation to take a hazardous or counterproductive path).

Revisions to the Orienting Activity (Word Processor)

We rewrote the orienting activity (word processor fonts). It ties too tightly to the lecture to replace it completely, so instead we revised it and provided new feedback. The lecture emphasizes the surprising difficulty of this problem. There are too many fonts to test and there is no authoritative reference oracle. (As we use the term, a *reference oracle* is another program that can provide results that you can use to determine whether the program under test passed or failed.) Even though the lecture uses Word as a reference oracle, it is not automatable. The tester notices the OpenOffice font bug by visual inspection.

In practice, today, in dealing with a task like this, we would adopt a more technical approach. We would start with the recognition that font handling is now built into most operating systems. The well-designed program calls library functions to display, print, or otherwise use fonts. Fonts are defined in font definition files. These files may have errors, but they are errors in the font, not in the application that tries to use the font. If we were testing our own application, rather than the operating system's font files, we would not be interested in testing how the application works with all the fonts, one by one. Instead, we would probably do something like this:

1. Test the program with a few fonts to determine whether we could see any problems with visual comparison and inspection.

2. Examine the code to determine whether the program calls the same library functions no matter what font it uses. If we couldn't access the source code, we would try to develop technical methods to determine what functions the program was calling and would then automate a series of tests that (a) assign a font to some text and (b) check what functions were called when we tried to display or print the text. If the program consistently called the same functions, we would ultimately conclude that it probably always called the same functions and stop testing. This isn't as trustworthy as code inspection (the programmer might have built in a special case for some specific font, perhaps as an Easter Egg or as support for some type of malware) but it as good as we're going to get without code inspection.

3. Test against a few specific problems that our program might cope badly with, such as:

   - how it deals with oversize characters that want to run past the edge of the line (including characters that are big they are too wide to fit on the line)

   - how it copes with fonts that have bad definition files

   - how it copes when we type a string in one font and then change font for that string to a font that doesn't include all the characters in the string

In this solution, the partial oracle (check the library functions) simplifies the problem enormously. There is a risk that the operating system code handles a single font specially and badly, but we leave that to the people who test the O/S. There is a risk that this program has malware, but we would most effectively address this with source code inspection or reverse engineering, not with exhaustive testing. Having determined that font handling generally works, we narrow focus to the few things that might be screwy in this particular application. This is imperfect, it is incomplete, and it is probably good enough.

Replacement of the Application Activity (Consistency Heuristics)

Rather than asking students to use Bach & Bolton's consistency expectations to design tests, we now ask students to use these expectations to build arguments about bugs. How would you argue that this bug should be fixed?

This is true to our experience of the origins of these expectations (how Bach developed the initial list), we think it demonstrates the value of the ideas, and it doesn't encourage the students to think about test design in a way that we think is generally ineffective. We think the students would be much better served by thinking about test design in terms of an explicit mixture of techniques that include automation for any risks that can be cheaply and inefficiently managed that way.

Actually using partial oracles to design automated tests goes beyond the skill set we expect students in *Foundations* to achieve. However, we can expect students to think about how to do this. We encourage and evaluate that thinking using exam questions and the associated study guide. In the past, *Foundations'* emphasis on the consistency expectations was so intense that students tried to apply that to the exam questions as well.

Some Additional History And Perspective
- On the incompleteness of oracles
- Oracles are heuristics
- Bach and Bolton's consistencies
- Hoffman's approach

On The Incompleteness Of Oracles

Back when dinosaurs roamed the earth, some testasauruses theorized that a properly designed software test involves:

- a set of preconditions that specify the state of the software and system when you start the test
- a set of procedures that specify what you do when you do the test

■ comparison of what the software under test does with a set of postconditions: the predicted state of the system under test after you run the test. This set of postconditions make up the expected results of the test.

We can call the postconditions the oracle or we can say that a program that generates the expected results is the oracle, but in either case, the testasauruses said, good testing involves comparing the program's test behavior to expected results, and to do good testing, you need an oracle. (Fossils from this era are preserved in IEEE Standard 829 on software test documentation.[10]

Elaine Weyuker's (1980) On Testing Nontestable Programs shattered that view. Weyuker argued that "it is unusual for an oracle to be pragmatically attainable or even to exist".[11] Instead, she said, testers rely on partial oracles. For example:

■ A tester might recognize a result of a calculation as impossibly large even though she doesn't know what the exact result should be. (You might not know offhand what 1.465732 x 2.74312 is, but if a program said 7,000,000 you could reject that as obviously wrong without doing any calculations.)

■ A tester might recognize behavior as inappropriate, even if she doesn't know exactly how the program should behave.

Weyuker's paper wasn't widely noticed in the practitioner community. I don't think we appreciated the extent of this problem until the Quality Week conference in 1998, when Doug Hoffman[12] explained this problem and its implications this way:

Suppose that we specify a test by describing

■ the starting state of the system under test

■ the test inputs (the data and operations you use to carry out the test)

■ the expected test outputs

We can still make mistakes in interpreting the test results.

■ We might *incorrectly decide that the program passed the test because its outputs matched the expected outputs* but it misbehaved in some other way. For example, a program that adds 2+2 might get 4, but it is clearly broken in some way if it takes 10 hours to get that result of 4.

■ We might *incorrectly decide that the program failed the test because its outputs did not match the expected results*, but on more careful examination, we might realize that it did the right thing. For example, imagine testing to a network printer with the expectation that the printer will page a specific page within 1 minute—but during the test, another computer sent a long document to the printer and so it didn't actually get to the test document for a long time. This might be the exactly correct behavior under the circumstances, but it doesn't match the expectation.

Most testers, doing manual testing, would probably not make either mistake. But an automated test would make both mistakes. So would a manual tester who was trying to exactly follow a fully-detailed script.

---

10 http://en.wikipedia.org/wiki/IEEE_829

11 http://www.testingeducation.org/BBST/foundations/Weyuker_ontestingnontestable.pdf p. 3

12 A Taxonomy for Test Oracles, http://www.softwarequalitymethods.com/Papers/OracleTax.pdf

Doug argued that both types of mistakes were inevitable in testing because no one could fully specify the starting state of the system and no one could fully specify the ending state of the system. There are too many potentially-relevant variables. For example, suppose in your 2+2 test, you do specify the expected time for the test to complete:

■ Did you specify the contents of the stack? What if the program adds stuff to the stack but doesn't remove it, or corrupts the stack in some other way?

■ Did you specify the contents of memory? Memory leaks are common bugs. And buffer overflows are a common example of a class of bug that corrupts memory.

■ Did you specify the contents of the hard disk? What if the program saves something or deletes something?

■ Did you specify what the printer would do during the test? What if the program sends something to the printer, even though it is not supposed to, or sends unauthorized email, etc.?

If you don't have experience thinking about the diversity of ways that something can go wrong, but you have a bit of technical savvy, the Hewlett-Packard printer diagnostics can be eye-opening. You can find documentation of these in Management Information Bases (MIB's) published by HP. I find these online here[13] but if this source goes away, you can find third party sites like OiDView. For example, the MIB file for the LaserJet 9250c runs 8506 lines, documenting 176 commands, many of them with many possible parameters. A program can go wrong in hundreds (or thousands) of different ways.

From a diagnostic point of view, imagine running a test and checking the state of the printer. For example, you might check how much free memory there is, or how long the last command took to execute, or the most recent internal error code. Each diagnostic command that you run changes the state of the machine, and so the results of the next diagnostic are no longer looking at the system as it was right after the test completed.

So in practical terms, even if you could fully specify the state of the system after a test (you can't, but pretend that you could), you still couldn't check whether the system actually reached that state after the test because each of the diagnostics that you would run to check the state of the system would change the state. The next diagnostic tests the machine that is now in a different state. In practical terms, you can only run a few diagnostics as part of a test (maybe just one) before the diagnostics stop being informative. IfÂ these diagnostics don't look for a problem in the right places, you won't see it. This is sometimes called the Heisenbug problem, in honor of the Heisenberg Uncertainty Principle.[14]

---

13 https://spp.austin.hp.com/SPP/Public/Sdk/SdkPublicDownload.aspx

14 http://en.wikipedia.org/wiki/Unusual_software_bug

Oracles are Heuristics

Hoffman argued that no oracle can fully specify the postcondition state of the system under test and therefore no oracle is complete. Given that an oracle is incomplete, you might use the oracle and incorrectly conclude that the program failed the test when it didn't or passed the test when it didn't. Either way, reliance on an oracle can lead you to the wrong conclusion.

A decision rule that is useful but not always correct is called a heuristic.

My favorite presentations of the ideas underlying Heuristics were written by Billy V. Koen. See a wonderful historical article that he wrote for BBST[15] and his book (I prefer the shorter and simpler ASEE early edition used in introductory engineering courses[16] but the current version is widely respected.[17])

15 http://www.testingeducation.org/BBST/foundations/Koen_EngineeringMethod.pdf
16 http://www.abebooks.com/servlet/SearchResults?an=koen&sts=t&tn=Definition+of+the+Engineering+Method
17 http://www.abebooks.com/servlet/SearchResults?an=koen&sts=t&tn=Discussion+of+the+Method

The Bach / Bolton Consistency Heuristics

Imagine running a test. The program misbehaves. The tester notices the behavior and recognizes that something is wrong. *What is it that makes the tester decide this is wrong behavior?*

In Bach's view (as I understand it from talking with him and teaching about this with him), what happens is that the tester makes a comparison between the behavior and some expectations about the ways the program should (or should not) behave. These comparisons might be conscious or unconscious, but Bach posits that they must happen because every explanation of why a program's behavior has been evaluated as a misbehavior can be mapped to one of these types of consistency.

Bach created a list of these expectations, which he calls consistency heuristics or oracle heuristics. His list (now his and Bolton's) is designed to cover every type of consistency-expectation that testers rely on. If they realize the list is incomplete, they add a new type.[18]

For the sake of argument, I will assume that this list is complete, i.e. that every rationale that a tester provides for why a program is misbehaving can be mapped to one of these 8 types of consistency.

I have seen it argued (mainly on Twitter) that this is the "right" list. That every other oracle can be mapped to this list (this oracle tests for this type of inconsistency) and therefore they are all special cases. If you know this list, the argument goes, you can derive (or imagine) (or something) all the oracles from it.

As far as I know, there is no empirical research to support the claim that testers in fact always rely on comparisons to expectations or that these particular categories of expectations map to the comparisons that go on in testers' heads.

- That assertion does not match my subjective impression of what happens in my head when I test. It seems to me that misbehaviors often strike me as *obvious* without any reference to an alternative expectation. One could counter this by saying that the comparison is implicit (unconscious) and maybe it is. But there is no empirical evidence of this, and until there is, I get to group the assertion with Santa Claus and the Tooth Fairy. Interesting, useful, but not necessarily true.

- The assertion also does not match my biases about the nature of concept formation and categorical reasoning.

  - As a graduate student, I studied cognition with Professor Lee R. Brooks.[19] Some of his most famous work was on nonanalytic concept formation.[20] For introductory overviews to this

18 http://www.developsense.com/blog/2009/12/structures-of-exploratory-testing/
19 http://www.science.mcmaster.ca/Psychology/lb.html
20 http://scholar.google.com/scholar?hl=en&as_sdt=0,10&q=brooks+nonanalytic+concept+formation

work, see his 1978 chapter In Rosch & Lloyd's classic *Cognition & Categorization*[21] or his paper with Larry Jacoby (1984) on Nonanalytic cognition.[22]

- A traditional view of cognition holds that we make many types of judgment on the basis of rules that put things into categories—something is this or that because of a set of rules that we consult either consciously or unconsciously. Bach and Bolton's consistencies are examples of the kinds of categories that I think of when I think of this tradition.

- A very different view holds that we make judgments on the basis of similarity to exemplars[23]. (An exemplar is a memorable example.) A person can learn arbitrarily many exemplars. Experts have probably learned many more than nonexperts and so they make better evaluations.[24]

- One of the most interesting experiments in Lee's lab required the experimental subject to make a judgment (saying which category something belonged to) and explain the judgment. The subjects in the experiments described what they said were their decision rules to explain each choice. But over a long series of decisions, you can ask whether these rules actually describe the judgments being made. The answer was negative. The subject would describe a rule that recently he hadn't followed and that he would again not follow later. Instead, the more accurate predictor of his decisions was the similarity of the thing he was categorizing to other things he had previously categorized. It appeared that unconscious processing was going on, but it was nonanalytic (similarity-based), not analytic (rule-based). I found, and still find, this line of results persuasive.

A list can be useful as a heuristic device, as a tool that helps you consciously think about a problem, whether the list describes the actual underlying psychology of testing or not.

But if it is to be a good heuristic device, it has to be more useful than not. As a tool for teaching oracles as part of test design, my experience is that the consistency list fails the utility criterion.

I don't have any scientific research to back up my conclusion, just a lot of personal experience. But when dealing with a heuristic device that is not backed up by any scientific research (just a lot of personal experience), I get to rely on what I've got.

---

21 http://www.amazon.com/Cognition-Categorization-Eleanor-Rosch/dp/0470263776/
22 http://books.google.com/books?hl=en&lr=&id=p5X51gkLKOwC&oi=fnd&pg=PA1&dq=brooks+nonanalytic+concept+forma tion&ots=gTFMTiulFs&sig=opMByI-Adnug-97CGwdT49_a8wE
23 http://www.springerlink.com/content/p1m5x6020346q711/
24 http://en.wikipedia.org/wiki/Expertise

Doug Hoffman's Approach

I first saw Doug talk about oracles in 1998, at Quality Week. That was the start of a long series of publications[25] on oracles and the use of oracles in test automation. Along with the papers, I have the benefit of having taught courses on test automation with Doug and having talked at length with him while he struggled to get his ideas on paper.

Doug made two key points in 1998:

- All oracles are heuristic (we've already covered that ground)

---

25 http://softwarequalitymethods.com/html/papers.html#taxonomy

■ There are a lot of incomplete oracles available. Given that we have to rely on incomplete oracles (because no oracles are complete), we should think about what combinations of oracles we can use to learn interesting things about the software.

Doug's work was so striking that we opened the Fifth Los Altos Workshop on Software Testing[26] with it. That meeting became an intense, 2-day long, moderated debate between Doug and James Bach. We learned so much about managing difficult debates in that meeting that we were able to create what I think of as the current structure of LAWST, adopted in LAWST 6.

---

26 http://lawst.com/

4

LESSON 4: PROGRAMMING FUNDAMENTALS AND COVERAGE

Lesson Introduction

Lesson 4 introduces several topics from the fundamentals of computing:

- How computers store numbers and text. What it means to overflow the storage reserved for a piece of data.

- How computers do arithmetic. The basics of binary storage and binary calculations.

- The nature of floating-point arithmetic. Why floating-point calculations introduce errors as a matter of design. Why testers need to be aware of this so that they don't make fools of themselves by insisting that tiny errors in floating-point calculations are bugs.

- The main data types. You will only learn their names and the most basic facts about them here (including a very few examples of ways that programs go wrong using them), but this might be more than you knew before joining the class.

- The main control structures in programs. A control structure is a programming concept that controls how program execution proceeds from one place in the code to another. We include interrupts and exceptions in this set, and a few examples of how programs get into trouble with each of these.

This is basic software vocabulary. Most programmers expect most testers to understand these terms and concepts. Many bugs are easier to imagine (and to plan tests for) if you understand these concepts. Many programmers' responses on bug reports are incomprehensible if you don't understand these concepts—at least at a very basic level.

In previous versions of this course, we had assumed that most testers were familiar with these concepts. Not necessarily *knowledgeable* about them, but familiar with the ideas. When we published study guides (lists of all the questions that we considered candidates for inclusion in one of our exams), we included questions that we felt were asking students to apply basic testing knowledge and skill. But when those questions assumed that students were familiar with any of the concepts covered in Lesson 4, our students repeatedly taught us, in their pre-exam questions to us and in their performance on their exams, that we were assuming more than they knew. To address the knowledge gaps that intruded even into questions that we didn't consider technical at all, we decided to create a Lesson with this material.

Our goal of improving testers' computing-related literacy was one of two reasons we created this Lesson.

The other was to build a bridge from the material covered so far (Lessons 1-3) and the more technical issues in Lessons 5 and 6:

Lesson 5 is about the amount of testing you can, or should do, or have done. Lecture 6 extends the discussion of how we measure how much testing we've done to an introduction to measurement theory (the foundations of software engineering metrics).

Many of the discussions of the adequacy or completeness of testing are focused on programs' control structures. For example, did your tests cover every statement in the program? Every way that the program could get from there to here? These "did your tests cover every..." questions are formally described as questions of structural coverage. You can't understand what people are talking about unless you know something about the basic control structures in programs. You can't evaluate whether these would be useful measures of your testing work and you can't explain effectively to anyone else why you think they would be useful measures, or not-useful measures, unless you know the basics of control structures.

Lesson 4 provides the basics and briefly describes the most popular measurements of structural coverage.

Readings

The following readings are required:

- Kaner, C. (1995). Software negligence and testing coverage. Software QA Quarterly, 2, 18. Retrieved from http://www.kaner.com/pdfs/negligence_and_testing_coverage.pdf
- Marick, B. (1997). How to Misuse Code Coverage. Retrieved from http://www.testingeducation. org/BBST/foundations/Marick_coverage.pdf

The following readings are recommended:

- Goldberg, D. (1991). What Every Computer Scientist Should Know About Floating-Point Arithmetic. ACM Computing Surveys, 23(1), 5–48.

- Kahan, W. & Severance, C. (1998), "An interview with the old man of floating point." http://www.eecs.berkeley.edu/~wkahan/ieee754status/754story.html and http://www.eecs.berkeley.edu/~wkahan/

- Marick, B. (undated). Experience with the Cost of Different Coverage Goals for Testing. Retrieved from http://www.testingeducation.org/BBST/foundations/Marick_experience.pdf

- Petzold, C. (2000). Code: The Hidden Language of Computer Hardware and Software (First Paperback ed.). Microsoft Press.

Orientation: Testing An Integer Square Root Function

Note: This is really an orientation to both Lessons 4 and 5. We typically assign it at the start of Lesson 4 but some students find it more useful after experiencing Lesson 4. If you are studying this book on your own, and have little programming background, we suggest that you try this task at the start of Lesson 4 but don't look at the notes in the back of the book. Try it again after Lesson 4 as you move into Lesson 5. How have your answers changed? How confident are you in the new ones? Then watch the lecture, and then look at the notes in the back.

Please try this task before viewing the Lesson 4 lecture or the Lesson 5 lecture. Capture your first impressions. Make notes on what questions you think are easy (and what the easy answers are) and what you think are hard. Don't get bogged down. If you find yourself getting stuck, make notes on what is confusing you and move on. Try to limit yourself to 30 minutes on this task.

After you post your own answers, please review answers from at least two other students and post comments on their answers. How did their analyses differ from yours? Did they make assumptions that differed from yours? How do those differences change how you and they would test?

Here is the task...

Imagine testing a program that includes an Integer Square Root function. This type of function reads a 32-bit word that is stored in memory, interprets the contents as an unsigned integer and then computes the square root of the integer. It returns the result as a floating-point number. For example, it might calculate the square root of the integer, 3, and return the floating-point number 1.732050808.

1. What values can you input to this function?

2. Can you imagine any invalid inputs to this function, inputs that should cause the function to return an error message?

3. If you were to test *all* of the inputs to this function, how many tests would there be?

4. How long do you think it would take you to run all these tests?

5. How would you test this function? Describe your thinking about your possible test strategies.

6. Would you add more tests if this function was in a life-critical program and you wanted to be sure it had no bugs? How many more tests? Which ones? Why these?

7. If the program computed the square root of 4 and reported 1.9999999999999999, would that be a passing result or a failure? How close would the answer have to be to 2.0 for the result to be a pass? Why?

In an instructor-led class, the instructor might also ask you these two questions or some like them:

- Have you ever done this type of testing? If so, when? Please describe your experience.
- Have you ever used tools that would do this type of testing? If so, what tools? How would you use them for this task?

Slides And Notes

SLIDE 142

Welcome to this fourth lecture of the *Foundations of Software Testing*.

BLACK BOX SOFTWARE TESTING:
FOUNDATIONS: LECTURE 4.
PROGRAMMING FUNDAMENTALS
& COVERAGE

CEM KANER, J.D., PH.D.
PROFESSOR OF SOFTWARE ENGINEERING
FLORIDA INSTITUTE OF TECHNOLOGY

REBECCA L. FIEDLER, M.B.A. PH.D.
PRESIDENT: KANER, FIEDLER & ASSOCIATES

JAMES BACH
PRINCIPAL, SATISFICE INC.

This work is licensed under the Creative Commons Attribution License. To view a copy of this license, visit http://creativecommons.org/licenses/by-sa/2.0/ or send a letter to Creative Commons, 559 Nathan Abbott Way, Stanford, California 94305, USA.

These notes are partially based on research that was supported by NSF Grants EIA-0113539 ITR/SY +PE: "Improving the Education of Software Testers" and CCLI-0717613 "Adaptation & Implementation of an Activity-Based Online or Hybrid Course in Software Testing." Any opinions, findings and conclusions or recommendations expressed in this material are those of the author(s) and do not necessarily reflect the views of the National Science Foundation.

142

SLIDE 143

Today's central question is how to assess coverage of our tests.

OVERVIEW: FUNDAMENTAL TOPICS

- Why are we testing? What are we trying to learn? How should we organize our work to achieve this? *Information objectives drive the testing mission and strategy*

- How can we know whether a program has passed or failed a test? *Oracles are heuristic*

- How can we determine how much testing has been done? What core knowledge about program internals do testers need to consider this question? *Coverage is a multidimensional problem*

- Are we done yet? *Complete testing is impossible*

- How much testing have we completed and how well have we done it? *Measurement is important, but hard*

143

SLIDE 144

TODAY'S READINGS

- Cem Kaner (1995), "Software Negligence & Testing Coverage." http://www.kaner.com/pdfs/negligence_and_testing_coverage.pdf
- Brian Marick (1997), How to Misuse Code Coverage http://www.exampler.com/testing-com/writings/coverage.pdf

Useful to skim:

- Michael Bolton (2008), "Got you covered." http://www.developsense.com/articles/2008-10-GotYouCovered.pdf
- David Goldberg (1991), "What every computer scientist should know about floating point arithmetic", http://docs.sun.com/source/806-3568/ncg_goldberg.html
- William Kahan & Charles Severance (1998), "An interview with the old man of floating point." http://www.eecs.berkeley.edu/~wkahan/ieee754status/754story.html

  http://www.eecs.berkeley.edu/~wkahan/

- Brian Marick (1991), "Experience with the cost of different coverage goals for testing", http://www.exampler.com/testing-com/writings/experience.pdf
- Charles Petzold (1993), *Code: The Hidden Language of Computer Hardware and Software.* Microsoft Press

Your class may use other readings, but we had these in mind when creating this lecture.

144

We have two primary references, one by Brian Marick on the abuse of structural code coverage measures and one of mine that describes alternatives to the structural measures.

SLIDE 145

Testers repeatedly make fools of themselves by saying things to programmers that demonstrate their deep ignorance of how computers and programs work.

Today's lecture gives me an excuse to give you a refresher on the basics of computing: how programs store and use data and execute instructions. You cannot understand structural code coverage measures without understanding these basics.

COMPUTING FUNDAMENTALS

Why teach this material now?

- Most discussions of "coverage" in testing involve structural coverage. To understand what people are talking about
  - what these types of coverage actually measure
  - what types of tests people emphasize in order to achieve coverage
  - what risks are **not** addressed by these types of coverage

  you need a bit of knowledge of data representation and program structure.

145

SLIDE 146

I can't go into depth in this material—I have only part of one lecture, before getting back to the nature and challenges of coverage measurement.

I'm hoping that for some of you, this lecture will give you a starting point, to go read more about the foundations of computing.

Charles Petzold's book, CODE, is an excellent starting point. Petzold uses history to explain the why of many of the choices that underlie the design of computers and programming languages. This is a very readable book. You should read it.

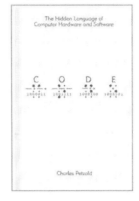

COMPUTING FUNDAMENTALS:
READ THIS BOOK

The Hidden Language of Computer Hardware and Software

C O D E

Charles Petzold

146

SLIDE 147

We're going to start by considering how computers store data and do arithmetic.

HOW DO COMPUTERS STORE DATA?

- Basic storage and arithmetic (Decimal)
  - Decimal numbers
  - Addition
  - Overflow
  - Integers vs floating point
- Basic storage and arithmetic (Binary)
  - Representation
  - Addition
  - Overflow
  - Floating point
- Alphanumeric and other characters

147

SLIDE 148

And that starts with how we do arithmetic.

We work with a 10-digit number system. We have 10 distinct numerals, 0 through 9.

DECIMAL NUMBERS

Digits: We have 10 of them
So we can count:
1, 2, 3, 4, 5, 6, 7, 8, 9, 10

But instead of

1, 2, 3, 4, 5, 6, 7, 8, 9, 10

We use the following Decimal numerals:

0, 1, 2, 3, 4, 5, 6, 7, 8, 9

http://www.flickr.com/photos/stnstic/1362089/

148

SLIDE 149

We can represent any number as a power of 10 or a sum of powers of 10.

Thus, nine hundred and fifty four means

Nine hundred – that's 9 times 100

Plus fifty – that's five times ten

Plus four

_____

_____

_____

_____

_____

_____

DECIMAL NUMBERS

Decimal arithmetic:

- "decimal" refers to 10 (like counting on your 10 fingers)
- Base 10 arithmetic represent numbers as a sum of powers of 10:
    - 10^0 = 1
    - 10^1 = 10
    - 10^2 = 10 x 10 = 100
    - 10^3 = 10 x 10 x 10 = 1000

$10 = 1 \times 10^1 + 0 \times 10^0$

$954 = 9 \times 10^2 + 5 \times 10^1 + 4 \times 10^0$

(Special case: 0 = 0)

149

SLIDE 150

We use the same information when we add numbers.

So when we add the 6 and the 2 in six-hundred-and-54 plus two-hundred-and-43, we know we are adding 600 and 200.

_____

_____

_____

_____

_____

_____

_____

ADDING DECIMAL NUMBERS

Consider

$654 = 6 \times 10^2 + 5 \times 10^1 + 4 \times 10^0$

$243 = 2 \times 10^2 + 4 \times 10^1 + 3 \times 10^0$

To add them,

- Add 4×10^0 and $3 \times 10^0 = 7 \times 10^0$
- Add 5×10^1 and $4 \times 10^1 = 9 \times 10^1$
- Add 6×10^2 and $2 \times 10^2 = 8 \times 10^2$

So, 654 + 243 = 897

150

SLIDE 151

When we add, we can overflow a digit.

If you add two one-digit numbers, sometimes you get a one-digit result. For example, 6 plus 3 is 9

But you can also get a result that is too big for one digit. For example, 6 plus 7 is too many for 10 fingers. We need another digit.

_____

_____

_____

_____

_____

_____

OVERFLOW

Consider the following 1-digit decimal numbers.

6   = 6×10^0

7   = 7×10^0

To add them,

- 6 + 7 is larger than the largest decimal numeral
- 6 + 7 = 6 + (4 + 3)

        = (6 + 4) + 3

        = 10 + 3

        = $1 \times 10^1 + 3 \times 10^0$

        = 13

        a 2-digit decimal number

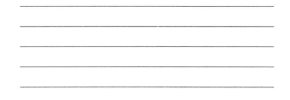

We "carry the 1".
That is, we add
1 times
the next higher power of 10

151

_____

_____

_____

SLIDE 152

Rather than trying to supplement our fingers with toes, let's switch to number boxes. Each box has 10 sides, labeled 0 through 9.

Working with two boxes makes it possible to represent numbers between 00 and 99.

_____

_____

_____

_____

_____

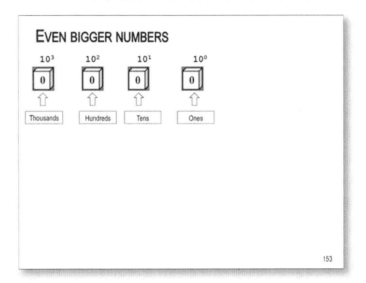

SLIDE 153

With four boxes, we can represent four digits.

_____

_____

_____

_____

_____

_____

_____

_____

_____

_____

_____

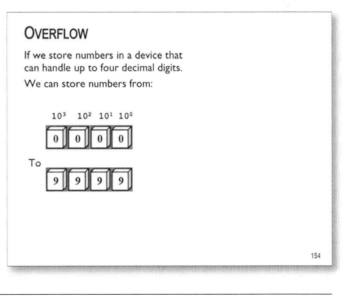

SLIDE 154

And that lets us store numbers up to 9 thousand 9 hundred ninety nine.

_____

_____

_____

_____

_____

_____

_____

_____

_____

_____

_____

_____

_____

_____

_____

SLIDE 155

We can show addition with these number blocks this way.

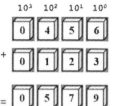

SLIDE 156

And here's what we have with overflows.

8 plus 3 is too big for one block, so it becomes 11, one for the ones block and one for the tens block.

7 plus 5 would be twelve, but we're carrying the 1, so this becomes 13, three for the tens block and one carried to the hundreds block.

SLIDE 157

Everything works fine until we have a sum bigger than 9999.

Computers store integers in a fixed number of digits, just like these four boxes.

If we add two big enough integers together, the sum is too big to store, and we get an integer overflow.

SLIDE 158

We can also represent fractions this way. Along with number blocks for ones, tens and hundreds, we can have number blocks for 1-tenths, 1-hundredths and 1-thousands.

_____

_____

_____

_____

_____

_____

_____

WE CAN ALSO REPRESENT FRACTIONS

Base 10 arithmetic represent numbers as a sum of powers of 10:

- 10^{-3} = 1 / 1000
- 10^{-2} = 1 / 100
- 10^{-1} = 1 /10
- 10^{0} = 1
- 10^{1} = 10
- 10^{2} = 100
- 10^{3} = 1000

$0.02345 = 2 \times 10^{-2} + 3 \times 10^{-3} + 4 \times 10^{-4} + 5 \times 10^{-5}$
$0.2345 = 2 \times 10^{-1} + 3 \times 10^{-2} + 4 \times 10^{-3} + 5 \times 10^{-4}$
$2.345 = 2 \times 10^{0} + 3 \times 10^{-1} + 4 \times 10^{-2} + 5 \times 10^{-3}$
$23.45 = 2 \times 10^{1} + 3 \times 10^{0} + 4 \times 10^{-1} + 5 \times 10^{-2}$
$234.5 = 2 \times 10^{2} + 3 \times 10^{1} + 4 \times 10^{0} + 5 \times 10^{-1}$
$2345. = 2 \times 10^{3} + 3 \times 10^{2} + 4 \times 10^{1} + 5 \times 10^{0}$

158

SLIDE 159

In fixed-point arithmetic, the decimal point is in the same place for every number. For example, in all of these, we use the decimal point to mark the boundary between the 10 to the zero digit (the one's digit) and the 10 to the -1 digit (the one-tenths).

_____

_____

_____

_____

FIXED POINT REPRESENTATION

In a fixed-point representation, the decimal point stays "fixed" (same place) no matter how large or small the number.

$0.02345 = 2 \times 10^{-2} + 3 \times 10^{-3} + 4 \times 10^{-4} + 5 \times 10^{-5}$
$0.2345 = 2 \times 10^{-1} + 3 \times 10^{-2} + 4 \times 10^{-3} + 5 \times 10^{-4}$
$2.345 = 2 \times 10^{0} + 3 \times 10^{-1} + 4 \times 10^{-2} + 5 \times 10^{-3}$
$23.45 = 2 \times 10^{1} + 3 \times 10^{0} + 4 \times 10^{-1} + 5 \times 10^{-2}$
$234.5 = 2 \times 10^{2} + 3 \times 10^{1} + 4 \times 10^{0} + 5 \times 10^{-1}$
$2345.0 = 2 \times 10^{3} + 3 \times 10^{2} + 4 \times 10^{1} + 5 \times 10^{0}$
$23450.0 = 2 \times 10^{4} + 3 \times 10^{3} + 4 \times 10^{2} + 5 \times 10^{1}$
$234500.0 = 2 \times 10^{5} + 3 \times 10^{4} + 4 \times 10^{3} + 5 \times 10^{2}$

159

SLIDE 160

Fixed-point arithmetic is a lot like integer arithmetic.

With integers, there is a fixed number of digits. They are all whole numbers, no fractions. For example, in 9999, there are four significant digits.

With fixed-point numbers, we can have fractions. For example, with currency, we can have dollars and cents. The decimal point divides the dollars from the cents, where a cent is 1 one-hundredth of a dollar.

However, we still have a fixed number of significant digits.

FIXED POINT REPRESENTATION

Fixed point representation in a computer is essentially the same as integer storage.

- We have a limited set of number blocks and we can't go beyond them.
- We call these our "significant digits"
- The difference is that we get to choose (once, for all numbers) where the decimal point goes.
- For example, $1234.56 is a **six-significant-digit** fixed-point number. We cannot represent a number larger than $9999.99 or currency subdivisions finer than a penny (1/100th).

160

_____

_____

_____

_____

SLIDE 161

With fixed-point arithmetic, we can decide what range of numbers we want to look at, in effect moving the decimal point.

For example, here's a recent income statement from Microsoft. Their revenue was 62,484,000 *thousands* of dollars. This is not 62 million dollars, it is 62 million thousand-dollars. All of the numbers in the income statement are in the same units, thousands of dollars.

The decimal point is still fixed. But now it is always between thousands of dollars and fractions of thousands instead of between ones of dollars and fractions of ones.

FIXED POINT REPRESENTATION

In fixed-point, we can choose where we place the decimal point.

Here for example: **"All numbers in thousands"**

SLIDE 162

We can represent a much larger range of numbers with floating point arithmetic.

In floating point arithmetic, we represent every number with two numbers, a mantissa and an exponent.

The mantissa includes the significant digits. In this example, they are 2, 3, 4, and 5.

To get the actual number, you multiply the mantissa by 10 to the exponent.

So 2.345 is represented as 2345 (the mantissa) by 10 to the -3. Both of these have the same value.

Similarly, 23.45 is the same as 2345 by 10 to the -2.

And two billion, three hundred and forty-five million is 2345 by 10 to the 6.

We still only have four significant digits, but the range of numbers we can work with is huge. We can have numbers in the billions or trillions or quadrillions or fractions in the 1-billionths or 1-quadrillionths or smaller.

FLOATING POINT

2.345

$= 2 \times 10^0 + 3 \times 10^{-1} + 4 \times 10^{-2} + 5 \times 10^{-3}$

$= 10^{-3} \times 2345$

$= 10^{-3} \times (2 \times 10^3 + 3 \times 10^2 + 4 \times 10^1 + 5 \times 10^0)$

- So we can represent "any" 4-digit number
  - as an Integer (a number with no decimal point)
  - multiplied by 10 to the appropriate power
- In 2345×10^{-3}
  - 2345 is called the *mantissa* or the *significand*
  - there are 4 *significant digits*
  - 10 is called the *base*
  - -3 is called the *exponent.*

$2,345,000,000 = 2345 \times 10^6$

A significant digit is a digit we allow to have a value other than zero.

SLIDE 163

To simplify how we read floating point numbers, there is a convention.

We write the mantissa with the decimal point after the most significant digit.

This way, all of the differences between two numbers in their order of magnitude show up in the exponent.

_____

_____

_____

_____

_____

FLOATING POINT

As a matter of convention, we usually show the mantissa with a decimal point after the most significant digit:

$$0.02345 = 2.345 \times 10^{-2}$$
$$2.345 = 2.345 \times 10^{0}$$
$$2345 = 2.345 \times 10^{3}$$
$$234500000 = 2.345 \times 10^{8}$$

- Each number has 4 significant digits
- Each has the same mantissa (2.345)
- Each has the same base
- Only the exponent is varying

163

SLIDE 164

Let's go back to our example of an integer overflow. We still have only four significant digits, so we can't store 13,777.

However, we can represent in floating point notation this as 1.378 times 10 to the fourth. We've rounded up the least significant digit to squeeze into a four-digit mantissa. The mantissa is 1.378.

_____

_____

_____

OVERFLOW AND FLOATING POINT

Now consider this example again…

The sum is **13777**, which overflows the 4 significant digits.
In floating point notation, it is
$$1.3777 \times 10^{4}$$
This is still too many digits, but we can round up:
$$1.378 \times 10^{4}$$

164

SLIDE 165

But there's still a problem. We've squeezed into a four-significant-digit mantissa, but where do we store the exponent? Without that, we have 1.378, not 1.378 times 10 to the fourth.

The solution is to add a new box for the exponent. So now, instead of storing four digits, we're storing five digits, but the first of these digits is for the exponent rather than for the mantissa.

There's only one additional detail.

The exponent can be negative as well as positive. Sometimes we multiply the mantissa by ten to the fourth and sometimes by ten to the minus fourth.

So let's add one more box, this time as a place to store the exponent's sign.

OVERFLOW, FLOATING POINT & ROUNDING

We still can't represent 1.378×10^{4} in four digits.

But what if we added a box for the exponent and a box for the exponent's sign?

$$= 10^{4} \times (1 \times 10^{0} + 3 \times 10^{-1} + 7 \times 10^{-2} + 8 \times 10^{-3})$$

In this way, we can represent a number

- as small as $10^{-9} \times 1.000$ (0.000000001) and
- as large as $10^{9} \times 9.999$ (9999000000.0).

165

SLIDE 166

There's a constraint in this that you should pay attention to.

Even though our numbers can span a huge range, they still have only four significant digits.

That means that a number like 12344 will look exactly the same, once it is stored, as 12340. There is no place for that last 4. There is no fifth significant digit.

SIGNIFICANT DIGITS AND PRECISION

We can represent a number
- as small as $10^{-9} \times 1.000$ (0.000000001)
- as large as $10^9 \times 9.999$ (9999000000.0)

However, we have only 4 significant digits.

Suppose we entered:
- 9999000000.0,
- 9999000001.0, and
- 9999499999.0

How will the computer store these?

In a floating point representation with 4 significant digits, all would be stored the same way, as 9.999×10^9

166

SLIDE 167

I often pose a puzzle to my students. I give them a function that computes the square root of 4 and ask if it would be a bug if the program reports a result of 1.999999999 instead of 2.

Almost all of the students say this would be a bug.

But suppose a program only stores four significant digits. What is the difference in representation between a number like 1.9999 and 2? Won't they be stored exactly the same way in memory?

Suppose that it would not be a bug to interpret 1.9999 as 2.

SIGNIFICANT DIGITS AND PRECISION

Which is the bigger error?

Saying that 2.000 is 1.9999?

OR

Saying that 1.99975 is 2.000?

167

What if we took the square root of 3.999? The actual square root of 3.999 is about 1.99975. In 4 digits, that would be stored exactly the same way as 1.9999, which would be stored exactly the same way as 2. So which is the bigger error? Saying that 1.99975 is 2 or saying that 2 is 1.9999?

Floating point arithmetic contains a fundamental limitation. Our calculations have rounding error. After a floating point operation like square root, we can't tell the difference between 1.9995, 1.9999, 2, or 2.0004. All of them end up stored in memory as 2.000 but in terms of the magnitude of the actual error, it would be a bigger mistake to call 1.99975 two than it would be to call two 1.9999.

SLIDE 168

We can add more precision to a number by storing more digits in the mantissa. When we distinguish between single precision and double precision and quadruple precision floating point arithmetic, mainly we're distinguishing between the number of digits in the mantissa.

Here are a few other ways to extend the range of floating point numbers.

Most floating point numbers add more digits in the exponent.

We also have negative floating point numbers as well as positive. To show this, we add another storage box for another sign. This one holds the sign of the mantissa instead of the sign of the exponent.

Thus, for example, minus one tenth – the number you get if you subtract one from point nine. Minus one tenth would be -1.0 x 10 to the minus 1.

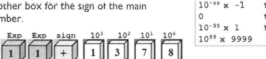

OVERFLOW, FLOATING POINT & ROUNDING

- If we want to represent a larger range of numbers, we can change the number of digits in the Exponent. With two digits, we can go from

    10^{-99} x 0001 to 10^{99} x 9999

- If we want negative numbers (in the significand) as well as positive, we can add another box for the sign of the main number.

```
10⁹⁹  x -9999  to
10⁻⁹⁹ x -1     to
0              to
10⁻⁹⁹ x 1      to
10⁹⁹  x 9999
```

SLIDE 169

So here's a puzzle to work on with your friends. It should be easy. But I'm not going to give you the answer.

Assume you have four significant digits and a sign bit for the mantissa, and two significant digits with a sign bit for the exponent.

What are your results for these two calculations?

_____

_____

_____

FLOATING POINT & ROUNDING ERROR

With this system for representing numbers,

a) What is the sum of
      1234 x 10^{10}
    + 5678 x 10^{-10} ?

b) What is the product of
      1234 x 10^{10}
    x 12 ?

    In that multiplication, assume we could never store more than 4 digits at any time.

SLIDE 170

Modern computers don't usually store numbers as decimal digits.

They store numbers in bits instead. Bits are binary digits.

_____

_____

_____

_____

_____

_____

BINARY NUMBERS

A simpler approach to digits:
Instead of counting from 0 to 9 (decimal), consider counting from 0 to 1 (binary).

Our binary digits are
0 and 1.
We call binary digits
"bits".
We also call the
physical portion of
computer memory
needed to store
a 0-or-1 a 'bit'.

http://www.flickr.com/photos/jsfield/2761629984

SLIDE 171

Instead of decimal arithmetic, computers do binary arithmetic.

For the next few slides, I'll keep showing you number boxes, but these boxes are binary instead of decimal. They can have a 0 or a 1, that's it.

Here, we see the decimal number 15 represented in binary.

1 times 2 to the three, plus 1 times 2 to the two plus 1 times 2 to the 1 plus 1 times 2 to the zero. Decimal 15 is the same as binary 1111.

SLIDE 172

Here are some other binary conversions. For example decimal 132 is binary 1 zero zero zero zero 1 zero zero.

_____

_____

_____

_____

_____

_____

_____

_____

_____

SLIDE 173

We can add binary numbers just like we added decimal numbers, except that we overflow a lot more quickly.

In decimal, five plus five is one-zero. We call that ten.

In binary, one plus one is one-zero. We call that two.

We can also write this as 0000 0010, which is how we show 2 within an 8-bit binary number.

_____

_____

_____

_____

_____

_____

BINARY ARITHMETIC

Binary refers to 2 (like counting with one finger that goes up or down)

Base 2 arithmetic represent numbers as a sum of powers of 2:

- $2^0 = 1$
- $2^1 = 2$
- $2^2 = 4$
- $2^3 = 8$

$15 = 1 \times 2^3 + 1 \times 2^2 + 1 \times 2^1 + 1 \times 2^0$

171

BYTES (8 BITS)

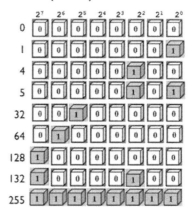

172

ADDING BINARY NUMBERS

Consider 8-bit binary numbers:

```
    1+1 = 00000001    (1)
        + 00000001    (1)
        = 00000010    (2)
```

- Just like 5+5 = 10 (carry the 1) in decimal arithmetic (because there is no digit bigger than 9), 1+1 = 10 in binary (because there is no digit bigger than 1)

```
17 + 15 = 00010001    (17)
        + 00001111    (15)
        = 00100000    (32)
```

173

SLIDE 174

The biggest number you can store in 8 bits is 255. Add anything to 255 and, if you're working in 8-bits, you get an overflow.

Some programmers still work with 8-bit numbers, even on computers with 64-bit words. Their goal is to fit their code and data into the tiniest amount of space possible. Occasionally, this goal is necessary because processors designed to control equipment sometimes come with very little memory. Whether the restriction to 8-bit arithmetic is necessary or just someone showing off, the risk of overflow with 8-bit integer arithmetic is very high. If you think calculations might be only 8 bits, or only 16, you need to test for overflows.

> ### OVERFLOW
>
> The biggest number you can fit in a byte is 11111111 = 255.
>
> ```
> · 255 + 1  = 11111111   (255)
>            + 00000001   (1)
>            = overflow   (256)
> ```
>
> - To deal with larger numbers, we either have to work with larger areas of memory (such as 16-bit or 32-bit words) or we have to work with floating point.
> - We'll address both soon...
> - But first, let's consider positives and negatives
>
> "In computing, word is a term for the natural unit of data used by a particular computer design. A word is simply a fixed sized group of bits that are handled together by the system. The number of bits in a word (the word size or word length) is an important characteristic of computer architecture."
>
> http://en.wikipedia.org/wiki/Word_%28computing%29
>
> 174

SLIDE 175

As with decimal numbers, we can have negatives as well as positives. In binary, we reinterpret the first bit as the sign bit. So instead of standing for two to the seventh, a 1 in the top bit means the number is negative.

> ### UNSIGNED VERSUS SIGNED
>
> Rather than interpreting the first (leftmost) bit in a binary number as a digit, we can interpret it as a sign bit.
>
>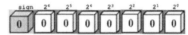
>
> - 00000001 is 1
> - 01111111 is 127
> - 10000000 is -128
> - 11111111 is -1
>
> http://en.wikipedia.org/wiki/Two%27s_complement
>
> 175

SLIDE 176

I've mentioned word sizes a few times. The central processor or arithmetic processor chip fetches data from memory in chunks. Older processors typically fetched 8 bits or 12 bits at a time. Newer processors typically fetch 32 or 64 bits at a time. Whatever is the natural working size for a computer is what we call its word size. If a computer typically operates on 64 bits of memory at a time, it's a 64-bit computer, with a 64-bit word size.

> ### 8, 16, 32 & 64-BIT WORDS
>
> - Computers read memory several bits at a time.
> - A *word* is the amount of memory typically read in one fetch operation.
>   - The Apple 2 computers read memory 1 byte at a time. Its word size was 1 byte
>   - The original IBM computers read memory in blocks of 16 bits at a time. Their word size was 16 bits
>   - Most modern computers operate on 32 or 64 bits at a time, so their word size is 32 or 64 bits.
>
> 176

SLIDE 177

The size of an integer, the number of significant digits, is often determined by the programming language rather than the computer's chip. That makes it possible for us to run the same program and have the same precision of calculation on many different types of computers.

For any particular computer, what the programming language treats as an integer might span less or more than one computer word of memory.

WORDS

- A computer with a 32-bit word size can operate on smaller blocks of memory.
  - It might work with 8 or 16 bits
  - Unless you are testing new chips in development, the program is **unlikely** to
    - read or work with the wrong number of bits
    - read or write one too many or one too few bytes (it will read 8, not 7 or 9)

177

SLIDE 178

Because integers are different sizes in different programming languages, we often talk about MinInt and MaxInt. MinInt is the smallest value an integer can take on this system or in this language. MaxInt is the largest value.

INTEGERS

Textbook examples for integers typically use 8-bit or 16-bit words
- With 16 bits, MaxInt is
  - 32767 with signed integers
  - 65535 with unsigned integers
- MinInt is
  - -32768 if integers are signed
  - 0 if integers are unsigned

> It is usually a mistake to assume you know the value of MaxInt. Even if you know it today, the system will change and MaxInt will change with it. Design your tests (and code) using MinInt and MaxInt, not numeric constants.

178

SLIDE 179

Java supports four types of integers, spanning 8 through 64 bits. I've also seen integers with 12-bits, 24-bits, 48-bits, and 128-bits.

When you do test design, do most of your work with general limits, MinInt and MaxInt instead of locking yourself down to an exact number of bits. Document your tests in terms of the general limits too. Fill in specific numeric constants when you have to, but understand that the more tied your test designs, test docs and test code are to these numeric constants, the faster they will become obsolete, the harder they will be to

---

INTEGERS: JAVA

	Size		Range	
	Bytes	Bits	MinInt	MaxInt
byte	1	8	-128	127
short	2	16	-32,768	32,767
int	4	32	-2,147,483,648	2,147,483,647
long	8	64	-9,223,372,036,854,775,808	9,223,372,036,854,775,807

179

---

reuse on another program or another system, and the harder they will be to modify if the programmers change integer precision on the software under test.

SLIDE 180

Floating point arithmetic in binary is essentially the same as floating point in decimal.

In a 32-bit word, the top bit is the sign bit for the mantissa. The next 8 bits are a signed byte for the exponent. Then the mantissa, for 23 binary digits of precision. This works out to about 10 decimal significant digits.

_____

_____

_____

FLOATING POINT (SINGLE PRECISION)

32-bit number

- Leftmost bit: sign bit
  - 0 is positive
  - 1 is negative
- Next 8 bits: exponent
  - -127 to 127   (see note)
- Next 23 bits: mantissa (aka significand)
  - $1.175494351 \times 10^{-38}$ to
  - $3.402823466 \times 10^{38}$

Note: Exponent values of 0 and 255 have special meanings. For details, see discussions of the IEEE specification for floating point numbers. For our purposes, the exact details don't matter. Assume that an exponent of 0 behaves in the usual way, i.e. $N^0 = 1$.
Read:
- http://docs.sun.com/source/806-3568/ncg_goldberg.html
- Petzold, *Code*, Chapter 23.

180

SLIDE 181

We can also have double-precision arithmetic, using 64 bits. This gives 52 significant binary digits.

_____

_____

_____

_____

_____

_____

_____

_____

_____

FLOATING POINT (DOUBLE PRECISION)

64-bit number

- Leftmost bit: sign bit
- Next 11 bits: exponent
- Next 52 bits: mantissa

181

SLIDE 182

Along with binary and decimal, we often talk about hexadecimal numbers. In a hexadecimal digit, the values run from 0 to 15 instead of 0 to 9 in a decimal digit or 0 to 1 in a binary.

_____

_____

_____

_____

_____

_____

_____

HEXADECIMAL NUMBERS

Decimal	Binary	Hexadecimal	Decimal	Binary	Hexadecimal
0	0000	0	16	00010000	10
1	0001	1	17	00010001	11
2	0010	2	31	00011111	1F
3	0011	3	32	00100000	20
4	0100	4	63	00111111	2F
5	0101	5	64	01000000	40
6	0110	6	100	01100100	64
7	0111	7	112	01110000	70
8	1000	8	128	10000000	80
9	1001	9	144	10010000	90
10	1010	A	160	10100000	A0
11	1011	B	176	10110000	B0
12	1100	C	192	11000000	C0
13	1101	D	208	11010000	D0
14	1110	E	224	11100000	E0
15	1111	F	255	11111111	FF

182

_____

_____

_____

_____

SLIDE 183

We can store characters in memory, not just numbers. We encode them. The most widely discussed encoding scheme is ASCII, the American Standard Code for Information Interchange.

ASCII encodes letters, numbers, and some other characters like spaces and exclamation marks. For example, the code for 2 is 50.

ASCII was invented for teletypes, so it only encodes a few characters—it stores everything in 8 bits. And some of the things it encodes are actually teletype commands, like ring the bell or make a vertical tab.

> **ALPHANUMERIC REPRESENTATIONS: ASCII**
> - American Standard code for Information Interchange
> - Encoding for teletypes
>   - Code 7 says to ring the TTY bell
>   - Code 11 calls for a vertical tab
> - Codes 0 to 31 are commands (non-printing characters)
> - Code 32 is for Space character
> - Code 33 is for !
> - Code 47 is for /
> - Codes 48 – 57 are for digits 0 to 9
> - Codes 65 – 90 for A to Z
> - Codes 97 – 122 for a to z
>
> http://www.asciitable.com/
> http://en.wikipedia.org/wiki/Unicode
>
>
>
> http://www.flickr.com/photos/ajmexico/4669611994/
>
> 183

Another encoding standard is called Unicode. Unicode stores characters in 16 bits and handles many languages..

SLIDE 184

Let's sum up. When a program reads a 32-bit word from memory, it interprets those bits. It might interpret them as an integer, a floating point number, a sequence of letters, or in some other way. There is no way to tell, from the 32-bit pattern, what type of data was stored.

The program's interpretation of a word of data as integer might be correct or we might have a bug—someone stored letters but the program reads them as a number.

> **SAME DATA, DIFFERENT MEANINGS**
> - What a bit pattern in memory means depends on how the program reading it interprets it
> - The same bit pattern might be
>   - An integer
>   - A floating point number
>   - A character or sequence of characters
>   - A command
>   - An address (identifies a location in memory)
> - The same pattern in the same location might be read differently by different functions
>
> 184

SLIDE 185

Along with storing individual numbers or characters, we can store data structures. Think of a data structure as a collection of numbers or characters, deliberately organized in a specific way.

My goal in mentioning these is just to make you aware of them. Most data stored in most programs is stored in data structures.

To learn more about these, take a data structures course. This is one of the early courses in the computer science curriculum. It will tell you when and why one structure is more useful than another, and what risks of bugs or slow processing come with each structure.

In the slides that follow, I'll often note errors that are common when dealing with a given data structure. These are not necessarily the most common or the most important errors. These are what came to my mind as examples that you'd probably understand, that might help you envision the variety of testing issues associated with data structures.

DATA STRUCTURES

- A data structure is a way of organizing data. We select a data structure to optimize some aspect of how software will work with it
- So far, we've seen primitive data types
  - Integers, floating point numbers, characters, bits
- We can group primitives together in meaningful ways, such as:
  - Strings
  - Records
  - Arrays
  - Lists

> This scratches the surface.
> The goal is merely to familiarize you with some of the variety of ideas.

185

SLIDE 186

The simplest structure is the string. A sequence of characters.

DATA STRUCTURES: STRING

- A sequence of characters
- Each character comes from the same alphabet (set of acceptable symbols)
- Commonplace operations:
  - Search for a substring
  - Replace one substring with another
  - Concatenate (add one string to another. For example,

  `One ⊕ string = Onestring`)
  - Calculate length
  - Truncate

> Common errors
> - Overflow
> - Match or mismatch

186

SLIDE 187

Records are another structure. When you enter values into several fields in a dialog, you're probably filling in a record.

_____

_____

_____

_____

_____

_____

_____

_____

_____

_____

DATA STRUCTURES: RECORD

- Related data, stored together
  - First name
  - Last name
  - Street address
  - City
  - State
  - Country
  - Postal code
  - Identification number
- One record refers to one person
- Each part is called a _field_
- We might show (or input) all the fields of a record in a dialog

Common Operations

- Search among many records (e.g. an array of records)
- Retrieve a record on basis of values of some fields
- Replace values of some fields
- Sort records

Common errors

- Write to or retrieve wrong record or wrong fields
- Store wrong data
- Overflow or underflow

187

SLIDE 188

An array is a sequence of the same type of data.

In an array A of integers, if you ask for A[0], you would get the first element in the sequence. A[2] would return the third element in the list.

You can also have an array of records. For example, you easily could retrieve the 43rd tax return from a database of tax returns, if these records were stored in an array.

DATA STRUCTURES: ARRAY

- Linear sequence of variables of the same type. Each variable in the array is an _element_.
- Examples
  - a[ ] is an array of integers, so
    - a[0] and a[1] etc. are all integers
  - b[ ] is an array of records.
    - b[3].lastName yields the lastName field associated with record number 3
- Common operations
  - Read, write, sort, change

Common errors

- Read / write past end of the array
- Read uninitialized data
- Read / write the wrong element

188

SLIDE 189

Lists are like arrays but more general. For example, we can have a list of lists and each list could point to a different set of records. Maybe one list would contain tax returns and another list would contain mortgage records.

When we store a collection of data, we want to be able to find it later. Each type of data structure makes some types of searches easier and some types of changes easier. A structure that is very fast for some tasks can be painfully slow for others.

Especially in real-time programs, like games, and in programs that work with large amounts of memory, a lot of work goes into optimizing data structures, to achieve the right tradeoff between speed of the most important operations and the amount of space required in memory or on disk.

DATA STRUCTURES: LIST

Like arrays,

- A collection of variables of the same type
- We can read/write an individual variable, such as a single record in a list of records

Unlike arrays,

- The individual variables might be different sizes. For example, lists of different-length lists.
- Retrieval is not necessarily by element number
  - Elements in the list are linked to previous/next elements via pointers
  - Search for match to a field or combination of fields
- To reach a given element, might have to move through the list until you reach it

Common errors

- Search forward when relevant element is behind current place
- Read/write past end of list
- Incorrectly specify or update pointer to next or previous element

189

SLIDE 190

So far, we've studied data, mainly how the computer stores and retrieves data.

It's time to switch our focus to control. Control structures tell the computer what to do next.

CONTROL STRUCTURES

We'll consider only a few:

- Sequence
- Branch
- Loop
- Function (method) call
- Exception
- Interrupt

190

SLIDE 191

The simplest structure is the sequence. Just keep executing the next command.

CONTROL STRUCTURES: SEQUENCE

- A program includes a list of statements.
- If you start executing a sequence, you execute all of its statements
- Example

```
SET A = 5
SET B = 2
INPUT C FROM KEYBOARD
PRINT A + B + C
```

191

SLIDE 192

A branch is a decision point. The computer evaluates a logical expression, like X equals Y. This is true if X does equal Y and false if X does not equal Y.

If the expression is true, the program does one thing, it goes down one branch. If the expression is false, the program does something else.

CONTROL STRUCTURES: BRANCH

- The program decides to execute
  - one statement (or sequence)
  - rather than another
  - based on the value of a logical expression (logical expressions can evaluate to True or False)
- Example

```
INPUT C FROM KEYBOARD
IF (C < 5)
    PRINT C
ELSE
    PRINT "C IS TOO BIG"
```

- Note: "logical expressions" are also often called "Boolean expressions."

Common errors

- In a complex branch (CASE or a sequence of IF's), falling through the branches to an inappropriate default because a special case was missed.
- Incorrect branching because the logical expression is complex and was mis-programmed

192

SLIDE 193

A loop is a sequence that repeats.

_____

_____

_____

_____

_____

_____

_____

_____

_____

_____

CONTROL STRUCTURES: LOOP

- The program repeats the same set of instructions until an exit criterion is met
- Example
  ```
  SET A = 5
  WHILE (A < 5) {
    PRINT A
    INPUT A FROM KEYBOARD
  }
  ```
- The exit criterion is (A ≥ 5). The loop continues until the user enters a value ≥ 5 at the keyboard.

Common errors
- Infinite loop
- Loop exercises one time too many or too few
- Out of memory
- Huge data files, printouts, emails, because loop runs unexpectedly many times
- Too slow because it executes a poorly-optimized block of code thousands of times.

193

SLIDE 194

A function is a self-contained task. For example, we could send a number to a square root function, which would return the square root of that number.

Programmers work extensively with library functions. A library function is often supplied by someone else and, allegedly, has been thoroughly tested. The library might come with your programming language, or you might buy a specialized library like a graphics library.

CONTROL STRUCTURES: FUNCTION CALL

A function (or method or procedure or module) is self-contained

- Can be called from other parts of the program
- Takes an action and/or returns a value
- Examples
  - PRINT is the name of a method that sends its input data to the printer
  - R = SQUAREROOT (X)
    shows a function (SQUAREROOT) that accepts value X as input and returns the square root of X as a new value for R.

Common errors
- Memory leak
- Unexpectedly changes global data (or data on disk or data in memory referenced by address)
- Fails without notifying caller or caller ignores a failure exit-code

194

SLIDE 195

Exceptions are get-me-out-of-here commands. For example, if you try to write to the disk and the disk crashes, the driver, the program that controls transfer of data to the disk, will issue an exception and stop trying to write data to the disk.

Some common exceptions that you might have run into include divide-by-zero messages (as the program crashes), out of memory messages (as the program crashes) and general protection fault, which usually means that the program tried to write data to a protected part of memory and the operating system is shutting down the program.

CONTROL STRUCTURES: EXCEPTION

While executing a command, there is a failure. For example, while attempting to print, the printer shuts off or runs out of paper. The Exception returns from the failed task with information about the failure.

- Example
  ```
  TRY {
    PRINT X
  } CATCH (OUT OF PAPER) {
    ALERT USER AND WAIT
    THEN RESUME PRINTING
  } CATCH (PRINTER OFF) {
    ABANDON THE JOB
    ALERT USER
  }
  ```

Examples
- Divide by zero (invalid calculation)
- Access restricted memory area.

Common error
- Exceptions often leave variables or stored data in an unexpected state, files open, and other resources in mid-use resulting in a failure later, when the program next tries to access the data or resource

195

Notice the pattern here. If something causes an exception to be thrown while a program is running, and the program doesn't do its own error handling for this exception, the operating system will catch the exception and put the program out of its misery.

An exception can leave the program in a messy state. When an exception is thrown inside a method and some other part of the program handles the method, that part has no idea whether the program finished whatever loop it was in, finished storing its data on the disk, released unused memory to the operating system, and so on. Exception handling that is not skillfully managed causes a lot of hard to reproduce failures.

SLIDE 196

An interrupt is just a signal that some type of event has happened. There are hardware interrupts and software interrupts. In either case, the computer responds by stashing a few key pieces of data into temporary storage, such as the current location of the currently running program. Then the computer runs an interrupt handler, determines how to respond to the event that generated the interrupt, deals with it, and comes back to the main program, reloading all the temporary data.

> **CONTROL STRUCTURES: INTERRUPT**
>
> - A *hardware interrupt* causes the processor to save its state of execution and begin execution of an interrupt handler. These can occur at any time, with the program in any state.
> - *Software interrupts* are usually implemented as instructions that cause a context switch to an interrupt handler similar to a hardware interrupt. These occur at a time/place specified by the programmer.
>
> Interrupts are commonly used for computer multitasking, especially in real-time computing. Such a system is said to be interrupt-driven.
>
> *Interrupt handlers are code. They can change data, write to disk, etc.*
>
> **Examples of hardware interrupts**
> - Key pressed on keyboard
> - Disk I/O error message coming back through the driver
> - Clock signals end of a timed delay
>
> **Common errors**
> - Race condition (unexpected processing delay caused by diversion of resources to interrupt)
> - Stack overflow (interrupt handler stores program state on the stack—too many nested interrupts might blow the stack)
> - Deadly embrace: You can't do anything with B until A is done, but you can't finish A until you finish servicing B's interrupts
>
> 196

To the main program, it's as if nothing ever happened. But these background events, serviced by interrupts, might actually be critical to the program. For example, the printer might be taken offline just as the program is trying to print to it. Or a key piece of data is changed just as the program is about to use it.

SLIDE 197

Now that we've looked at storage and control, we can finally talk about coverage.

The coverage question is, How much have you tested?

Coverage answers are usually proportions or percentages. I've tested half the code. I've tested all the printers.

> **COVERAGE**
>
> - Extent of testing of certain attributes or pieces of the software under test.
> - Example
>   - How many statements have we tested?
>   - Generally, we report a percentage
>   - Number tested, compared to
>   - Number that could have been tested
> - *Extent (or proportion) of testing of a given type that has been completed, compared to the population of possible tests of this type.*
>
> 197

SLIDE 198

When programmers and computer science professors talk about coverage, they are usually talking about structural coverage.

I should correct this, by saying that computer scientists often teach additional coverage measures. Amman and Offutt provide a solid discussion of graph coverage. Paul Jorgensen gives a good introduction to dataflow coverage.

STRUCTURAL CODE COVERAGE

Coverage you can measure by focusing on the control structures of the program

Examples
- Statement coverage
  - Execute every statement in the program
- Branch coverage
  - Every statement and every branch
- Multi-condition coverage
  - All combinations of the logical expressions

Ammann & Offutt (2008), *Introduction to Software Testing*
Jorgensen (2008, 3rd ed), *Software Testing: A Craftsman's Approach*
http://www.exampler.com/testing-com/writings/iview1.htm
http://sqa.fyicenter.com/art/EXPERIENCE_WITH_THE_COST_OF_DIFFERENT_COVERAGE_GOALS_FOR_TESTING.html
http://www.bullseye.com/coverage.html

198

SLIDE 199

But the common discussions, including discussions in standards, focus on simple descriptions of a program's flow of control. So let's look at these first.

STRUCTURAL COVERAGE

IEEE Unit Testing Standard is 100% Statement Coverage and 100% Branch Execution

(IEEE Std. 982.1-1988, § 4.17, "Minimal Unit Test Case Determination")

Most companies don't achieve this (though they might achieve 100% of the code they actually write.)

Several people seem to believe that complete statement and branch coverage means complete testing. (Or, at least, sufficient testing.)

199

SLIDE 200

You achieve 100% statement coverage if you test every statement in the program.

We can achieve 100% statement coverage of this little program with one test.

STRUCTURAL COVERAGE: EXAMPLES

```
INPUT A FROM KEYBOARD
INPUT B FROM KEYBOARD
IF (A < 5) {
     PRINT A
     }
IF (B == "HELLO") {
     PRINT B
     }
```
- Statement coverage
  - Execute every statement in the program
  - Tests
    - Enter 4 for A and "HELLO" for B

200

SLIDE 201

You achieve branch coverage if you test every statement and every branch.

It takes two tests to achieve 100% branch coverage of this program. Notice that we have to test with B is not "Hello" even though there is no code specifically written for the not-hello case, because branch coverage requires us to take every branch that we can take.

Stunningly many programmers and consultants think that we achieve complete code coverage if we achieve 100% branch coverage. This is silly.

From a structural point of view, the most glaring error in this reasoning comes from interrupts. The operating system can shift control from your program to the interrupt handler at any time, at any point in your program, for as long as it wants. The state of the system can change in ways that are important to you, between the time that your code swaps out to the interrupt handler and the time it starts back up. The other software can change data on disk, change data in memory, tie up resources, and delay your processing so that other things can happen before you're ready for them. These can all cause failures. They have all caused failures in systems that I've worked on.

Interrupts look like branches to me. We can try to rationalize ignoring them because they're hard to test. We can't see them in the code. And besides, the programmer didn't intentionally write them into the code. So we can say these aren't the branches we're talking about when we talk about code coverage.

But there's something wrong with calling your testing complete coverage if there's a way to cause failures and you aren't going to test it.

SLIDE 202

Continuing with structural coverage (and ignoring our interrupts), the next level up is multi-condition coverage. This checks all of the combinations of the logical expressions. We don't just check the true branch and the false branch for each individual expression. We check them together. Here we have two IF statements. We can branch-cover them with 2 tests, but multi-condition coverage requires 4 tests.

There are ways to optimize multi-condition coverage, to achieve essentially the same results with fewer tests. But we'll usually need more tests than branch coverage.

STRUCTURAL COVERAGE: EXAMPLES

```
INPUT A FROM KEYBOARD
INPUT B FROM KEYBOARD
IF (A < 5) {
      PRINT A
      }
IF (B == "HELLO") {
      PRINT B
      }
```

- Branch coverage
    - Every statement and every branch
    - Tests
        - Enter 4 for A and "HELLO" for B
        - Enter 6 for A and "GOODBYE" for B

> An interrupt forces a branch to the interrupt handler. Can we seriously claim 100% branch coverage if we don't test branches for every interrupt from every instruction?
>
> (Problem: we probably can't do all these tests…)

201

STRUCTURAL COVERAGE: EXAMPLES

```
INPUT A FROM KEYBOARD
INPUT B FROM KEYBOARD
IF (A < 5) {
      PRINT A
      }
IF (B == "HELLO") {
      PRINT B
      }
```

Multi-condition coverage
- All combinations of the logical expressions

A	B
4	HELLO
4	GOODBYE
6	HELLO
6	GOODBYE

202

SLIDE 203

Simple structural coverage measures are useful, but they are incomplete.

Here's a simple example program that illustrates the problem. The program asks for two inputs, A and B, then it prints A over B. You can achieve 100% branch coverage of this program with one test. Give it 2 for A and 1 for B, it will print you a 2 and you're done.

But what happens if you give it zero for B instead of 1. What happens when it tries to print 2 divided by zero?

Structural testing is blind to any data values that aren't specifically checked by the program. There's no test for B equals zero. There's no code for B equals zero. So we don't add any coverage if we test with B equals zero.

> **COMPLETE COVERAGE?**
>
> Consider the following program:
>
> ```
> Input A   // the program accepts any
> Input B   // integer into A and B
> Print A/B
> ```
>
> A test with A =2 and B =1 will cover:
> - every statement
> - every branch
>
> However, this testing misses a serious error:
> - What test is missing?
> - What bug is missed?
>
> > In a study by Brian Marick, 43% of failures were traced to faults of omission (missing code rather than wrong code) http://www.exampler.com/testing-com/writings/omissions.html
>
> 203

SLIDE 204

Error handling accounts for a high percentage of the code in many programs. The divide by zero bug we just looked at is a simple example of the absence of error handling code.

Tests designed to maximize structural coverage are blind to the absence of error detection and error handling.

They won't notice if a program isn't designed to check whether a set of calculations will use up all available memory. The program will crash out of memory instead. They won't notice a failure to detect that an incoming message has a huge data structure that will overrun the temporary storage area that receives the message. These temporary storage areas are called input buffers. Buffer overruns are the most commonly exploited security vulnerability in web applications. If you rely on structural coverage, you won't notice that you have no buffer protection code. You'll just get hacked.

> **COMPLETE COVERAGE?**
>
> The last example shows that even if we obtain "complete coverage" (100% statement or branch or multi-condition coverage), we can still miss obvious, critical bugs.
>
> This is because these measures are blind to many aspects of the software, such as (to name just a few):
>
> - Unexpected values (e.g. divide by zero)
> - Stability of a variable at its boundary values
> - Data combinations
> - Data flow
> - Tables that determine control flow in table-driven code
>
> - Missing code
> - Timing
> - Compatibility with devices or other software or systems
> - Volume or load
> - Interactions with background tasks
> - Side effects of interrupts
> - Handling of hardware faults
> - User interface errors
> - Compliance with contracts or regulations
> - Whether the software actually delivers the benefits or solves the problems it was intended to deliver/solve
>
> 204

Tests designed to maximize structural coverage are blind to plenty of other risks too. They won't notice that the program is unusably slow, incomprehensible, incapable of delivering promised benefits, or incompatible with widely used video cards.

_____

_____

_____

_____

_____

_____

SLIDE 205

Branch coverage is useful. Nothing I say today should make you suspect that I think branch coverage is not useful.

Programmers who have the discipline to achieve 100% branch coverage of the code they write probably find a lot more bugs than programmers who don't think about coverage when they do their testing.

When I teach programming courses, I insist that my students learn to use a coverage monitor and achieve high branch coverage. In my advanced course, students who don't do this get zeros on their assignments.

> **GOOD TOOLS FOR STRUCTURAL COVERAGE**
>
> - There are fine tools for this that are free and easy to use, such as Emma (and EclEmma which is integrated into Eclipse)
>
>   http://www.eclemma.org/
>   http://emma.sourceforge.net/
>
> - Programmers can easily check coverage when they test their code
> - Black box testers find it hard to check structural coverage
>
> 205

These tools are free or cheap, easy to get, and they help you find bugs. When you write code, you should use them.

Some people try to encourage black box testers to use these tools as they run black box tests. There are expensive tools that can help with this. As a black box tester, I have never found structural coverage tools helpful.

SLIDE 206

Years ago I was managing development of a new release of a desktop publishing program. The VP of Development asked me what code coverage our testing had achieved. I didn't know. She asked again a few days later and I said, before we can ship this, we have to pass compatibility testing with about 80 printers. At the moment, we work with 10. What I'm worried about today is when we're going to work with more printers.

After that, the VP stopped asking me how many lines of code we'd tested and asked instead how many printers worked.

> **OTHER COVERAGES**
>
> Structural coverage looks at the code from only one viewpoint.
>
> Structural coverage might be the only family of coverage measures you see in programmers' textbooks or university research papers, but we've seen many other types of coverage in real use.
>
> **Coverage assesses the extent (or proportion) of testing of a given type that has been completed, compared to the population of possible tests of this type.**
>
> Anything you can list, you can assess coverage against.
>
> | Track coverage of the things that are most important to your project, whether these are the "standard" coverage measures or not.
>
> For 101 examples, see Kaner, Software Negligence & Testing Coverage.
> http://www.kaner.com/pdfs/negligence_and_testing_coverage.pdf
>
> 206

Percentage of printers is just as good a coverage measure as percentage of statements.

Another important coverage measure on that project involved a long list of word processors and graphics programs. We could read data from any of them, or at least that's what our advertising said, so we had to test all of them.

Also, many programs on our platform had problems reading or writing files that were exactly 2 to the N bytes long. So we wanted to test every type of file that we wrote at every one of the sizes we were worried about.

These are three examples of coverage:

- Device compatibility coverage
- Input file format coverage

- Output file format-and-size coverage

They're coverage because we can figure out how many tests we want to run and then figure out what percentage of these we have covered so far.

If you can imagine all of the tests we could run, and then consider what percentage of these we have covered so far, that percentage would be our true coverage.

Unfortunately, the total number of possible tests is infinite, so our percentage of true coverage will always be zero.

SLIDE 207

Brian Marick is one of the early authors of code coverage tools. He wrote a well-known open source monitor for programs written in C and was then hired as a consultant to write the kernel for many commercial coverage tools. He also consulted to companies who used these tools. He wrote about the problems he saw in a paper called *How to Misuse Code Coverage*.

When you measure someone's performance, they do things that make them look better according to that measure. If you count how many statements I've tested,

> **COVERAGE AS A MEASUREMENT**
>
> *People optimize what we measure them against, at the expense of what we don't measure.*
>
> - Driving testing to achieve "high" coverage is likely to yield a mass of low-power tests.
> - Brian Marick discusses this in "How to Misuse Code Coverage," http://www.exampler.com/testing-com/writings/coverage.pdf
>
> For more on measurement distortion and dysfunction, read Bob Austin's book, *Measurement and Management of Performance in Organizations.*
>
> 207

I'll add tests to cover more statements, but that doesn't mean that I'll add good tests. Coverage doesn't measure how powerful my tests are—how well designed they are to expose bugs. It only measures how many statements they've touched.

What Brian saw was that companies would tell their programming staff to write tests that achieved 90% coverage, and they would. But the tests weren't necessarily any good. People shifted focus from writing powerful tests to writing tests that gave good coverage numbers. So they might have more tests, but in the process, they might find fewer bugs.

Measuring code coverage is a lousy way to tell how close you are to being done. Knowing that you have achieved 90% branch coverage does not tell you how thoroughly you have tested. However, this doesn't make branch coverage useless. It only makes it bad for the purpose of deciding how close your testing is to complete.

A different use of code coverage is to identify areas of the program that you haven't yet tested or have tested only lightly.

Testing from the outside, it's easy to miss things. There are plenty of reports of coverage measurements showing that a project's test plan reached only 35% of the code. When you identify the 65% that you've missed, you can design tests to plug the gaps you consider important.

_____

_____

_____

_____

_____

_____

SLIDE 208

Well, that's it for today. Next time, we'll take our work on coverage down a little different path, estimating the number of tests we can run under various circumstances, and confronting again the impossibility of running everything.

_____

_____

_____

_____

_____

_____

LET'S SUMMARIZE

Today we took a high-level tour of some of the basic programming concepts:

- How computers store different types of data
- Binary arithmetic and the challenge of rounding errors in floating point arithmetic
- Flow of control in the program (control structures)
- Evaluation of the breadth of testing ("coverage").

208

SLIDE 209

_____

_____

_____

_____

_____

_____

_____

_____

_____

_____

_____

_____

BLACK BOX SOFTWARE TESTING FOUNDATIONS

END OF LECTURE 4

CEM KANER, J.D., PH.D.
PROFESSOR OF SOFTWARE ENGINEERING
FLORIDA INSTITUTE OF TECHNOLOGY

REBECCA L. FIEDLER, M.B.A. PH.D.
PRESIDENT: KANER, FIEDLER & ASSOCIATES

JAMES BACH
PRINCIPAL, SATISFICE INC

This work is licensed under the Creative Commons Attribution License. To view a copy of this license, visit http://creativecommons.org/licenses/by-sa/2.0/ or send a letter to Creative Commons, 559 Nathan Abbott Way, Stanford, California 94305, USA.

These notes are partially based on research that was supported by NSF Grants EIA-0113539 ITR/SY +PE: "Improving the Education of Software Testers" and CCLI-0717613 "Adaptation & Implementation of an Activity-Based Online or Hybrid Course in Software Testing." Any opinions, findings and conclusions or recommendations expressed in this material are those of the author(s) and do not necessarily reflect the views of the National Science Foundation.

209

_____

_____

_____

_____

_____

_____

_____

_____

_____

_____

_____

_____

_____

_____

_____

_____

Authors' Reflection On Lesson 4

Testers sometimes embarrass themselves by demanding a level of accuracy from programs that they can't have. Floating-point arithmetic is subject to rounding errors.

Floating-point numbers are stored in a finite amount of memory and so two numbers that are actually different might be stored as having an identical value. For example, the computer might store 1.0000000001 and 1.0000000002 as 1.0000000000. In practical terms, every number that would be stored as 1.0000000000 is equivalent to that number, because the program will turn it into that number before doing anything else with it.

- Some testers will knowledgeably insist that the programmer increase the precision of their data types and calculations. For example, they might argue that the programmer should switch from single-precision to double and give examples of why this is important in the current program. Such a tester might be asking for a change that will be dismissed as impractical but the argument will probably be treated with respect.

- Other testers will ask for greater precision without understanding what they are asking for. They seem to insist that no calculations should have rounding errors, ever. For floating-point calculations, this is unreasonable. The tester who asks for something like this is announcing that he doesn't know anything about computer arithmetic. That damages the credibility of their bug report on this issue and it might damage the credibility of most of their other reports. That is, some programmers and some managers will have less respect for a tester who seems completely ignorant of how a program stores numbers and does calculations.

If you're going to argue about the accuracy of a program's calculations, we want you to be perceived as the knowledgeable tester, not the clueless one. We think this Lesson helps with that.

Similarly, many testers talk about "coverage" without understanding anything about how programs work. How can someone who doesn't know a branch from a loop talk about "path coverage"? The tester might be able to speak the words, but if she doesn't know what a path is then very little of what she has to say about coverage will be taken seriously.

The most significant problem in *Foundations Versions 1 and 2* was that we expected students to know more about the fundamentals of programming and of computer arithmetic than they actually knew, or knew how to apply.

In *Foundations 3*, we created Lesson 4 to address this. It appears to be working. It is not complete—some students continue to have difficulty. We didn't expect this Lesson to work for everyone and it doesn't, but it seems to be working as well as we'd hoped. At this point, we don't have any unexpected disappointments to report or ideas for revisions for *Foundations 4*.

5

LESSON 5: IMPOSSIBILITY OF COMPLETE TESTING

Lesson Introduction

Lesson 5 considers what it means to achieve complete testing. Lesson 4 introduced the concept of coverage. Some people come to our course believing that they can achieve complete testing by achieving complete structural coverage. This lesson demonstrates how severely mistaken this view is.

We expect you to remember six things from this lesson:

- Two key definitions:

  - Two tests are *distinct* if one test would expose a bug that the other test would miss.

  - To achieve *complete testing*, you have to run every distinct test.

- Two key examples:

  - In the *MASPAR square root example*, testers had to run all 4,294,967,296 tests to find the function's two bugs.

  - In the *Telenova stack overflow example*, covering all branches and statements and independent sub-paths was not enough. To replicate a system-killing bug in the field, testers had to create sequences that were so long and so complex that it would be impossible to find all bugs like this in the lab. The lecture (the video, not the slides) pointed out that Telenova's staff ultimately built a simulator that fed the program long sequences of inputs and checked the system's state with diagnostics. They found many other bugs using this long-random-sequence testing that would only show up only intermittently in the field but be serious when they did show up. The lecture drew a sequence diagram for the stack overflow bug. It looked just like the sequence diagram of a famous example in Glen Myers' *Art of Software Testing*. Myers showed that to test all sequences through his simple little program would take over 100 trillion tests. To find Telenova's other long-sequence bugs would have taken even more tests.

- One key formula:
  - If V_1 through V_k are k independent variables, and if N_i is the number of possible values of variable V_i, then the number of combination tests of all the variables together is $N_1 * N_2 * ... * N_k$.

- One conclusion:
  - *Complete testing is impossible and therefore all of testing involves tradeoffs.* Testing involves many tasks, such as designing and running tests, writing effective bug reports, documenting test ideas, creating test tools, etc. The amount of time needed to do all of these is infinitely greater than the time testers have. You only have time to do a small sample of this work and the time you spend on one task will no longer be available for the others. Inflexible directives, like "You must write down an expected result for every test", are unreasonable because they demand a huge amount of work on one testing task without considering what other testing tasks will be left undone as a result. The optimal tradeoffs will vary on a project-by-project basis.

Readings

The following reading is required:
- Kaner, C. (1997). The impossibility of complete testing. Washington Software Association, QA SIG. Redmond, WA. Retrieved from http://www.kaner.com/pdfs/impossible.pdf

The following readings are recommended:
- Black, R. (2002, Nov/Dec). Factors that Influence Test Estimation. STQE Magazine. Retrieved from http://www.stickyminds.com/sitewide.asp?Function=edetail&ObjectType=ART&ObjectId=5992. Supplement available at http://www.rbcs-us.com/documents/TestEstimation%28supplement%29.pdf.

- Kaner, C. (1996). Negotiating testing resources: A collaborative approach. 9th International Software Quality Conference (Quality Week). San Francisco. Retrieved from http://www.kaner.com/pdfs/qweek1.pdf

- Kelly, M. (2007, November 17). Estimating testing using spreadsheets. Michaeldkelly.com: software testing, development, coaching and consulting. Retrieved from http://michaeldkelly.com/blog/2007/11/17/estimating-testing-using-spreadsheets.html

Orientation: Testing An Integer Square Root Function

This is the same activity we presented at the start of Lesson 4. If you haven't done it yet, do it now.

If you did it back then, you might have noticed that the Lesson 4 lecture addressed some parts of the activity, such as the ways integers are stored in memory and the accuracy of floating-point calculations.

However, it didn't consider how many tests it would really take to check all the inputs to the function or whether that is a reasonable set of tests to run. We consider those types of questions in Lesson 5. Even if you have tried this activity already, you might find it interesting to try those parts of the activity again so that you have a recent experience of considering these questions, and thus a basis for comparing the ideas you had with the ideas in the lecture.

The point here is not necessarily to get the "right" answers. It is to get you thinking about the questions so that, mentally, you will be better prepared for the lecture's treatment of the topic. You will be better prepared to understand the lecture and, if you disagree with its conclusions, better equipped to argue with them.

Slides And Notes

SLIDE 210

Welcome to this fifth lecture of the *Foundations of Software Testing*.

_____

_____

_____

_____

_____

_____

_____

_____

_____

_____

> **BLACK BOX SOFTWARE TESTING FOUNDATIONS: LECTURE 5**
>
> **THE IMPOSSIBILITY OF COMPLETE TESTING**
>
> CEM KANER, J.D., PH.D.
> PROFESSOR OF SOFTWARE ENGINEERING
> FLORIDA INSTITUTE OF TECHNOLOGY
>
> REBECCA L. FIEDLER, M.B.A. PH.D.
> PRESIDENT: KANER, FIEDLER & ASSOCIATES
>
> JAMES BACH
> PRINCIPAL, SATISFICE INC
>
> This work is licensed under the Creative Commons Attribution License. To view a copy of this license, visit http://creativecommons.org/licenses/by-sa/2.0/ or send a letter to Creative Commons, 559 Nathan Abbott Way, Stanford, California 94305, USA.
>
> These notes are partially based on research that was supported by NSF Grants EIA-0113539 ITR/SY +PE: "Improving the Education of Software Testers" and CCLI-0717613 "Adaptation & Implementation of an Activity-Based Online or Hybrid Course in Software Testing." Any opinions, findings and conclusions or recommendations expressed in this material are those of the author(s) and do not necessarily reflect the views of the National Science Foundation.
>
> 210

SLIDE 211

I'm going to talk today about the impossibility of complete testing. And given that you can't test everything, I introduce a few basic parts of test estimation—how much *can* you test?

_____

_____

_____

_____

_____

_____

_____

_____

_____

> **OVERVIEW: FUNDAMENTAL TOPICS**
>
> - Why are we testing? What are we trying to learn? How should we organize our work to achieve this? *Information objectives drive the testing mission and strategy*
> - How can we know whether a program has passed or failed a test? *Oracles are heuristic*
> - How can we determine how much testing has been done? What core knowledge about program internals do testers need to consider this question? *Coverage is a multidimensional problem*
> - Are we done yet? *Complete testing is impossible* ⇐
> - How much testing have we completed and how well have we done it? *Measurement is important, but hard*
>
> 211

SLIDE 212

TODAY'S READINGS

Required:

- Doug Hoffman (2003). "Exhausting your test options" http://softwarequalitymethods.com/Papers/Exhaust%20Options.pdf

- Cem Kaner (1997), "The Impossibility of complete testing." http://www.kaner.com/pdfs/imposs.pdf

Useful to skim:

- Rex Black (2002), "Factors that influence test estimation", http://www.stickyminds.com/sitewide.asp?ObjectId=5992&Function=edetail&ObjectType=ART

- Michael Bolton (2009), "Blog: When do we stop a test?", http://www.developsense.com/blog/2009/09/when-do-we-stop-test

- Cem Kaner (1996), "Negotiating testing resources: A collaborative approach." http://www.kaner.com/pdfs/qweek1.pdf

- Mike Kelly, "Estimating testing using spreadsheets", http://www.michaeldkelly.com/archives/138

Your class may use other readings, but we had these in mind when creating this lecture.

212

Doug Hoffman's case study of testing the MASPAR computer and my paper on the impossibility of complete testing are our primary readings. The supplementary readings introduce estimation.

SLIDE 213

Last time, I demonstrated that "complete" structural coverage doesn't mean complete testing.

COVERAGE ...

Last time, we considered some structural coverage measures and realized that

complete coverage
doesn't mean
complete testing

| Question: | What do we have to do, to achieve complete testing? |
| Answer: | We can't achieve complete testing. We might be able to achieve adequate testing... |

213

SLIDE 214

To achieve complete testing, we would have to reach a point where we know that we've found all the bugs. This would require running every distinct test.

_____

_____

_____

_____

_____

_____

_____

COMPLETE TESTING

- Two tests are **distinct** if one test would expose a bug that the other test would miss.
- As we see it, for testing to be truly **complete**, you would have to:
  1. Run all distinct tests
  2. Test so thoroughly that you know there are no bugs left in the software
- It should be obvious (but it is not always obvious to every person) that the first and second criteria for complete testing are equivalent, and that testing that does not meet this criterion is incomplete.
- If this is not obvious to you, ask your instructor (or your colleagues) for help.

Incomplete Testing

We almost always stop testing before we know that there are no remaining bugs.

At this point, testing might be "finished" (we ran out of time), but if there are still bugs to be found, how can testing be considered "complete"?

214

SLIDE 215

To achieve complete testing, you'd have to test all the individual variables, all the combinations of values of the variables, all the ways you can order the tasks that you do with the program, all the hardware and software configurations you can run the program on and all of the variables, features and sequences that might interact with configuration, all the ways the program might be interrupted by other programs running at the same time, and all the ways people might use the program.

That's a lot of tests.

TO TEST EVERYTHING, YOU WOULD HAVE TO:

- Test every possible input to every variable (including output variables and intermediate results variables).
- Test every possible combination of inputs to every combination of variables.
- Test every possible sequence through the program.
- Test every possible timing of inputs (check for timeouts and races)
- Test every interrupt at every point it can occur
- Test every hardware / software configuration, including configurations of servers not under your control.
- Test for interference with other programs operating at the same time
- Test every way in which any user might try to use the program.

Cem Kaner (1997), The Impossibility of Complete Testing, http://www.kaner.com/pdfs/imposs.pdf

215

SLIDE 216

So let's get started by looking at individual variables.

The usual approach is to test variables with a few values. We should check normal operation and error handling, so we give it some values that the program should accept and process normally and we give it some values that are too big, too small, or too strange. Maybe we try a few special cases as well.

_____

_____

_____

_____

TO TEST EVERYTHING, YOU WOULD HAVE TO:

Test every possible input to every variable (including output variables and intermediate results variables).

- Test every possible combination of inputs to every combination of variables.
- Test every possible sequence through the program.
- Test every possible timing of inputs (check for timeouts and races)
- Test every interrupt at every point it can occur
- Test every hardware / software configuration, including configurations of servers not under your control.
- Test for interference with other programs operating at the same time
- Test every way in which any user might try to use the program.

Normally, we would sample the smallest and largest "valid" values (and the nearest "invalid" values). Or, if the values naturally subdivide into smaller groups, we'd sample one from each group (plus a few almost-valid values to check error handling.)

216

SLIDE 217

In preparation for this lecture, you probably analyzed a function that reads a 32-bit word from memory, interprets it as an unsigned integer, and reports its square root. There are 2 to the 32 possible inputs to this function, just over four billion.

None of these are invalid. No matter what you intend to store in this location of memory—letters, negative numbers, floating point numbers, whatever—No matter what you put there, a 32-bit word holds 32 ones and zeros and the function will read those 32 bits as a positive integer.

Similarly, if the function read 64 bits instead of 32, there would be 2 to the 64 possible values, which works out to a few quintillion.

> ### TEST EVERY INPUT
>
> - All the "valid" inputs
>   - How many valid inputs are there to a function that reads 32 bits from memory as an unsigned integer and takes the square root?
>   - How many valid inputs to a function that reads 64 bits as an unsigned integer?
> - Yes, of course we can sample. (We will often have to.)
>   - But optimizations, some calculation errors, and other special-case handling can go undetected if we don't check every possible input.
>
> 217

We can choose to test a small sample of these—compared to a billion or a quintillion, even a thousand tests is a small sample. No matter how we optimize that sample, we can't be sure that we've exposed all the bugs and therefore we can't consider this sample a complete test of the function.

Let me say this directly to experienced testers. You can use a data-sampling technique like domain testing – or maybe you studied this as boundary analysis and equivalence class analysis – you can test all of the values that this technique tells you to test, and if you do, that's probably a good set of tests. But it is not complete.

SLIDE 218

Doug Hoffman illustrated this in his report of testing built-in mathematical functions for the MASPAR computer. MASPAR is a superfast computer, with 64 thousand parallel processors.

The MASPAR designers expected their machines to be used for critical national security tasks. One of the applications I've heard mentioned is targeting nuclear missiles. It would be a good thing to get the math right on these computers.

> ### THE MASPAR EXAMPLE: TESTING THE "VALID" INPUTS
>
> Doug Hoffman worked on the MASPAR (the Massively Parallel computer, 64K parallel processors).
>
> The MASPAR has several built-in mathematical functions.
>
> The Integer square root function takes a 32-bit word as an input, interpreting it as an integer (value is between 0 and $2^{32}-1$). There are 4,294,967,296 possible inputs to this function.
>
> **How many should we test?**
>
> What if you knew this machine was to be used for mission-critical and life-critical applications?
>
> Doug Hoffman (2003). "Exhausting your test options" http:// softwarequalitymethods.com/Papers/ Exhaust%20Options.pdf
>
> 218

SLIDE 219

MASPAR had built-in floating point functions. One of them read a 32-bit word as an integer and computed its square root.

When I ask students to estimate how long it would take to run the four billion tests, most tell me it would take an impossibly long time. This includes students with years of testing experience.

Knowing that there are too many tests to run, most people would test the smallest and largest number, 0 and 4,294,967,295.

Some people would also test powers of 2: 1, 2, 4, 8, 16 and so on. In terms of bit patterns, these numbers have 31 bits set to

MASPAR

- To test the 32-bit integer square root function, Hoffman checked all values (all 4,294,967,296 of them). This took the computer about 6 minutes to run the tests and compare the results to an oracle.
- There were 2 (two) errors, neither of them near any boundary. (The underlying error was that a bit was sometimes missed, but in most error cases, there was no effect on the final calculated result.) Without an exhaustive test, these errors probably wouldn't have shown up.
- What about the 64-bit integer square root? How could we find the time to run all of these? If we don't run them all, don't we risk missing some bugs?

- To test all combinations of 32 bits, there are 2^{32} tests
- These 2^{32} tests required 6 minutes of testing.
- To test all combinations of 64 bits, there are 2^{64} tests.
  $$2^{64} = 2^{32} \times 2^{32}$$
- For this, we'd need
  $$2^{32} \times 6 \text{ minutes,}$$
  i.e. (24 billion) minutes.
- This is clearly impossible, so we MUST sample, even though this might cause us to miss some bugs.

219

0 and one bit set to 1. There are 32 tests with 1 bit set. What differs is which of the 32 bits is set. There are 32 more tests with 31 bits set to 1 and the odd bit set to 0. These 64 tests plus 0 (all bits 0) plus 232 1 (all bits 1) make up most of the tests that most people would run. Some people add random numbers or their favorite numbers or other values they suspect, but very few people suggest more than 100 tests.

Rather than assuming this was an impossibly big task, Hoffman decided to check how long it would take. The answer was only 6 minutes, so he tested them all.

Two tests failed. Two tests out of 4 billion failed.

Neither test input was anywhere near any boundary value. None of the 66 tests that I described would have exposed these two bugs.

So how can you find these bugs? Either you test exhaustively or you stumble over them by luck, where maybe luck is defined as a huge random sample, plus luck.

Now consider testing the 64-bit square root function. There are 2^{64} tests instead of 2^{32}. Testing them all would take over 24 billion minutes—about 49 thousand years of computer time.

And even if you could line up enough computers for this testing, you'd also want to test 64-bit multiply, 64-bit divide, and all the other built-in math functions.

You can't run this many tests. So even if it is possible that there are more bugs and even if this computer will be used to target nuclear missiles, the best you can do in testing is run large samples.

There are other strategies for improving the reliability of software, such as careful code reviews or test-driven programming, but from a black box testing viewpoint, there are more tests to run than you can find time to run.

_____
_____
_____
_____
_____
_____
_____
_____
_____
_____
_____

SLIDE 220

Hoffman's tests focused on a function that read data from a known location in memory. He didn't consider how data got into that location.

When you test human input, you have a lot more opportunities for misbehavior. For example, when you enter a number, you can edit while you type. You can type 123, then backspace and replace it with 456. Some programs can be confused and receive this as 123456 instead of 456 or as something else.

Another amusing type of input problem happens when you type very quickly or very slowly or when other computer activity is draining processor time. The program might misread your fast input.

Or it might time you out. Try this on your phone—start dialing, enter 6 digits and wait. After about a minute, the system times out. You get an error tone or message. What if you dial your 7th digit just as the system is about to time you out? This was a common source of bugs in phone systems. There are time-out intervals in most multi-user systems and in many other real-time systems.

Timeouts cause more mischief when you are entering several values into a dialog, or data into several dialogs. What does the program do with your partial set of data?

> **TESTING EVERY INPUT**
>
> Along with the simple cases, there are other "valid" inputs
>
> - Edited inputs
>   - The editing of an input can be quite complex. How much testing of editing is enough to convince us that no additional editing would trigger a new failure?
> - Variations on input timing
>   - Try entering data very quickly, or very slowly. Enter data before, during and after the processing of some other event, or just as the time-out interval for this data item is about to expire.
>   - In a client-server world (or any situation that involves multiple processors) consideration of input timing is essential.
>
> 220

SLIDE 221

We have other risks to consider when the variable we're testing is a result variable instead of an input variable.

For example, suppose we multiply two numbers together. The inputs might be valid, but together, they might overflow the result. We have to design tests that try to force overflow of the internal data type and, if the value will be displayed or printed, we want to overflow the space reserved for displaying or printing that value.

> **INVALID INPUTS TO INDIVIDUAL VARIABLES**
>
> - **Normally**, we look for boundaries, values at the edge of validity (almost invalid, or almost valid):
>   - If an input field accepts 1 to 100, we test with -1 and 0 and 101.
>   - If a program will multiply two numbers together using integer arithmetic, we try inputs that, together, will drive the multiplication just barely above MaxInt, to force an overflow.
>   - If a program can display a 9-character output field, we look for inputs that will force the output to be 10 characters.
>
> 221

SLIDE 222

Underflows also cause failures. If you just press return at a data entry dialog, without entering anything, you've given the program an empty string. No data. Some programs fail badly with empty strings.

And then there are Easter Eggs. Easter Eggs are hidden surprises in programs. If you type just the right sequence of characters at just the right place in the program, the program might give a special response. Some eggs are jokes. Others have included departing programmers' criticisms of the company, abusive language, and even animations of dancing naked women. Your company might not want to ship a product with these.

> **INVALID INPUTS TO INDIVIDUAL VARIABLES**
>
> • **However**, there are additional possibilities. For example...
>   – Extreme values can cause overflows or underflows.
>   * An enormous input string might overflow the area reserved for input, overwriting other data
>   * An empty input string might cause a there's-no-input failure such as a null pointer exception.
>   – These types of errors do happen accidently, but buffer overflows are also the most commonly exploited vulnerability by malicious code (or coders)
>
> And there are OTHER possibilities, like
> **Easter Eggs.**
>
> 222

Testing for Easter Eggs at the user interface is another sampling problem. Any sequence of keystrokes could bring up an Easter Egg. You can't test for them all.

SLIDE 223

Finally, let's consider clearly invalid input. Some testers, and many programmers, don't bother testing for inputs that they don't expect people to do.

In 1997, on the USS Yorktown (a somewhat famous cruiser in the United States) a seaman entered a zero into a data entry field that no one ever expected to see a zero in. The resulting divide by zero error took down the ship's systems and left the Yorktown dead in the water, at sea, for almost three hours.

People will do things that you don't expect. Maybe they're tired, or they don't

> **EXTREME VALUES EXPOSE ERROR-HANDLING WEAKNESSES**
>
> "No user would do that."
> really means
> "No user I can think of, who I like, would do that on purpose."
>
> • Who aren't you thinking of?
> • Who don't you like who might really use this product?
> • What might good users do by accident?
>
> Obviously, we can't test every possible invalid value (there are infinitely many). We have to sample...
>
> 223

understand the system, or they expect the system to do something that the system designer didn't think of, or they dropped something on the keyboard. Or maybe they are intentionally trying to do something that you don't approve of. Your system has to cope with these inputs because they will happen.

But you can't test for all of them.

And that's the point.

Even when you are testing one variable at a time, you probably can't test everything that people can throw at that field. You can test a lot. And it can be useful to know how long a thorough test would take because sometimes, you will decide to run that huge set of tests, like Hoffman did. But most of the time, the best you can do is a sample.

SLIDE 224

And even if you could test each individual variable completely, the program doesn't usually operate on just one variable at a time. It works with several.

_____

_____

_____

_____

_____

_____

_____

TO TEST EVERYTHING, YOU WOULD HAVE TO:

- Test every possible input to every variable (including output variables and intermediate results variables).

Test every possible combination of inputs to every combination of variables.

- Test every possible sequence through the program.
- Test every possible timing of inputs (check for timeouts and races)
- Test every interrupt at every point it can occur
- Test every hardware / software configuration, including configurations of servers not under your control
- Test for interference with other programs operating at the same time
- Test every way in which any user might try to use the program.

> Even if we ignore invalid variable values, the number of input combinations we can test gets impossibly large quickly.
>
> Several techniques are available to guide our sampling of these inputs.

224

SLIDE 225

Here's an example that took me by surprise. My staff and I tested a program extensively for printer compatibility. In a different series of tests we tested compatibility with different video cards. We also tested print preview quite often. What we failed to test was the combination of high resolution printing with high resolution video with the print preview feature. That combination ran customers' systems out of memory and crashed them.

AN EXAMPLE

- Program printed user-designed calendars
  - Printing to high-resolution printers worked well
  - Displaying to a high-resolution monitor worked well
  - "Print preview" of a high-resolution printout to a high-resolution monitor crashed Windows.
- The variables here are configuration variables: what printer, what video card, how much memory, etc.

> The program worked well with each variable, when we tested them one at a time.
>
> But when we tested them together, the system crashed.

225

SLIDE 226

When you test variables together, we call that combination testing.

If you test three variables together – let's call them V1, V2 and V3, and V1 has N1 possible values and V2 has N2 possible values and V3 has N3 possible values, then the total number of combination tests is N1 x N2 x N3.

THE BASIC COMBINATION RULE

Suppose there are K independent variables, V1, V2, ..., VK.

Label the number of choices for the variables as N1, N2 through NK.

The total number of possible combinations is

$N1 \times N2 \times \ldots \times NK$.

226

_____

_____

_____

_____

_____

_____

_____

_____

_____

SLIDE 227

We call combination testing configuration testing when we test combinations of things that make up the environment of the program, for example, combinations of devices, versions of system software, and communications with external servers.

So if we test with 40 printers and 20 video cards, there are 800 configurations. What if we also test how much available memory there is – suppose we test a level we consider barely enough and second level that has lots of free memory? Now we have 40 x 20 x 2 = 1600 configurations to test.

SLIDE 228

As you consider more variables, and test them together, the total number of tests gets very large very quickly.

_____

_____

_____

_____

_____

_____

_____

_____

_____

SLIDE 229

Configuration testing is just one example of combination testing. Other combinations involve data.

I worked with a word processor once that had a memory leak. If you selected some text and made it bold, then italic, everything worked. But if you made it italic first, then bold, the appearance on the screen was the same but memory was corrupted. Combination errors can be very surprising and seem unreasonable.

Let's go back to Hoffman's square root test. He tested on function that accepted 2 to the 32 inputs. Lets test formulas. We'll start

APPLY THE BASIC RULE TO OUR CONFIGURATION EXAMPLE

- V1 is the type of printer (we're ignoring printer driver versions). N1 is the number of printers we want to test. (40 has been realistic on many projects. We've worked on projects with over 500)
- V2 is the type of video card. N2 is the number of types of video cards we want to test (20 or more is realistic.)
- Number of distinct tests = N1 x N2

Number of printers	Number of video cards	Number of tests
2	2	4
3	3	9
5	5	25
40	20	800

Suppose we add a third variable (V3): how much free memory is available in the computer.

Now we have

N1 x N2 x N3 tests

227

THE BASIC COMBINATION RULE

Suppose we test

- N1 printers, with
- N2 versions of their printer driver
- N3 video cards, with
- N4 versions of their driver
- N5 amount of free memory
- N6 versions of the operating system
- N7 audio drivers
- N8 mouse drivers
- N9 keyboard drivers
- N10 types of connections to the Net

= N1 x N2 x N3 x N4 x N5 x N6 x N7 x N8 x N9 x N10 distinct tests

228

IT'S NOT JUST CONFIGURATION TESTING

- Booked a several-segment (several country) trip on American Airlines on a special deal that yielded a relatively low first-class fare.
- AA prints a string on the ticket that lists all segments and their fares.
- Ticket agents at a busy airport couldn't print the ticket because the string was too long. The usual easy workaround was to split up the trip (issue a few tickets) but in this combination of flights, splitting caused a huge fare change.
- It took nearly an hour of agent time to figure out a ticketing combination that worked.

- How many variables are in play here?
- How many combinations would you have to test to discover this problem and determine whether it happens often enough to be considered serious?

229

with a simple one, a square rrot of one number tiems a square root of another. That's 2 to the 32 times 2 to the 32 combinations. Now imagine testing a calculator. How many different formulas can you test?

Other combinations of data can yield divide by zero, overflow, or serious rounding errors.

In the example discussed on the slide, a complex travel plan overflowed the output fields on an airline ticket, creating a big tie-up at the airport ticket counter.

SLIDE 230

There are testing techniques that optimize sampling, so that you run a small set of combination tests and have a good chance of finding most or all of the combination-related errors. With the 1600 tests of printer with video card with memory configurations, a common sampling heuristic called all-pairs would yield 80 tests. We'll discuss these in more detail in the test design course, but for now, understand that the 80 tests would probably find most of the bugs, but the remaining 1520 tests are distinct. This sampling could easily miss a failure that occurs only on a low memory system with this particular printer and that particular video card.

> ### COMBINATIONS
> - The **normal** case when testing combinations of several independent variables is to adopt a sampling scheme. (After all, we can't run **all** these tests.)
> - For example, with 40 printers and 20 video cards, you might cut back to 50 tests:
>   - One test for every printer (40 tests)
>   - Test each video card at least once (test printer and video together, you still have only 40 tests)
>   - Add a few more tests to check specific combinations that have caused technical support problems for other products.
> - Variants on this sampling scheme are common. Some (the combinatorial tests, such as "all-pairs") are widely discussed.
>   - In our example of 40 printers x 20 video cards x 2 levels of memory, all-pairs would reduce the 1600 tests to a sample of 800.
>
> **As with all other tests, though, any combination you don't test is a combination that might trigger a failure.**
>
> 230

SLIDE 231

Our next challenge involves errors that occur in time, when the program does this after that.

> ### TO TEST EVERYTHING, YOU WOULD HAVE TO:
> - Test every possible input to every variable (including output variables and intermediate results variables).
> - Test every possible combination of inputs to every combination of variables.
>
> *Test every possible sequence through the program.*
>
> - Test every possible timing of inputs (check for timeouts and races)
> - Test every interrupt at every point it can occur
> - Test every hardware / software configuration, including configurations of servers not under your control.
> - Test for interference with other programs operating at the same time
> - Test every way in which any user might try to use the program.
>
> 231

SLIDE 232

We need some vocabulary.

When I speak of a path, I mean a sequence of steps in a program from program start to program end.

I say sub-path to refer to shorter sequences.

Many other people use the word path generally, to mean a full path or a subpath.

_____

_____

_____

_____

PATHS AND SUBPATHS

A path through a program
- starts at an entry point (you start the program)
- ends at an exit point (the program stops)

A sub-path
- starts and ends anywhere

A sub-path of length N
- starts, continues through N statements, and then stops

232

SLIDE 233

I'm going to draw paths using flowcharts.

Flowcharts are currently out of fashion, but I know many testers who find them easier to read, so I use them here.

In a flowchart, we show a branch with a diamond shape. Here, we branch from A to B or C.

_____

_____

_____

_____

SOME NOTATION

 Do task "A". "A" might be a single statement or a block of code or an observable event.

 Do task "A" and then do "B" or "C". This is a basic branch

Do task "A" and then do "B" and then loop back to A

233

SLIDE 234

Flowgraphs are more fashionable today. To turn our diagrams into flowgraphs, just replace all the diamonds and boxes with circles.

_____

_____

_____

_____

_____

_____

_____

_____

SOME NOTATION

 Do task "A". "A" might be a single statement or a block of code or an observable event.

 Do task "A" and then do "B" or "C". This is a basic branch

 Do task "A" and then do "B" and then loop back to A

Vocabulary Alert

If we replace the boxes and diamonds with circles and call them "nodes" and call the lines "edges," we have a "directed graph."

Directed graphs have useful mathematical properties for creating test-supporting models (e.g. state models).

For a detailed introduction written for testers, read Paul Jorgensen's (2008) *Software Testing: A Craftsman's Approach* (3rd Ed.)

234

_____

_____

_____

SLIDE 235

Here's a little program. What would it take to test it?

_____

_____

_____

_____

_____

_____

_____

_____

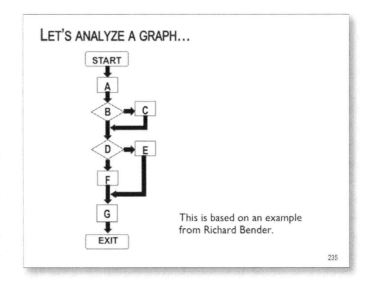

LET'S ANALYZE A GRAPH...

This is based on an example from Richard Bender.

235

SLIDE 236

We can test all the statements and all the branches with two tests. One takes us from A to B to C to D to F to G. The other takes us from A to B to D to E to G.

This is complete branch coverage. Is it enough?

_____

_____

_____

_____

_____

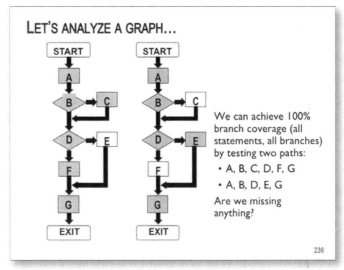

LET'S ANALYZE A GRAPH...

We can achieve 100% branch coverage (all statements, all branches) by testing two paths:
• A, B, C, D, F, G
• A, B, D, E, G
Are we missing anything?

236

SLIDE 237

Simple path models, like branch coverage, ignore the program's data. If a data value doesn't cause a branch, it is irrelevant.

But programs use data, they do things with data, so the value of the data is not irrelevant. It's important.

People who think data is important often work with data flow diagrams. These show when the program assigns a value to a variable and when that value of that variable is used.

I'm not going to draw traditional data flow diagrams, but the chart on this slide can show data flows.

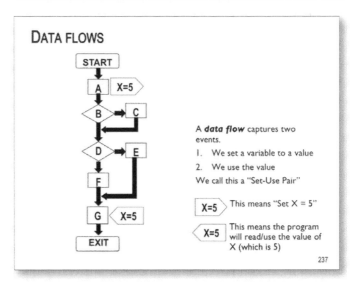

DATA FLOWS

A **data flow** captures two events.
1. We set a variable to a value
2. We use the value
We call this a "Set-Use Pair"

X=5 〉 This means "Set X = 5"

X=5 〉 This means the program will read/use the value of X (which is 5)

237

Look at step A. The program sets X to 5. Then the program uses X at point G. I'm going to suppose we print the value of X at G. So we can ask, what value does it print?

SLIDE 238

When we set a value at A and use it at G, A and G form a set-use pair. Similarly, We set X to 7 at C and use it at G, so C-G is a set/use pair. E/G is our third set/use pair on this diagram.

In this test, the set/use pair that is active is C/G. We set X to 5 at A but we reset it to 7 at C. When we print X at G, we print a 7.

_____

_____

_____

_____

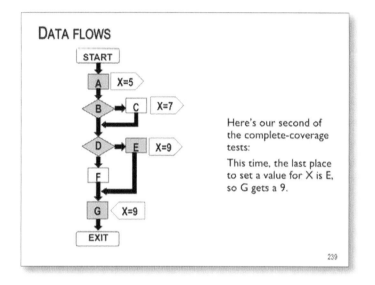

SLIDE 239

In the second test, EG is the set/use pair.

_____

_____

_____

_____

_____

_____

_____

_____

_____

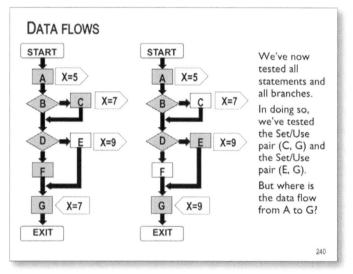

SLIDE 240

Between these two tests, we have complete branch coverage, but we don't have a test for the A/G set use pair.

_____

_____

_____

_____

_____

_____

_____

SLIDE 241

For that third set/use pair, we need a third test.

_____

_____

_____

_____

_____

_____

_____

_____

_____

DATA FLOWS

To test that third data flow, we need to test a third path. This one will do it.

START

A — X=5

B → C — X=7

D → E — X=9

F

G — X=9

EXIT

241

SLIDE 242

In the example so far, we assumed that G does something very simple with X, like printing it. But what if G did something more complicated, like dividing some other number by X? In that case, the specific value of X would be very important.

Whenever you test a variable, it's important to ask how the program will use the value of that variable, and test the variable with different values, to best test the different uses.

Testing for consequences – considering what the program does with a variable whenever you set the variable – testing for consequences is one of the things that sets skilled testers apart from juniors.

DATA FLOWS: CAUTION

When you test data flows, it's not enough to set X and use it.

You must consider how X is used:

- What does the program do with X?
- What values of X might be troublesome for that use?
- Does the program use X in combination with other variables? What values of X would be troublesome with those variables?
- Does the program based another variable on X or on a calculation that uses X? What trouble can **that** variable cause?

Test the **consequences** of the use.

242

SLIDE 243

Let's look at our next example for testing sequences.

_____

_____

_____

_____

_____

_____

_____

_____

_____

_____

_____

TO TEST EVERYTHING, YOU WOULD HAVE TO:

- Test every possible input to every variable (including output variables and intermediate results variables).
- Test every possible combination of inputs to every combination of variables.

Test every possible sequence through the program.

- Test every hardware / software configuration, including configurations of servers not under your control.
- Test every way in which any user might try to use the program.

We're still in the middle of this every-possible-sequence analysis...

243

SLIDE 244

This is a famous example from Glen Myers. We start the program at A and all the branches lead to X. At X, we either loop back to A or we exit. If we reach X for the 20th time, we always exit.

_____

_____

_____

_____

_____

_____

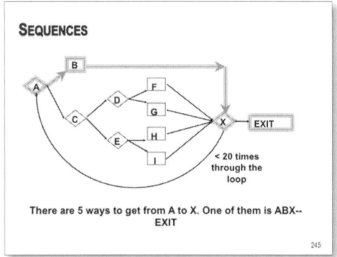

NEXT EXAMPLE

< 20 times through the loop

This example shows there are too many paths to test in even a fairly simple program.
This is from Myers, *The Art of Software Testing*.

244

SLIDE 245

Let's look at the paths through this program.

One goes from A to B to X.

_____

_____

_____

_____

_____

_____

_____

_____

_____

SEQUENCES

< 20 times through the loop

There are 5 ways to get from A to X. One of them is ABX--EXIT

245

SLIDE 246

Another from A to C to D to F to X.

_____

_____

_____

_____

_____

_____

_____

_____

_____

_____

_____

_____

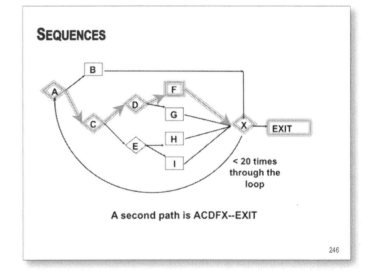

SEQUENCES

< 20 times through the loop

A second path is ACDFX--EXIT

246

_____

_____

_____

_____

SLIDE 247

And A to C to D to G to X.

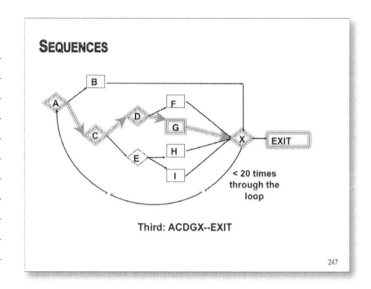

SLIDE 248

And A to C to E to H to X.

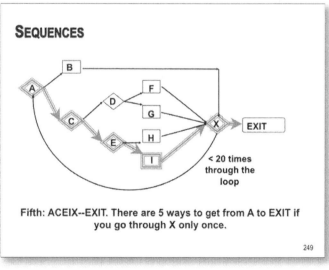

SLIDE 249

Or from A to C to E to I to X. So there are 5 ways to get from A to X.

If we only go through the loop once, we exit as soon as we reach X. This gives 5 paths.

SLIDE 250

But you don't have to exit the first time you hit X. You can go to X up to 20 times, looping back to A.

_____

_____

_____

_____

_____

_____

_____

_____

SLIDE 251

Here, we see a path that goes from A to C to E to H to X, then back to A then to B to X and to the exit.

This is one of the 25 paths in which we exit the second time we hit X.

_____

_____

_____

_____

_____

_____

SLIDE 252

We can count up the possible paths using the combination rule that we studied a few slides ago.

Imagine a variable V1 which holds the path from A to X. V1 has five possible values.

Now imagine V2 which holds the path from A to X the second time through the loop. V2 has five values.

We have 20 Vs because we can go through the loop up to 20 times. The N for each V is 5, V1 has N1 = 5 paths, V2 has N2 = 5 paths and so one.

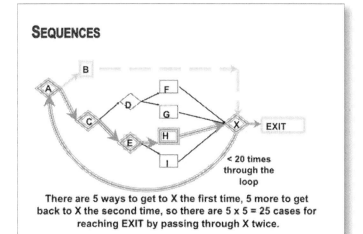

SEQUENCES

But you can go through X more than once. Here's another path. ACEHXABX--EXIT.

250

SEQUENCES

There are 5 ways to get to X the first time, 5 more to get back to X the second time, so there are 5 x 5 = 25 cases for reaching EXIT by passing through X twice.

251

SEQUENCES

ANALYZING MYERS' EXAMPLE

There are

- 5 ways to get to X once, then EXIT.
- 5 x 5 ways to get to X twice, then EXIT
- 5 x 5 x 5 ways to get to X three times, then EXIT.

In total, there are $5^1 + 5^2 + ... + 5^{19} + 5^{20}$ = (approximately) 10^{14} = 100 trillion paths through the program.

(This applies the combination formula we looked at before. With variables V1, V2, etc., the number of combination tests is N1 x N2 x ... etc.)

Obviously, we can't test all these paths, so we need to select a sample.

A typical sample would probably include all 5 tests that get to EXIT once, at least one test that goes to EXIT all 20 times, an attempt to hit EXIT 21 times, and tests that check the pairs

- (pass through B, pass through F)
- (pass through G, pass through H)

and so on.

252

If we go through just once, we have five paths. If we go through twice, it is N1 x N2 paths. If we go through three times, there are N1 x N2 x N3 paths. That's about 100 trillion paths and this is a trivially simple program with one entry, one exit, and only one loop. Imagine the number of paths through a word processor or a telephone system.

SLIDE 253

Obviously, you can't test all these paths. Some people would test only six paths. Try each of the five ways to get from A to X. Then add a case that gets to X 20 times and exits automatically.

This covers every line, every branch, and every simple sub-path through the program.

But is it enough testing?

For example, suppose that we have a memory leak at F. If we go through F 10 times, the program crashes out of memory. Unless we're testing with a memory meter, we won't see a memory leak until the program misbehaves, like slowing down

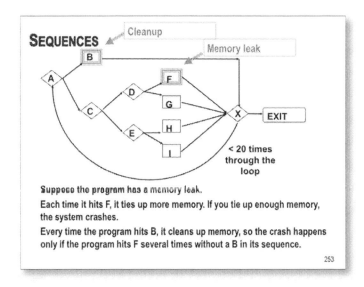

Suppose the program has a memory leak.

Each time it hits F, it ties up more memory. If you tie up enough memory, the system crashes.

Every time the program hits B, it cleans up memory, so the crash happens only if the program hits F several times without a B in its sequence.

drastically or crashing. So to find this bug, we'd have to run a test that passed through F 10 times. Any path that doesn't go through F ten times will miss this bug.

If you didn't suspect a memory leak, how many tests do you think you'd have to run before you stumbled on one that passed through F 10 times and crashed your program? It would be a lot of tests.

Now let's make the case more extreme.

Let's put a garbage collector in B. If you ever pass through B, the garbage collector checks for unused memory and gives it back to the operating system. This clears up the memory hogged by F. Now, the program will crash out of memory *only* if we pass through F ten times after the last time we passed through B.

Only a very small percentage of the 100 trillion tests that we could run would expose this bug, so unless we test with a very large sample, or are very lucky, we're going to miss this bug.

Let's make this case even more special. Suppose B is the most common choice from A and F doesn't happen very often in normal use. In this case, 10 F's in a row is going to be rare.

Do you think you would ever create a test that repeated F 10 times without passing through B?

SLIDE 254

When I teach this live, most students say no. This includes most professional testers when I teach this class to experienced testers. So if you said no, this test is too extreme, too specific, no one would ever run into this case in practice, you're in good company.

So let's sum up. I have demonstrated that we can't test every possible path, and I have found a way to show that, in theory, we could miss a very serious bug if we don't test all or almost all of the paths.

But, many people see this example as completely unrealistic. It would never happen in the real world. It is merely academic.

SEQUENCES

ANALYZING MYERS' EXAMPLE

This example is often treated as "academic" (purely theoretical), but this kind of problem can definitely show up in real life.

Here's a bug I ran into as a programmer, developing a phone system...

This is a good time to remember our rule about extreme cases. "No one would do that" doesn't mean "no one would do that." It means, "No one who I can currently think of would do that for any reason that I can currently imagine."

Testing is a humbling experience because it shows us time and time again how limited our imaginations really are.

SLIDE 255

In the real world, we actually did find exactly this bug.

This is the Telenova 1 phone system. I was one of the programmers. The phone had an LCD display and context-sensitive menus that could take you through all its features.

PHONE SYSTEM: THE TELENOVA STACK FAILURE

Telenova Station Set 1. Integrated voice and data.
108 voice features, 110 data features. 1984.

255

SLIDE 256

A person using our phone could put up to 10 people on hold at once. There was a fair bit of data associated with every call. When the user put a call on hold, we put the held-call's data structure on a stack. The phone displayed the hold queue—the list of calls on hold, and you could decide which call to reconnect to.

THE TELENOVA STACK FAILURE

Context-sensitive
display
10-deep hold queue
10-deep wait queue

256

SLIDE 257

One of our beta sites was a stock broker. In those days, stock brokers were like the Olympic athletes of telephone users. You'd visit a broker and see a desk full of phones. He set up trades over the phone. He'd have multiple calls going so that he could work on one deal while waiting on another. At peak times, the phones would ring so much, the broker would pick up a bunch of calls, put them on hold, and capture orders as quickly as he could.

The brokers loved our system. Instead of juggling handsets with one on this shoulder and one on that shoulder and different colors of phone to remind the broker which handset was which, we had one phone that could juggle 10 calls. Put on one headset and you could work all day without having to strain your neck and upper back trying to write while you worked on the phone.

Unfortunately, on busy days, sometimes one of our phones would crash. Then other phones would crash. Then others. Then the first phone would finish its twi minute rebooting cycle, come back on line, but it would crash again minutes later. And this could go on for an hour or longer.

> **THE TELENOVA STACK FAILURE**
>
> - Beta customer (a stock broker) reported random failures
> - Could be frequent at peak times
> - One phone would crash and reboot, then other phones crashed while the first rebooted
> - On a particularly busy day, service was disrupted all (East Coast) afternoon
> - We were mystified:
> - All individual functions worked
> - We had tested all statements and branches.
>
> 257

SLIDE 258

We finally figured out the problem.

Here's a simplified state diagram. You could have up to 10 calls on hold.

Your phone's usually at idle. Someone calls, your phone rings and you either pick it up, which puts your phone in the connected state, or you don't pick it up and eventually the caller will hang up and you go back to idle.

Once you're connected, you can talk for a while and hang up, or the caller can hang up. Either of these takes your phone to idle. Or you can put the caller on hold.

When you take a call off hold, we take the held call's data off the stack and put it in the current call record.

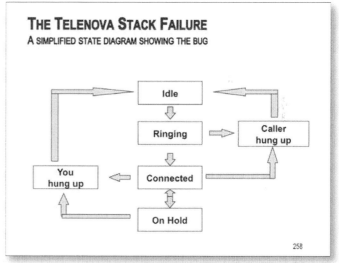

The Telenova Stack Failure — A Simplified State Diagram Showing the Bug

_____

_____

_____

_____

_____

_____

_____

_____

SLIDE 259

Suppose you put a call on hold but before you reconnect, the caller hangs up.

This was a rare case in the 1980's. Customer service standards on the phone were much higher. 90% of held calls were reconnected within two minutes, so not many people hung up while they were on hold. We handled the case pretty well. When the caller hung up, we took their name off the display, marked as available the outside line they called in on, we freed up the time slice allocated to the call, everything looked as though the call was gone. But the call record stayed on the stack. Inaccessible but not deleted. So the stack could fill up.

Telenova Stack Failure

259

SLIDE 260

You'd think we would have noticed this problem right away, because our testers worked with 10 held calls lots of times, and they did the caller-hangs-up thing, and didn't see a problem.

The problem was more subtle.

Originally, our code checked the stack every time we added or removed anything. This would have caught this bug. Unfortunately, this took so much system time that we had to pull it out. By then, we were confident that the handling of the call waiting and hold stacks worked, so we expected never to see a stack problem.

THE TELENOVA STACK FAILURE

Ultimately, we found the bug in the hold queue
* Up to 10 calls on hold, each adds record to the stack
* Initially, the system checked the stack when any call was added or removed, but this took too much system time. So we dropped our checks and added these
  - Stack has room for 20 calls (just in case)
  - Stack reset (forced to zero) when we knew it *should* be empty
* The error handling made it almost impossible for us to detect the problem in the lab. Because a user couldn't put more than 10 calls on the stack (unless she knew the magic error), testers couldn't get to 21 calls to cause the stack overflow.

260

Just in case a bug was introduced later, we made the stack bigger, big enough for 20 call records even though the system would only have at most 10 held calls. So if garbage ever did get on the stack, we still had room for the real calls. Then we added a stack reset command to a few places where the stack was supposed to be empty, like the idle state. This made sure that, if there ever was garbage on the stack, it got cleared off quickly.

This shouldn't have been necessary because the hold stack worked, but we put it in just in case, because in defensive programming, you anticipate the possibility that someone will put a bug into the code later when they change a feature, and you want to automatically detect that future failure if it ever happens and recover from it.

Sometime over the next year, one of us made the bug, and this defensive code made it harmless and invisible for almost everyone.

SLIDE 261

The bug put us in a situation that looks just like our diagram from Myers. Every time you hit F, there's another record worth of garbage on the stack. If you get to B, the garbage gets cleared up. There's only a problem if you have so many hangups-on-hold before getting to B that the total of hangup calls and real calls on hold exceeds 20. Then you overflow the stack.

When the stack overflows, the phone transfers its held calls—the real ones—to some other phones. This is called hold forwarding. You've probably been hold-forwarded. You call someone, wait a long

SEQUENCES

The stack bug was just like this program, with a garbage collector at B (the idle state) and a stack leak at F (hang up from hold). If you hit F *N* times without touching B, when you try to put a *21-Nth* call on hold, you overflow the stack and crash.

261

time on hold, then you might hear a click, maybe the music on hold changes, and someone else answers the phone and says who are you and what do you want?

So, when phone one crashed, it hold-forwarded its held calls to phone two and if two's stack is full, to phone three. Maybe this gives phone two a full stack. On the next held call, phone two crashes and dumps its calls on phone three, which will crash and dump its calls to phone four. Eventually—two minutes later—phone one comes back into service and everybody dumps their calls to phone one, refilling its stack and setting it up to crash again soon.

This is called a rotating outage. In a rotating outage, error handling from one subsystem triggers a failure in the next, and the next and the next, until finally, error handling in the last one triggers another failure in the first system, starting the sequence over again. In our phone system, the outage will finally clear when the pace of calls slows enough to let the phones get to idle every now and again. But during really busy times, that might not happen for hours.

SLIDE 262

We were really lucky with this bug. All it did was cost a beta site some money. Things could have been much worse.

Once we understood this bug, we could imagine realistic scenarios under which this rotating outage in our system would prevent potential customers of ours from giving help under life-critical circumstances. In retrospect, we were lucky that this bug hadn't killed anyone.

I want to tie this back to coverage. I've talked about this bug in a lot of meetings and classes. Every now and again, some pompous fool stands up and tells me that

TELENOVA STACK FAILURE

This example illustrates several important points:

- Simplistic approaches to path testing can miss critical defects.
- Critical defects can arise under circumstances that appear (in a test lab) so specialized that you would never intentionally test for them.
- When (in some future course or book) you hear a new methodology for combination testing or path testing, I want you to test it against this defect. If you had no suspicion that there was a stack corruption problem in this program, would the new method lead you to find this bug?

262

we must not have achieved full statement or branch coverage, because if we had, we would have found the bug.

We did achieve full branch coverage of this code. I know that because I was one of the programmers and I know what I tested. The other programmers did extensive, careful checking too.

But that doesn't matter because hitting every line and every branch once won't expose this bug.

Several of us did maintenance in this area. When I worked on this, I *did* test abandoned held calls. With my debugger running, I put a call on hold, hung up the held call, and looked at the stack. Problem is, even though the stack got corrupted, it got reset by the error handler so fast that I never noticed it. I never imagined that I might need to abandon several held calls before I got back to idle, so I never ran that test.

This is a long-sequence bug. That is, it shows up only after a long series of events. Ultimately, Telenova built a simulator for long sequence testing and had impressive results. A lot of the problems people think of as irreproducible are probably long-sequence.

SLIDE 263

But for now, it's time to sum up.

Testers are asked to do many different tasks. Along with testing, they're expected to troubleshoot bugs and write great failure reports, write documentation for their tests, participate in code reviews, create test tools, help technical support staff understand how to work around the product's bugs, review user documentation, and so on. But if the basic testing time required is infinite, that doesn't leave much time for all these other activities. Any time you spend on one activity, you can't spend on any of the others. It's easy to say that testers should

> ### SUMMING UP
>
> Testers live and breathe tradeoffs.
>
> **The time needed for test-related tasks is infinitely larger than the time available.**
>
> Time you spend on
> - analyzing, troubleshooting, and effectively describing a failure
>
> Is time no longer available for
> - Designing tests
> - Documenting tests
> - Executing tests
> - Automating tests
> - Reviews, inspections
> - Supporting tech support
> - Retooling
> - Training other staff
>
> 263

always fully document each test, but the real-life decision is more complex if documentation time takes away time for code inspections or bug report writing or some other worthy activity.

In the face of an infinite set of tasks, statements that testers always have to do this or always have to do that are unreasonable. Every task is subject to a tradeoff—what is the value of this task, compared to the values of all the other tasks that could be done in that time instead?

You might try to solve the tradeoff by hiring more testers, but in the face of an infinitely large set of testing tasks, you'll run out of money and testers and still have tests that haven't been run, automated, documented, or evaluated, and you still have to decide what testing tasks to do and what not.

This is probably the hardest problem in software testing.

_____

_____

_____

_____

_____

_____

_____

_____

_____

_____

_____

SLIDE 264

BLACK BOX SOFTWARE TESTING:
FOUNDATIONS

END OF LECTURE 5

CEM KANER, J.D., PH.D.
PROFESSOR OF SOFTWARE ENGINEERING
FLORIDA INSTITUTE OF TECHNOLOGY

REBECCA L. FIEDLER, M.B.A. PH.D.
PRESIDENT: KANER, FIEDLER & ASSOCIATES

JAMES BACH
PRINCIPAL, SATISFICE INC

This work is licensed under the Creative Commons Attribution License. To view a copy of this license, visit http://creativecommons.org/licenses/by-sa/2.0/ or send a letter to Creative Commons. 559 Nathan Abbott Way, Stanford, California 94305, USA.

These notes are partially based on research that was supported by NSF Grants EIA-0113539 ITR/SY +PE:"Improving the Education of Software Testers" and CCLI-0717613 "Adaptation & Implementation of an Activity-Based Online or Hybrid Course in Software Testing." Any opinions, findings and conclusions or recommendations expressed in this material are those of the author(s) and do not necessarily reflect the views of the National Science Foundation.

264

Authors' Reflection On Lesson 5

I created many of the slides for this lesson by importing some from earlier courses I had created and others from James Bach. The mixture of ways we describe things has created some terminological confusion in class.

In particular, the slide "Complete coverage doesn't mean complete testing" has caused unnecessary confusion. It sounds cute to say "complete coverage isn't complete coverage" (which is what this slide is really saying). But the reader has to understand why that is true or the words make no sense. The student who doesn't already understand the material doesn't get the joke. It just confuses them.

What we've discovered is that students who don't understand the "complete coverage isn't complete testing" slide will often make up counterproductive definitions for themselves of complete coverage and complete testing. That hurts their learning of the rest of the material.

I'm sorry about that confusion. It's not what was intended.

If you are not clear on the terminology, perhaps this will help:

- COVERAGE means the extent of testing of a given type that has been completed, compared to the population of possible tests of that type. (Slide 198)

- COVERAGE is a measurement. It assesses the extent (or proportion) of testing of a given type that has been completed, compared to the population of possible tests of this type. (Slide 207)

- COMPLETE COVERAGE means the same thing as COMPLETE TESTING. You would have to achieve 100% of all types of tests, which is impossible. Otherwise put, you would have to test so thoroughly that you could be certain that there are no bugs in the software that you don't know about. (Slide 215).

- COMPLETE COVERAGE OF A CERTAIN KIND means you have covered 100% of that kind of test. For example, if you achieve complete printer coverage, you have tested all the printers that could conceivably be tested with your program. If you achieve complete statement coverage, you have tested all the statements in the program. (Slide 207)

- COMPLETE CODE COVERAGE or COMPLETE STRUCTURAL COVERAGE is sometimes what programmers or academics mean when they say "complete coverage." Complete structural coverage includes such ideas as complete statement coverage, complete branch coverage, complete multicondition coverage or complete path coverage (see slides 199-204). As we argue in Lectures 4 and 5, "complete code coverage" is not the same thing as complete testing (and it is not the same thing as complete coverage). (Slide 204-207)

- COMPLETE TESTING means the same thing as COMPLETE COVERAGE. You would have to achieve 100% of all types of tests, which is impossible. Otherwise put, you would have to test so thoroughly that you could be certain that there are no bugs in the software that you don't know about. (Slide 215).

6

LESSON 6: INTRODUCTION TO MEASUREMENT

Lesson Introduction

Lesson 6 introduces you to software metrics. This is a necessarily brief introduction. The lesson presents four key concepts:

- *Measurement:* the empirical, objective assignment of numbers to attributes of objects or events according to a rule derived from a model or theory with the intent of describing them;

- *Construct validity:* the basis for believing that a measure actually describes the attribute. For example, the question, "Why do you think a tester's bug count is a measure of her skill as a tester?" is a challenge of the construct validity of bug counts as a description of skill. According to the lecture (and to research published by Kaner & Bond), very few papers or books on software metrics evaluate the construct validity of the metrics they suggest. The lecture implies (and we believe) that very few of the software engineering metrics, including testing metrics, have any construct validity;

- *Surrogate measures:* A surrogate measure ascribes numbers to attributes but without the benefit of an underlying model or theory. In practice, we use surrogate measures when we don't know how to measure an attribute, but we think the surrogate is correlated with the attribute. Surrogates often measure a narrow aspect of an attribute. For example, a tester's bug count might be one aspect of their skill or productivity but it misses how interesting those bugs are, how well described the bug reports are, how hard-to-find those bugs were, how well the tester crafted or used tools to find bugs like this, how well the tester covered the area of the program the bug was found in, how well the tester coaches other testers, etc. If we focus too much on bug counts, we might cause testers to spend less time on these other aspects, which might be more important than the bug counts.

■ *Measurement dysfunction:* People will optimize their behavior to improve the scores they get when they are measured. This normal human behavior is what makes management-by-measurement possible. What you measure guides how they allocate their time, attention, and improvement-efforts. If you measure the wrong things, they work on the wrong things. Sometimes, measuring something can make the attribute worse than it would have been if there had been no measurement. This is measurement dysfunction.

The lesson presents two examples involving bug counts. One is the risk (we think, futility) of using bug counts to measure the skill (productivity, effectiveness, value) of testers. The other is the risk of using bugs-per-week as a measure of project progress, and in particular of using this in conjunction with a statistical model that is easily proved to be completely invalid.

Some of you may be tempted to interpret this lecture as a condemnation of all metrics or all test-related metrics. It's not. Rather, this is more like a lesson on gun safety. There are legitimate reasons for owning and using guns. But if you don't know how to use them safely, very bad things will happen.

Readings

The following reading is required:

■ Kaner, C., & Bond, W. P. (2004). Software engineering metrics: What do they measure and how do we know? Retrieved from http://testingeducation.org/BBST/foundations/Kaner_Bond_metrics2004.pdf

The following readings are recommended:

■ Bolton, M. (2009, January 19). Meaningful metrics. Developsense Blog. Retrieved from http://www.developsense.com/blog/2009/01/meaningful-metrics/

■ Hoffman, D. (2000). The Darker Side of Metrics. Pacific Northwest Software Quality Conference. Portland, Oregon. Retrieved from http://www.softwarequalitymethods.com/SQM/Papers/DarkerSideMetricsPaper.pdf

■ Kaner, C. (2013). Practical Approaches to Software Metrics. http://kaner.com/pdfs/PracticalApproachToSoftwareMetrics.pdf

■ Kaner, C. & Kabbani, N. (2012). Software Metrics: Threats to Validity. Conference of the Association for Software Testing. Slides at http://testingeducation.org/BBST/metrics/MetricsValidityLecture2012.pdf. Video at http://testingeducation.org/BBST/metrics/CAST2012Metrics.mp4

■ Simmons, E. (2000). When Will We be Done Testing? Software Defect Arrival Modeling Using the Weibull Distribution. Pacific Northwest Software Quality Conference. Portland, OR. Retrieved from http://www.pnsqc.org/proceedings/pnsqc00.pdf

Orientation: What Makes A Measurement?

Please spend up to an hour researching and writing your answer to this question.

If you are in an instructor-led course, post your answer in the course forum and review two other students' work. How were their answers similar to yours, how where they different? What did you learn from them and how would you change your answer now that you have seen those other ideas?

Please watch the lecture and consider your answer again after that. Don't read the feedback in the back of the book until after you have watched the lecture and considered how you would revise your answer in the light of it.

Here is the question...

Kaner and Bond define measurement as follows: "Measurement is the empirical, objective assignment of numbers to attributes of objects or events (according to a rule derived from a model or theory) with the intent of describing them."

Consider this case:

A professor decides to base the grades in her class on the height of her students. The taller the student, the higher the grade. Grades will be assigned on a 1-100 scale. The tallest student earns 100, all other students are given a score that matches the ratio (expressed as a percentage) of their height to the tallest student's height.

    a. Is this a measurement under this definition?

    b. Justify your answer to (a)

    c. Briefly describe three advantages or problems with this proposed measure.

    d. On balance, do the advantages outweigh the problems for using this as a measure?

Slides And Notes

SLIDE 265

Welcome to this sixth lecture of the *Foundations of Software Testing*.

_____

_____

_____

_____

_____

_____

_____

_____

_____

BLACK BOX SOFTWARE TESTING FOUNDATIONS: LECTURE 6

MEASUREMENT

CEM KANER, J.D., PH.D.
PROFESSOR OF SOFTWARE ENGINEERING
FLORIDA INSTITUTE OF TECHNOLOGY

REBECCA L. FIEDLER, M.B.A. PH.D.
PRESIDENT: KANER, FIEDLER & ASSOCIATES

JAMES BACH
PRINCIPAL, SATISFICE INC

This work is licensed under the Creative Commons Attribution License. To view a copy of this license, visit http://creativecommons.org/licenses/by-sa/2.0/ or send a letter to Creative Commons, 559 Nathan Abbott Way, Stanford, California 94305, USA.

These notes are partially based on research that was supported by NSF Grants EIA-0113539 ITR/SY +PE:"Improving the Education of Software Testers" and CCLI-0717613 "Adaptation & Implementation of an Activity-Based Online or Hybrid Course in Software Testing." Any opinions, findings and conclusions or recommendations expressed in this material are those of the author(s) and do not necessarily reflect the views of the National Science Foundation.

265

SLIDE 266

Today we look at a few key concepts from measurement theory.

_____

_____

_____

_____

_____

_____

_____

_____

_____

_____

_____

OVERVIEW: FUNDAMENTAL TOPICS

- Why are we testing? What are we trying to learn? How should we organize our work to achieve this? *Information objectives drive the testing mission and strategy*

- How can we know whether a program has passed or failed a test? *Oracles are heuristic*

- How can we determine how much testing has been done? What core knowledge about program internals do testers need to consider this question? *Coverage is a multidimensional problem*

- Are we done yet? *Complete testing is impossible*

- How much testing have we completed and how well have we done it? *Measurement is important, but hard*

266

SLIDE 267

TODAY'S READINGS

No required reading. Useful to skim:

- Robert Austin (1996), *Measurement and Management of Performance in Organizations.*
- Michael Bolton (2007), What Counts? http://www.developsense.com/articles/2007-11-WhatCounts.pdf
- Michael Bolton (2009), Meaningful Metrics, http://www.developsense.com/blog/2009/01/meaningful-metrics/
- Doug Hoffman (2000), "The Darker Side of Software Metrics", http://www.softwarequalitymethods.com/Papers/DarkMets%20Paper.pdf.
- Cem Kaner & Walter P. Bond (2004), "Software engineering metrics: What do they measure and how do we know?" http://www.kaner.com/pdfs/metrics2004.pdf
- Erik Simmons (2000), "When Will We Be Done Testing? Software Defect Arrival Modelling with the Weibull Distribution", www.pnsqc.org/proceedings/pnsqc00.pdf

267

We don't have any required readings today. We're too close to the end of the course.

SLIDE 268

My goal is to introduce you to a theoretical framework for questions like "how much testing have we done?" These are measurement questions. We can learn a lot about them by studying the theory of measurement.

_____

_____

_____

_____

_____

_____

WHAT BRINGS US TO THIS TOPIC?

We seem to be asking quantitative questions, or questions that can be answered by traditional, quantitative research, such as:

- How much testing have we done?
- How thorough has our testing been?
- How effective has our testing been? Are we meeting our information objectives? Do we need to adopt a different strategy?
- How much testing is enough?
- Are we done yet?

These are important questions.

But they are difficult.

We can't teach you how to answer them today. (We're working on that course...)

We <u>can</u> introduce you to the reasons that the popular, simplistic measures are often dysfunctional.

268

_____

_____

_____

_____

SLIDE 269

The first thing to understand about measurement is that it's not about counting things. Knowing how many branches we've covered or how many tests we've run or how many bugs we've found doesn't answer the questions we want answered, like:

How good is this product? or
How much testing do we have left? or
How competent is this programmer?

> ## BASICS OF MEASUREMENT
> - It's not about counting things
>   - **It's about estimating the value of something**
> - We don't count bugs because we care about the total number of bugs. **We count bugs because we want to estimate:**
>   - the thoroughness of our testing, or
>   - a product's quality, or
>   - a product's reliability, or
>   - the probable tech support cost, or
>   - the skill or productivity of a tester, or
>   - the incompetence of a programmer, or
>   - the time needed before we can ship the product, or
>   - something else (whatever it is)…
>
> 269

SLIDE 270

To turn our numbers into answers, we need a model that tells us how and why we can use our numbers to estimate the answers to our questions.

> ## MEASUREMENT
>
> Measurement is the empirical, objective assignment of numbers to attributes of objects or events (according to a rule derived from a model or theory) with the intent of describing them.
>
> Kaner & Bond discussed several definitions of measurement in Software engineering metrics: What do they measure & how do we know?
>
> http://www.kaner.com/pdfs/metrics2004.pdf
>
> 270

SLIDE 271

The starting point for measurement is the attribute, the thing we're trying to measure. For example, when we ask how good is this product, our attribute is product quality.

We might use many different types of data to estimate a value of that attribute, but the reason we're collecting those data is to get an estimate of this attribute—product quality.

Once we know what type of information we're looking for, our next question is how to get it? In practice, we probably use one or more measuring instruments.

> ## MEASUREMENTS INCLUDE
> - the ATTRIBUTE: the thing you want to measure.
> - the INSTRUMENT: the thing you use to take a measurement
> - the READING: what the instrument tells you when you use it to measure something
> - the MEASURED VALUE or the MEASUREMENT is the READING
> - the METRIC: the function that assigns a value to the attribute, based on the reading
> - We often say METRIC to refer to the READING or the SCALE
>
> If you're not sure what you're trying to measure, you probably won't measure it very well.
>
> 271

SLIDE 272

Let's work through these ideas with an example.

Suppose you're going to use a projector when you give a presentation. You'll project your slides onto a screen. How wide is that screen?

If what you're really trying to find out is how wide the screen is, that's your attribute.

We can use a tape measure as our instrument. Suppose we get a reading of 40 with the tape. We interpret that as meaning the screen is 40 inches wide.

MEASUREMENT: TRIVIAL CASE

Attribute:	Width of the projector screen
Instrument	Tape measure
Reading	40 inches (from the tape measure)
Metric	inches on tape = inches of width

Flikr: D. Sharon Pruitt, http://www.flickr.com/photos/pinksherbet/3209939998

272

SLIDE 273

Even this very simple case can help us see some of the challenges of measurement.

_____

_____

_____

_____

_____

_____

_____

_____

_____

_____

MEASUREMENT: TRIVIAL CASE

Even simple measurements have complexities:
- Measurement error (random variation in reading the tape)
- Precision of the measurement (inches? miles?)
- Purpose of the measurement
- Scope of the measurement (just this one screen?)
- Scale of the measurement (what you can read off the tape)

273

SLIDE 274

Let's start with measurement error. When you stretch a tape measure across a screen and get 40 inches, do you hold the tape perfectly level? Perfectly taut? If you took the measurement again, would you get exactly the same number the second time?

What I mean by measurement error is the random variation we get when we take a measurement.

_____

_____

_____

_____

MEASUREMENT ERROR

- Measure the same thing 100 times and you'll get 100 slightly different measurements
- Frequently, the distribution of measurement errors is Gaussian (a.k.a. Normal)

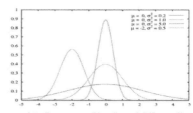

http://commons.wikimedia.org/wiki/Image:Normal_distribution_pdf.png

274

_____

_____

_____

_____

SLIDE 275

The next challenge is precision. If you get a tape measure that shows distance in miles, all it will tell you about a 40 inch screen is that the width is a lot less than a mile. Your measurement won't be precise enough. On the other hand, it rarely makes sense to measure a distance of a mile with an instrument that counts inches.

_____

_____

_____

_____

PRECISION OF MEASUREMENT

What are the units on your measuring instrument?

- inches? yards?
- if your tape measure has a mark every mile (like mile markers on the highway), do you think your measurements will be accurate to the nearest inch?
- how accurate is your measurement of a 1 mile road:
  - measured in inches with a 36-inch yardstick
    - high precision, but
    - high measurement error

275

SLIDE 276

I think of precision and variation as technical issues. They're important, but we usually have straightforward methods for dealing with them.

Figuring out why you are taking this measurement is a harder question. Why do you want to know the width of this projector? Why do you care what the quality of this product is?

Asking about your purpose often leads you to realize that you don't actually care about this attribute. You're actually trying to find out something else.

For example, suppose you were trying

PURPOSE OF THIS MEASUREMENT

Why do you care how wide the projector screen is?

- estimate the size of text that will appear on the screen and thus its visibility?
- decide whether it will fit in your truck?
- reserve a room that isn't too small for the screen?
- estimate and control manufacturing error?
- chastise someone for ordering a screen that is too big or too small?

To control manufacturing error (width of the screen), you usually want high consistency and precision of measurements.

Try using a "five-why" analysis to figure out your underlying purpose.

http://en.wikipedia.org/wiki/5_Whys

276

to figure out whether people could read the text on your slides. You start by asking "how wide is this screen?" But then you ask about purpose, "why do I want to know how wide this screen is?" And you answer, "I want to estimate how big the letters will be when I project my slides." "Why do you want to know how big the letters will be?" You answer, "I want to know whether people can read my slides."

AHA! This is a very different question and knowing the screen width might not answer it. In a small room, with people sitting very close to the screen, the screen doesn't have to be very big for people to read it. But in a very large room, the screen has to be bigger.

The number you really want to know is how big the letters will be to a person who sits as far away from the screen as they can sit, in the room where you will make your presentation. In other words, you want to measure your slide's letter sizes, in degrees of visual angle, a certain distance from the screen.

This sequence of asking why again and again to get to your underlying goal is often called "5 whys" or five-why analysis. (e.g. http://en.wikipedia.org/wiki/5_Whys)

Sometimes, you can understand your purpose completely with one answer. Why do I need to know how wide this is? Answer: I want to roll up the screen and move it in my truck. If the rolled-up screen is longer than 6 feet, it won't fit. In that case, we don't need to ask more questions, and we don't need to be very precise. Even if we measured the screen as 50 inches instead of the correct 40, a huge measurement error, we would reach the correct conclusion that this screen will fit in the truck.

SLIDE 277

If we are moving one screen in one truck on one day, we only need to measure one screen. But suppose instead, we're trying to understand whether there is too much manufacturing variation in these screens. In this case, we will measure the widths of many screens. We might draw a conclusion about the variability of an entire factory's manufacturing process. This is a much broader scope.

As a software example, suppose we were trying to estimate the quality of a program. We might be interested only in that program. We might be interested in all programs written by this specific person or team of programmers. We might be interested in all programs made by this company

> ### SCOPE OF THE MEASUREMENT
> - Just this one screen?
> - Just screens in this building?
> - Just screens from this manufacturer?
> - Just screens manufactured this year?
>
> As the scope broadens, the more variables come into play, introducing more causes for measurement error.
>
> 277

SLIDE 278

We'll close this simple example by considering our scale of measurement.

The tape measure told us that the screen is 40 wide. Forty doesn't mean much until we add the units of measurement, 40 inches. Our scale is length, as measured in inches.

> ### SCALE OF MEASUREMENT
> The "scale" attaches meaning to the number.
> For example, we can read "40" from the tape measure, but that doesn't tell us much: **40 what?**
> In this case, our scale is "inches."
> We know several things about inches:
> - We have an agreed standard for how long an inch is. We can check a tape measure against that standard.
> - Every inch is the same as every other inch. They are all the same length.
> - Three inches is three times as long as one inch
>
> 278

SLIDE 279

Our scale of measurement is critically important. Without it, our measurements are like a width of 40—meaningless because we don't know 40 of what?

The scale of measurement from a tape measure is so obvious that many people find it hard to think about scale with this example.

So here is another example.

Suppose we present noises to a person and ask how loud they are.

We can measure the physical sound pressure level of these noises. The scale is called decibels. For example, quiet

> ### SCALE OF MEASUREMENT
> It is easy to count things, but **unless we have a model that:**
> - maps the count to a scale, and
> - maps that scale to the scale of the the underlying attribute
>
> we won't know how to interpret the count. It will just be a number.
>
>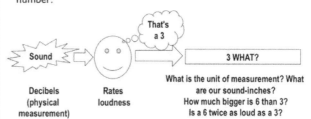
>
> 279

conversation in a quiet room is about 40 decibels. If you are near a busy road, loud traffic noise is about 80 decibels. If you're near a jackhammer breaking up that road, 100 decibels.

Now, let's present these sounds to a person.

Our goal is to estimate perceived loudness — how loud different noises seem to people. There are many applications of this information. For example, companies have used it to design much better speaker systems.

We'll use a person as our measuring instrument. This is the only instrument we *can* use. When you hear a sound, only you know how loud that sound seems to you and that's what we're trying to find out.

So play a sound and ask a person how loud it is. The person says three to a quiet sound, and 6 to a louder sound.

What do three and six mean?

With inches, 6 inches is twice as long as 3 inches. Is that how it works for sounds? Is a 6-rated sound twice as loud as a 3-rated sound? Probably not.

SLIDE 280

Numbers don't always have all the properties we expect of numbers.

With inches, they do. 6 inches is twice as big as 3 inches and 600 inches is twice as big as 300. That defines a ratio scale.

_____

_____

_____

_____

_____

_____

_____

SCALE OF MEASUREMENT

Ratio Scale:

a / b   = (k * a) / (k * b)   (for any constant, k)

e.g., the tape measure

    20 inches / 10 inches
  = 200 inches / 100 inches

S.S. Stevens (1946), "On the theory of scales of measurement" *Science*, http://web.duke.edu/philosophy/bio/Papers/Stevens_Measurement.pdf

280

SLIDE 281

But consider temperature. Is 100 degrees Fahrenheit twice as hot as 50 degrees? If so, then when we convert temperatures from Fahrenheit to Centigrade, 37.8 degrees centigrade should be twice 10 degrees centigrade.

Obviously, that's not true.

Our common units for temperature are not ratio scaled. They are interval scaled. What an interval scale means is that differences between numbers are consistent. So the difference between 100 degrees Fahrenheit and 75 is the same as the difference between 75 and 50. In Fahrenheit, the difference is 25 degrees in both cases. If you convert to centigrade, the difference is 13.9 degrees in both cases.

SCALE OF MEASUREMENT

Interval Scale:

a - b   = (k + a) - (k + b)

e.g., Fahrenheit or Centigrade temperatures

- These have no true zero, so ratios are meaningless
    - 100° Fahrenheit = 37.8° Centigrade
    - 50° Fahrenheit = 10.0° Centigrade
    - 100 / 50   ≠ 37.8 / 10
- But intervals are meaningful
    - The difference in temperature between 100 and 75 Fahrenheit is the same as the difference in temperature between 75 and 50 (25° Fahrenheit and 13.9° Centigrade) in each case.
- We can have an interval scale when we don't have (don't know /use) true zero
- (compare to Kelvin temperature scale, which has true zero).

Multiplying interval-scale numbers is meaningless.

(A product of two interval-scale numbers has no unambiguous mathematical meaning.)

281

SLIDE 282

A third kind of scale is ordinal. All we know about ordinal numbers is that 2 is smaller than 3. We don't know how much smaller, just smaller. If you tell me you ran fifth in a race, that means you ran faster than the sixth-place person and slower than the fourth-place person, but I don't know how much faster.

Imagine that we're evaluating staff. We might know that Jane is a better programmer than Joe and decide to pay her more, but how much more? If our measurements are ordinal, we can say that Jane is a better programmer, but we probably can't say by how much. We can't say that Jane deserves twice what Joe gets because she's twice as good. Not if our measurements only give us ordinal information.

Being able to rank our programmers from best to worst, might be as precise as we can get.

> **SCALE OF MEASUREMENT**
> **Ordinal Scale**
> If a > b and b > c, then a > c
>
> e.g. winners of a race or a cooking contest
> • 1st place is better than 2nd place
> • 2nd place is better than 3rd place
> • How much better?
>   – Better.
>
> > Adding or multiplying ordinal-scale numbers is meaningless.
>
> 282

SLIDE 283

Finally, we have nominal scales. Two things are different if they have different names.

Which one is better? We don't know better. We just know different.

_____

_____

_____

_____

_____

_____

_____

> **SCALE OF MEASUREMENT**
> **Nominal Scale**
> a = b (a and b have the same name) if and only if a and b are the same
>
> e.g. names of people or companies
> • Joe is Joe
> • Joe is not Susan
> • If Joe runs in a race and has a "2" on his back, that doesn't mean he is faster or slower than Susan (she has a "1" on her back). It just means that
>   – Joe has the label "1"
>   – Susan has the label "2"
>
> > Ranking or adding or multiplying nominal-scale numbers is meaningless.
>
> 283

SLIDE 284

In software engineering, none of our measurements are as straightforward as reading inches from tape measures. We can't even agree on how to measure the size of a program.

_____

_____

_____

_____

_____

_____

> **NON-TRIVIAL MEASUREMENT**
>
> Relationship between attributes and measuring instruments are often **not** straightforward.
> Some Attributes:
> • quality
> • reliability
> • productivity
> • supportability
> • size of a program
> • predicted schedule
> • speed of a program
> • predicted support cost
> • complexity of a program
> • extent of testing done so far
> • quality of testing done so far
> • completeness of development
>
> > What's the tape measure for this attribute?
>
> 284

SLIDE 285

That brings us back to our structure for thinking about measurements. And to our most important starting point, the attribute.

What do we think we mean by the size of a program or the skill of a programmer? Not how we measure it, but what are we really trying to measure? If we don't understand what attribute we are trying to measure, how can we know if our measure of it is any good?

MEASUREMENTS INCLUDE

- the ATTRIBUTE: the thing you want to measure.
- the INSTRUMENT: the thing you use to take a measurement
- the READING: what the instrument tells you when you use it to measure something
- the MEASURED VALUE or the MEASUREMENT is the READING
- the METRIC: the function that assigns a value to the attribute, based on the reading
- We often say METRIC to refer to the READING or the SCALE

If you don't know what you're trying to measure, you won't measure it well.

And you can do a lot of damage in the process.

285

SLIDE 286

Measurement theorists often talk about the validity of a measurement. If we want to measure programmer skill this way, is that measurement valid? Does it really tell us about programmer skill?

My first doctorate was in psychophysics—this field applies measurement theory to subjective magnitudes, like how loud something sounds or how hot something feels. I've read about theory of measurement in many fields: chemistry, economics, medicine, physics, psychology, sociology and so on. Every other field that I have studied has a more sophisticated approach to measurement and pays more attention to validity than computer science and software engineering. We spend lots of time arguing how to write programs to count things efficiently. We spend almost no time on the measurement validity of those counts.

CONSTRUCT VALIDITY (MEASUREMENT VALIDITY)

Construct validity:

- **Does this measure what I think it measures?**
  - Does this measure the attribute?
  - (Social scientists often say "construct" where I say "attribute")
- Most important type of validity
- Widely discussed in measurement theory
  - But our field routinely skips the question, "what is the attribute"
  - search ACM's Digital Library or IEEE portal for "construct validity" or "measurement validity"

Valid metrics are extremely useful.

Invalid metrics cause dysfunction.

286

SLIDE 287

In software engineering, most of our measurements are surrogate measures.

Suppose you don't understand how to measure an attribute. Often, that's because you don't have a clear idea of what the attribute is. But you think that something you can count easily is probably correlated with that attribute. You don't have a strong model of causation to relate this something that you are counting to the attribute and you don't know how strong the correlation is between your something and the attribute.

If you use that something as your measure of the attribute, you are using a surrogate measure.

SURROGATE (OR PROXY) MEASURES

"Many of the attributes we wish to study do not have generally agreed methods of measurement. To overcome the lack of a measure for an attribute, some factor which **can be** measured is used instead. This alternate measure is presumed to be related to the actual attribute with which the study is concerned. These alternate measures are called surrogate measures."

Johnson, M.A. (1996) *Effective and Appropriate Use of Controlled Experimentation in Software Development Research*, Master's Thesis (Computer Science), Portland State University.

A widely used opportunity for disaster

287

SLIDE 288

We use bug counts as surrogates for all sorts of things. How good a tester is, how good a programmer is, how close the program is to being finished, how good the program is, how expensive technical support will be, and so on.

_____

_____

_____

_____

_____

SURROGATE (OR PROXY) MEASURES

Example

• We don't know how to measure tester productivity

• So let's count bugs

   – Bugs are our surrogate for productivity

   – We assume that they must be correlated with productivity

   – And they're easy to count

288

SLIDE 289

Surrogate measures often lead to predictable problems.

For example, when companies measure productivity of testers by counting their bug reports, testers will spend lots of time reporting lots of bugs. But they won't spend much time on activities that don't directly increase their bug counts.

This can have a huge negative impact on collaboration within the test group and on the quality of work done by the testers.

Years ago, I led the testing of a project with enormous variation in bug counts per tester. Some testers reported over 100

PREDICTABLE MISCHIEF...

If we reward testers based on their bug counts, how much time will testers spend:

• Documenting their tests?

• Coaching other testers?

• Researching and polishing bug reports to make their bug easier to understand, assess and replicate?

• Running confirmatory tests (such as regression tests) that have control value (e.g. build verification) but little bug-find value?

• Hunting variants of the same failure to increase bug count?

Using surrogate measures can make things worse, while providing little useful information.

Yet, the ease of using them makes them quite popular.

289

bugs a month. One tester averaged four bugs per month. The one with four bugs a month designed tests that simulated real-life use of the program by experienced users. It took him a lot of time to figure out the details of something customers would try to achieve and to create all the necessary test data to make a representative-of-real-life-complexity test of it. He'd run the first test, then keep varying his test conditions until the system failed or he was satisfied that the system actually delivered the benefit he was checking. Most weeks, he got data corruption or a crash. No one else on my staff could test anywhere near as well for problems like these, and these were very important problems.

I've seen a lot of variations of bug counting to measure tester productivity or effectiveness. Some just count bugs. Others weight bugs by severity or value. But none that I have seen would have changed the weightings in my group enough to recognize this tester's impact on our projects.

If we had measured tester value with bug counts, he would have eventually changed his testing to improve his statistics. As a result, my staff would never have found several of the most important bugs that we reported, bugs that were either found by this tester or found by other testers who were coached or inspired by him.

SLIDE 290

It is normal human behavior to change how you work when you know how you are being measured.

This is how we manage people with measurement.

We expect people to change what they do to improve their measured results. We reward them for measured improvements and punish them for lack of improvement. In turn, they do less, and less well, on the things that we don't measure.

This creates serious risks. If we measure poorly, we can drive people to change their behavior in ways that improve their numbers but harm the project. Those risks are very pronounced with surrogate measures.

When we try to measure an attribute that we don't understand, when we use measures that we don't evaluate for construct validity, our measures *are* surrogate measures.

WE'VE SEEN THIS BEFORE (COVERAGE)

People optimize what we measure them against, at the expense of what we don't measure.

- Driving testing to achieve "high" coverage is likely to yield a mass of low-power tests.
- Brian Marick discusses this in How to Misuse Code Coverage, http://www.exampler.com/testing-com/writings/coverage.pdf
- What other side-effects might we expect from relying on coverage numbers as measures of **how close we are to completion of testing?**
- How is this different from using coverage measures to tell us **how far we are from an adequate level of testing?**

For more on measurement distortion and dysfunction, read Bob Austin's book, *Measurement and Management of Performance in Organizations.*

290

SLIDE 291

Here's another example with my favorite bad-but-common surrogate, bug counts. People use bug find rates to estimate the status of the project.

The idea is that if you're not finding bugs, maybe the program has run out of bugs—in which case, testing is complete.

So we can ask a status question—are we close to the point at which we won't find more bugs or are we still far away from it?

It's common for companies to create status reporting curves that show how many bugs have been found per week, or how many bugs are still open each week, or other weekly bug statistics. James Bach and I both created curves like these, so have plenty of our colleagues, and we'd use them again. They lead us to ask interesting questions and help us explain our thinking to other people on the project.

But it's important to recognize that curves don't actually tell you the state of the product. They only tell you what's being found by the test group.

Some people apply a theoretical reliability model to bug curves, and on the basis of the model, predict the week-to-week rate of bugs and the ultimate ship date of the software. Software projects often finish surprisingly late, so executives and project managers are thrilled with the idea of using relatively early project data to predict the eventual release date of the product.

> **ANOTHER EXAMPLE OF BUG COUNTING**
>
> - Some people think the Weibull reliability model can be applied as model of testing progress
> - They estimate likely ship date by using **bug-find rates** to estimate parameters of the Weibull curve.
>
> 291

SLIDE 292

The Weibull model is an example of the reliability models. The Weibull is the name of a famous probability distribution, like the normal distribution and the exponential distribution.

> **THE WEIBULL CURVE**
>
> New bugs found per week ("Defect arrival rate")
>
>
> Related measures:
>
> Bugs still open (each week)
>
> Ratio of bugs found to bugs fixed (per week)
>
> 292

SLIDE 293

A model relies on a set of assumptions—if the assumptions are incorrect, the model is inapplicable. Erik Simmons of Intel is one of the advocates of the Weibull model. He listed its key assumptions in one of his conference talks.

The problem is that these assumptions don't apply well to testing. There are problems with all of them. Here are three examples.

First, the model assumes that testing occurs in a way similar to the way the software will be operated. That's not true. Skilled testers will push the program harder than normal users to boost their chances of finding bugs. Second, the model assumes that bugs are equally likely to be encountered. That's not true. Some bugs show up almost every time you test the program. Others take show up rarely and take weeks to reproduce. Third, the model assumes that defects are corrected instantaneously, without introducing additional defects.

Oh come on! What is this model smoking?

> **WEIBULL MODEL ASSUMPTIONS**
>
> - Testing occurs in a way similar to the way the software will be operated.
> - All defects are equally likely to be encountered.
> - Defects are corrected instantaneously, without introducing additional defects.
> - All defects are independent.
> - There is a fixed, finite number of defects in the software at the start of testing.
> - The time to arrival of a defect follows the Weibull distribution.
> - The number of defects detected in a testing interval is independent of the number detected in other testing intervals for any finite collection of intervals.
>
> **These assumptions are wildly implausible as models of testing.**
>
> See Erik Simmons (2000), "When will we be done testing? Software defect arrival modeling with the Weibull distribution."
>
> 293

SLIDE 294

From a statistics point of view, the Weibull curve has a very flexible shape. If you have a set of data, any set of data, that has one peak and is either symmetrical or is skewed to the right, you can fit a Weibull curve to it.

Because a Weibull curve can fit the data, some people think they can apply the Weibull model. The difference between the curve and the model is that the model includes the theory that connects the meaning of the data to the curve.

> **THE WEIBULL MODEL**
>
> - An advocate of this approach asserts:
>
> *"Luckily, the Weibull is robust to most violations."*
>
> - From a purely curve-fitting point of view, this is correct: The Weibull distribution has a shape parameter that allows it to take a very wide range of shapes. If you have a curve that generally rises then falls (one mode), you can approximate it with a Weibull.
>
> 294

SLIDE 295

But we can't apply the model. We can't apply it because the model's assumptions, the theory that connects the data to the curve, are all wrong for software testing.

This is typical of surrogate measures. We don't have a theoretical justification for using a measure. Instead, we have a convenient set of data and some kind of plausibility argument, often a very fuzzy one, that we can use as our excuse for relying on this easy-to-collect data instead of doing the hard work necessary to come up with something better.

> **THE WEIBULL MODEL**
>
> - This illustrates the use of surrogate measures
>   - we don't have an attribute description or model for the attribute we really want to measure,
>   - so we use something else, that is convenient, and allegedly "robust", in its place.
>
> 295

SLIDE 296

I've seen the Weibull, and models like it, applied in practice. I've seen serious problems. Doug Hoffman has more experience than I do with clients who are more traditionally process-oriented and so he's seen models like this even more than I have. He wrote up some of his observations in *The Dark Side of Software Metrics*.

The problem is that the model is not just descriptive. People try to change the project schedule by changing the shape of the bug curve. Executives pay attention to the model and put pressure on the people who generate the bug curve.

> **SIDE EFFECTS (THE PREDICTABLE MISCHIEF) OF BUG CURVES**
>
> When development teams are pushed to show project bug curves that look like the Weibull curve, they are pressured
>
> - to show a rapid rise in their bug counts,
> - an early peak,
> - and a steady decline of bugs found per week.
>
> Under the model, a rapid rise to an early peak predicts a ship date much sooner than a slower rise or a more symmetric curve.
>
> In practice, project teams (including testers) in this situation often adopt dysfunctional methods, doing things that will be bad for the project over the long run in order to make the numbers go up quickly.
>
> **For more observations of problems like these in reputable software companies, see Doug Hoffman, *The Dark Side of Software Metrics*.**
>
> 296

They want lots of bugs found early in testing because they believe that an early peak in the bug find rate predicts an early completion date. They expect one peak and a steady decline in the bug rate after that, because that's what the model says.

SLIDE 297

Doug and I have seen testers cope with the pressure to maximize their start-of-project bug counts. They look for the cheap and easy bugs. Even if these bugs aren't very helpful to the project team, they make the numbers look good and keep the executives and the measurement bureaucrats from head office happy.

Unfortunately, when testers spend their early time finding bugs, they aren't spending it building or adapting tools, preparing for test automation, writing test plans, training new people on the project or doing anything else to be more efficient, more effective, or more accountable later in the project.

> ### WHAT IS THE PREDICTABLE MISCHIEF?
>
> **Early testing:**
>
> - Run tests of features known to be broken or incomplete.
> - Run multiple related tests to find multiple related bugs.
> - Look for easy bugs in high quantities rather than hard bugs.
> - Less emphasis on
>   - infrastructure,
>   - automation architecture,
>   - tools and documentation
> - More emphasis on bug finding. (Short term payoff but long term inefficiency.)
>
> The goal is to find lots of bugs early.
>
> Get to that peak in the curve right away.
>
> 297

SLIDE 298

Later in testing, the expectation is that testers will find fewer bugs each week.

Managers often define project milestones. For the project to meet a milestone, the development team has to show that the project satisfies certain criteria. For example, the milestone might require that a certain percentage of the features are implemented, that there is draft user documentation for X percent of these, and that the total number of not-yet-fixed serious bugs be less than N. On many projects, hitting a milestone is a big deal. For example, it might trigger a payment, a party, or a big announcement at a company meeting.

> ### AFTER THE PEAK
>
> After we get past the peak, the expectation is that testers will find fewer bugs each week than they found the week before.
>
> Based on the number of bugs found at the peak, and the number of weeks it took to reach the peak, the model can predict bugs per week in each subsequent week.
>
>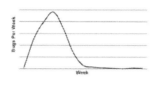
>
> 298

When a company adopts a mathematical model to predict milestones from bug find rates, you can imagine the pressure on testers to keep the total count of open bugs below N.

All the testers have to do is find only what they're expected to find.

_____

_____

_____

_____

_____

_____

_____

_____

_____

_____

SLIDE 299

A few years ago, I taught a course at a famous software company. They had an active metrics program, and "quality assurance" staff from head office would look at the project's numbers. Sometimes, when testers were finding too many bugs before a QA visit, the project manager would send them to a movie for the afternoon. The testers were amused and went along, until one week they were sent to the movies five times. That was the end of the movies. So, the next time head office's QA people were coming, local management hired me to teach a five-day testing class. It took us until the second day to realize that I was the new version of the movies.

> ### MORE PREDICTABLE MISCHIEF
> **Later in the project:**
> - Run lots of already-run regression tests
> - Don't look as hard for new bugs
> - Shift focus to status reporting
> - Classify unrelated bugs as duplicates
> - Close related bugs as duplicates, hiding key data about the symptoms / causes of a problem.
> - Postpone bug reporting until after a measurement checkpoint (milestone). (Some bugs are lost.)
> - Programmers ignore bugs until testers report them
> - Testers report bugs informally, keep them out of the tracking system
> - Project team sends testers to irrelevant tasks before measurement checkpoints.
> - More bugs are rejected, sometimes taken personally…
>
> **We expect fewer bugs every week.**
>
> 299

Another way testers keep their bug counts down before a milestone is to keep the bugs out of the database. Some groups use Post-It notes. They write a bug on a Post-It and stick it on the inside wall of one of the cubicles. Programmers stop by to look at the Post-Its. A Post-It bug can go into the bug tracking database when a programmer fixes it, because it doesn't boost the number of open bugs. After the milestone has been met, there's less pressure to keep bug numbers down, so the testers enter the backlogged bugs into the database.

I've seen some detailed bug count presentations from some metrics consultants. Some explain the value of milestones and of tracking performance against milestones by pointing to a motivational value of meeting a milestone. We know how motivating the milestone is because there is this big short-term jump in productivity. Testers find lots of new bugs right after they get motivated by meeting the milestone. Well, maybe there is a productivity spike. Or it maybe it's just be all those Post-It bug reports finally going into the database.

This type of mismatch between what happens in the project and what the head office's metrics people think is happening is one of the reasons Doug Hoffman finally wrote his paper on the dark side of software metrics.

There are lots of other reasons for a bug find rate to go down that don't involve intentional deception.

For example, many test groups create new tests every build but also reuse tests from previous builds. As the project goes forward, the testers use more of the old tests—this is called regression testing—and spend less time creating new tests. Old tests rarely expose new bugs—if there was a bug, the test would have already exposed it—so the more you rely on regression tests, the fewer bugs you'll find. People who believe the bug rate model is correct expect a declining bug rate over time, so when they see one, they see results that meet their expectations. They have no reason to look past the numbers to ask why the bug find rate is dropping.

There are lots of other variations on this theme—if we predict that testers will find fewer bugs each week, we won't be alarmed when we see fewer bugs each week, even if the drops are actually caused more by the testers doing non-testing activities like writing more status reports, training tech support staff, or polishing their test documentation.

SLIDE 300

I prefer a different model for bug rates.

In my model, I want the bug find rate to climb early in testing, but it's OK for the rate to climb slowly if people are doing work that will boost their productivity with more complex tests later.

Later in testing, I interpret a declining bug rate as a warning. It's time to try more powerful tests or to test other parts of the program or test more complex combinations of features. If one test technique isn't finding many bugs any more, it's time to try another one.

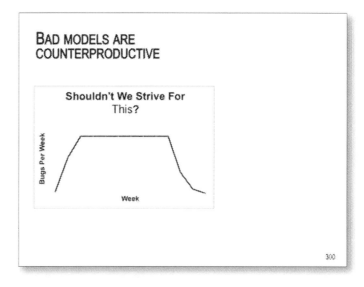

As the program gets more stable, you run more complex tests that take much more time to design, so bug find rates might fall. But as the program gets more stable, you can also run automated tests with long sequences of tasks—it takes a long time to program the test automation framework for high volume automated testing, but once it's running, the test automaton can generate millions of tests or test sequences, and under this style of testing, bug find rates might go up for a while.

Eventually, we run out of ideas for new tests, the bug find rate drops and we don't know how to substantially increase it. That's when to ship the product. Not because we are out of bugs, but because we don't know how to find the bugs that are left, so there is no point in delaying the release further.

SLIDE 301

A remarkable number of testing consultants tell us that it is better to use bad metrics than no metrics. Bob Austin's book takes this crazy idea on, working through the theory and practical disaster of measurement dysfunction.

> **DISTORTION AND DYSFUNCTION**
>
> *People optimize what we measure them against, at the expense of what we don't measure.*
>
> - A measurement system yields **distortion** if it creates incentives for a person to make the measurements **look better** rather than to optimize for achieving the organization's actual goals.
>
> - A system is **dysfunctional** if optimizing for measurement yields so much distortion that the result is a **reduction of value**: the organization would have **been better off with no measurement** than with this measurement.
>
> For more on measurement distortion and dysfunction, read Bob Austin's book, *Measurement and Management of Performance in Organizations.*

_____

_____

_____

_____

_____

_____

_____

_____

_____

_____

_____

_____

_____

_____

_____

SLIDE 302

So let me recap. I presented three examples of surrogate measures.

Using bug counts to assess tester effectiveness

Using code coverage to assess testing completeness

And using bug counts to assess the project's schedule.

All three are common and all three cause big problems. If all you have are surrogate measures, you are probably better off not using them.

That doesn't mean that we should never count bugs, or never look at code coverage.

My experience, Hoffman's experience, Marick's experience, Bach's experience is that we have all found these counts useful. But it definitely means that we need to be very careful in how we interpret these counts, and how we use them, and how we present them to management.

> ### RECAP: THREE EXAMPLES
> - Measuring the effectiveness of testing by counting bugs is fundamentally flawed. Therefore measuring the effectiveness of a testing strategy by bug counts is probably equally flawed.
> - Measuring code coverage not only misleads us about how much testing there has been. It also creates an incentive for programmers to write trivial tests.
> - Measuring progress via bug count rates not only misleads us about progress. It also drives test groups into dysfunctional conduct.
>
> 302

SLIDE 303

Eventually, we will develop trustworthy, validated quantitative measures for much of what we are interested in as project managers and test managers.

But until then, an alternative to using untrustworthy quantitative measures is to develop qualitative measures. This poses its own challenges, but so far, I've found the process of developing them, and the use of them, quite valuable. You'll see an example of this in the *Bug Advocacy* course's main assignment, when we evaluate the quality of bug reports that other testers have filed in Open Office.

> ### WHAT SHOULD WE DO?
> - This is a difficult, unsolved problem
> - General recommendations
> - Details to come in later courses
>
> Imagine evaluating employee performance:
> - Break down the job into a list of key tasks
> - For each of this person's key tasks, take a small sample (10?) of this person's work
> - Carefully evaluate each type of work, looking at the details.
> - **Then** you can rank performance, or assign metric summary numbers to the individual tasks.
> - And combine ratings across tasks for an employee profile.
>
> We'll study an example of task evaluation in the bug advocacy course.
>
> 303

SLIDE 304

BLACK BOX SOFTWARE TESTING: FOUNDATIONS

FINIS

CEM KANER, J.D., PH.D.
PROFESSOR OF SOFTWARE ENGINEERING
FLORIDA INSTITUTE OF TECHNOLOGY

REBECCA L. FIEDLER, M.B.A. PH.D.
PRESIDENT: KANER, FIEDLER & ASSOCIATES

JAMES BACH
PRINCIPAL, SATISFICE INC.

These notes are partially based on research that was supported by NSF Grants EIA-0113539 ITR/SY +PE: "Improving the Education of Software Testers" and CCLI-0717613 "Adaptation & Implementation of an Activity-Based Online or Hybrid Course in Software Testing." Any opinions, findings and conclusions or recommendations expressed in this material are those of the author(s) and do not necessarily reflect the views of the National Science Foundation.

304

Authors' Reflection on Lesson 6

This Lesson still needs work. We're still imagining what the replacement will look like but we're not yet ready to create it.

Here are my (Kaner's) main criticisms and concerns. Much of my reflection is based on recent success in Florida Tech's software metrics course (a course we teach to graduate students and undergraduate seniors in the Software Engineering program). I joined Pat Bond in wrestling with the design of that course when I first came to Florida Tech in 2000. We taught the courses together and separately, comparing notes and ideas for future iterations. Two years ago, I finally developed a version of the course that I liked and that got what I considered good work from good students. We learned a lot about what the students actually learn in the course and what simply bounces off. We learned a lot about the impact—and sometimes about the lack of impact—of not understanding some concepts well enough to explain them. What types of ignorance or confusion affect the students' most important work in the course (projects or research essays) and what doesn't?

- *Learning 1: Some of the material in this Lesson is unnecessary: too detailed and not important enough to be in a brief introduction.*

    In particular, I think the presentation of ordinal versus interval versus ratio numbers is important but, in an introduction to this topic, ineffective. The students don't learn it. Even the ones who memorize it don't learn it well enough to use it. There is probably other material that is equally hard to take out but equally inappropriate to leave in.

Another factor has been an evolution in my attitude toward metrics. I studied measurement theory in detail in the 1970s and 1980s. In the 1980s and 1990s, I was appalled by the sloppy and naive ways that software consultants and academics approached software metrics. My comments about this work were often disparaging, sometimes quite harsh. Behind this was a comfortable belief that, with a modest amount of work, my friends and I could do better. In raising the problems with other people's work, we weren't just being destructively negative. We were clearing the brush to make room for something better. My good friend, Hung Quoc Nguyen, reminded me of that in (I think it was) 2008. He reminded me that executives and managers have legitimate information needs. They need ways to characterize what is happening in their companies, in their projects and they especially need those when they are responsible for large groups (many projects) or large projects. You can learn a lot by walking around, watching people and talking with them, but as settings grow larger and more complex, personal observations are too incomplete and too prone to manipulation, luck, or misinterpretation. Good managers will use the best-quality metrics they can get, but if the only ones available are bad, that's what they'll use because they have no better alternative. As I tried my hand at doing better, and as I watched some of my colleagues roll out their own ideas (which sometimes seemed like old socks in new packaging), I realized that we are dealing with a hard problem. What I mean by a *hard problem* is a something that we're not likely to solve for a long time. In the interim, we have to make the best of what we've got or can develop. I actually went most of the way down that path in 1999, with presentations at *Consultants Camp* and at the *Pacific Northwest Software Quality Conference* that compared software metrics with the 150-year evolution of measurement theory and practice in psychophysics (the most measurement-oriented area of psychology). I suggested that it might be arrogant to think that in software engineering, we could solve fundamental theoretical problems an order of magnitude faster. Maybe in the meantime, we needed to think about how to do adequate work while we wait for our collective profession to eventually figure out how to do good work. By 2001 (*Lessons Learned in Software Testing*) I lost that thread. Hung reminded me of it.

I don't think the context-driven testing community (my community) has made any progress toward improving software metrics since 2001. It seems to me that instead, some of us have become better at talking about what is wrong with the state of the practice. Today, those talks are more commercially attractive (more places will pay a good speaker to give them). They are pretty much mainstream. Yes, yes. Bad bad bad. But after we come down from the pseudo-ethical posturing, what advice can we actually offer the manager who needs summaries of data that are interpretable and can help him run a business? In terms of our impact on the field, how is what we are doing helping the field move forward in a better way than it would without us? It was one thing to have not made progress by 2004, when I designed the first online version of *Foundations*. But it is not 2004 any more. It is 2014. How many years of our own unproductivity should we tolerate before it becomes time to show the *other* unsuccessful approaches a little more respect and see whether we can mine their work for anything that might be incrementally constructive?

> ■ *Learning 2: Too much of the tone of the lecture is too negative. Students do need to learn about dysfunction. They do need to learn about construct validity. They do need to learn that many metrics in use have no construct validity. But there has to be a balance. There has to also be constructive advice, suggestions of what to do. Without that, I think the Lesson reinforces our current place, which seems stuck in the glorification of progress-free negativity.*

A third source of insight was my study of quantitative finance. Starting in 2008, I spent several years in very detailed study of the data and modeling that financial professionals use to guide trillions of dollars of investment activity. The state of the data in that field is shocking. The numbers are ambiguous and often untrustworthy. The state of the metrics in that field is shocking. The good news is that there is a high level of model-building and careful, thorough model testing. A lot of good science is happening in this field. I enjoyed doing that type of work and teaching my students how to do it. But many of the measurements that the models are based on are simply untrustworthy. For example, the "price-to-earnings" ratio in finance is every bit as important as "number of hours worked on the project" in project management. Experienced testers are very conscious of the ways in which statistics like "hours worked" or "number of test cases" are gathered and reported. We don't trust them, for good reason. But what I learned is that in comparison to numbers like "price-to-earnings", our numbers are very good. I have never met anyone who was serious about quantitative finance who thinks they are working with great and trustworthy data. They know better. But they need some basis for managing the millions (or more) of dollars in their care and so they make do with what they've got.

> ■ *Learning 3: We need to learn more about how to cope with bad data. This is every bit as important as screaming about the fact that the data are bad.*

Another thing that I learned from quantitative finance is that even though the data are numeric, the analyses look for meaningful patterns over time. There is a great deal in common between what many financial analysts do and what qualitative analysts do in other fields. I didn't bother with multidimensional approaches to metrics (Balanced Scorecard, etc.) because these are often abused too. However, my best guess is that a multidimensional approach that relies on many different crummy measures and looks at patterns in their relationships over time will be the basis for genuine progress in the next decades.

> ■ *Learning 4: We should give the multidimensional approaches another look, accepting the fact that dysfunction comes when they are used naively or malignantly but asking whether someone who wants to get good information this way can follow a disciplined path to get good information.*

The final influence that I'll note here comes from my teaching of the statistics course at Florida Tech. My students are software engineering majors and computer science majors. They like to program. We can create simulations. We can study complex statistical problems with simulations.

Last year, I decided to introduce my students to the bug-count models from a different perspective. Rather than criticizing these models for making absurdly unrealistic assumptions about software projects (which is what I do in *Foundation's* Lesson 6), we ask what it would take to introduce a more realistic set of assumptions. I reread many papers on the bug-count models through new eyes, and read many additional papers.

- The models we see in the literature are what they are because the more realistic assumptions create mathematically intractable models. No one can derive the probability distributions for them.

- The beauty of simulation is that you can do a lot of the modeling numerically, without having to derive the underlying distributions. Generate a million simulated results and you can draw the curve pretty accurately.

Through the eyes of a modeler, I know that no model is ever accurate. They are always wrong. But some are close enough, in enough ways, to be useful. (George Box said this first.) Suppose that we simulate systems that have very complex and realistic assumptions, but for practical purposes the decisions they would have us make would almost always be the same as the decisions based on the crummy, unrealistic, but mathematically tractable exponential, Rayleigh and Weibull models that are popular today. I don't have data on this that I trust yet. All I have is the realization that this might be possible. If it is, then all of my attacks on this model for unrealism in its assumption are so much hot air.

- *Lesson 5: My real objection to the bug-count models is that they are subject to social abuse. That is, in several environments, Doug Hoffman and I have seen people change their behavior in counterproductive ways to make their projects' patterns conform to the models. What is worse is that these people often believed they were doing what the company wanted and that they were doing the right thing. Rather than distracting the reader with cheap shots on the models' assumptions, I should refocus my criticism on this and then pay more attention to the experience reports from people like Erik Simmons who still tell me (personal correspondence, 2013) that in environments they have seen, those risks are managed and the models are useful. Their experiences in their contexts and the dysfunction we've seen in other contexts can both be right. Maybe there is something to learn from the difference.*

Much from the Lessons here is driving the evolution of my metrics course, my software requirements course and my statistics course. These offer a semester of time rather than a single Lesson. I don't yet know what we can boil down from that work for the next generation of this work (*Foundations*).

FEEDBACK ON ORIENTATION ACTIVITIES

Introduction: The Answers At The Back Of The Book

You probably have experience with books that have solutions in the back. Here is the usual advice:

> *Look here after you do the activity, not before and not while you're doing it.*

In our case, that means, no peeking until after you have completed your peer reviews of other students' work and considered how you would revise your own if you had it to do over again.

We suggest that you also wait until after you have watched the lecture and thought about how you would change your answers now that you have seen the lecture.

Remember, these activities are low stakes. Most courses will give you feedback on them but not give you letter grades. (For example, at Florida Tech, students usually get 10 points for making a serious effort or no points. Intermediate values are rare.) These are designed to help you learn the material. If you take shortcuts, you'll learn less, with no corresponding added value.

The feedback we will provide here are not the answers. In some cases, there are no right answers. Instead, these are summaries of notes we've made about how people answered these questions in the past.

Orientation: Role Of The Testing Group

Please describe the role of the test group in your organization. (If you are not working for a company that has a test group, please describe the situation of the test group in some other company that you know.)

- What services does your group provide?

- Try to describe, in one relatively short sentence, the most important value that your group is designed or expected to provide to your company.

- Who does the manager of your group report to? (What is the role of that person? Are they primarily focused on customer support? Product development? Marketing? Corporate quality assurance? Some other function?)

- How large is your group and how does its size compare to the size of the development group(s) whose work you test? Is the balance of work, between you and them, reasonable?

- What are the key organizational challenges for your group? (When we say "organizational challenges, we're thinking about your roles, responsibilities, budget, ability to get training, ability to influence decision-making, etc.)

- How do you think this compares to the "typical" test group?

- How would you change this?

Our Notes

We see a broad diversity of answers in this activity. Students with no work experience and people who work in one company (or in a few companies that have essentially the same culture) might not realize how rich the variety really is. This activity helps students see that test groups operate in many different ways, working in many different situations. This is the reason we have to accept such a diversity of attitudes and practices in our field.

Pay special attention to the diversity of values. Some testers believe their responsibility is to protect the customer from bad products. Some believe their responsibility is to give the project manager good information. Some believe they are the company's process auditors. All of these beliefs might be correct. The interesting question is whether these people have the resources and authority to actually do what they say they have been tasked to do.

Experienced testers often write about how their company is undergoing change. They are changing their development practices to become more/less/differently agile and insourcing/outsourcing/crowdsourcing their security/testing/maintenance/support/coding/marketing. They are trying some new automation methodology that is guaranteed to put all testers out of work or change their life in some other way but it hasn't arrived/doesn't work/comes with an obnoxious consultant/runs slower than a turtle with a hangover. And they just got a new manager.

Not everyone in their company agrees with these changes. If you're new to the field and not yet used to this, welcome to testing! And as to the controversy, there's an old Yiddish proverb that translates as: "If everyone pulled in the same direction, the world would fall over." In our field, that's not such a big risk.

A useful exercise, whenever you consider a new process, is to think of two circumstances under which the process change would make things better, and two other circumstances under which it would make them worse. If you can't achieve that, maybe you don't yet understand the new process and what it changes.

Along with thinking about the implications of a process change or role change for your company, think about them for yourself. As your company changes, are you moving in a direction that is consistent with your interests and your ethics? Are you gaining new skills that make you more employable? Are you adding more value to the company, that make you less likely to be laid off? If not, then in a company undergoing many parallel transitions, maybe you should hunt around for another opportunity within the company that will support your career growth more effectively.

Finally, note the testers' own ideas for change. Many people don't get that far in their answer or aren't ready to share their thoughts. The ideas we do see, however, often show a lot of interesting insight.

Orientation: Testing A Word Processor

Your task is to determine whether text on the screen is displayed in the correct font.

Please answer these questions:

1. How could you determine whether the editor is displaying text in the correct typeface?

2. How could you determine whether the editor is displaying text in the right size?

3. How would you test whether the editor displays text correctly (in any font that the user specifies)?

Please describe your thinking about this problem in general and describe any specific strategies that you are considering.

Terminology Notes

A font is a set of characters of a single size of a typeface. For example,

- the font of this paragraph is Palatino, size 10 points

- the font of this paragraph is Palatino, size 12 points.

- the font of this paragraph is Palatino, size 14 points.

- the font of this paragraph is Gill Sans, size 10 points.

- the font of this paragraph is Gill Sans, size 12 points.

- the font of this paragraph is Gill Sans, size 14 points.

In these examples, *Palatino* and *Gill Sans* are the names of two *typefaces*. A program could display text in the correct typeface but the wrong size or the right size but the wrong typeface.

People normally talk about type sizes in terms of *points*. A point is approximately $1/_{72}$ of an inch. However, as you can see in the examples above, point sizes are not precisely mapped to sizes of letters. The letters in one 12-point font (such as Palatino) can be larger or smaller than the letters in a different 12-point font (such as Gill Sans).

For more on typefaces, fonts and point sizes, see

- https://en.wikipedia.org/wiki/Font

- https://en.wikipedia.org/wiki/Point_%28typography%29

- https://en.wikipedia.org/wiki/Computer_font

Some Things to Consider In Your Answer

If you are thinking of a strategy that would require an infinite amount of time, you can't do that. Try to think of a way to do this testing that you can actually finish.

You cannot test every possible font. There are tens of thousands of different fonts. If someone uses a font that you did not specifically test, how will you know from your testing whether the program will display that one correctly?

Computer fonts are supplied to the computer in files. Sometimes, the content of a font file contains errors. If the program appears to misbehave when it displays a set of characters in that font, how will you know whether the program is in the program or in the font file?

Our Notes

In our instructor-led courses, this is the first lab in which we give personalized feedback. We send these notes to the class as a whole to provide classwide feedback. This type of message hits the most common issues.

We also send short messages to individual students that make comments not covered in this general feedback. This approach lets us gives the most information to the most people in a timely manner.

Many of the answers we see are very short. That's fine. You should stay close to the recommended maximum times for orientation activities. You will usually get all of the potential learning benefit from the activity in that time, even if you don't write spectacular answers.

Our goal for orientation tasks is for you to wrestle with a problem as preparation for the lecture that follows. The instructional theory concept that leads us to orientation exercises is "readiness for learning." A student who isn't ready to appreciate the problems or puzzles that the lecture teaches how to solve will find a lecture too theoretical and miss the point and value of the lecture. We give orientation exercises to prepare you for the lecture. You don't need to solve the exercise. You just need to work on it enough to understand what makes it difficult, and think critically about what the lecture presents.

This activity was designed to highlight the difficulty of creating a good oracle. Students often settled for solutions that would work less well in practice than they might think.

There are too many fonts and characters for human review

The most common answers propose oracles that require a human to look at characters on the screen and evaluate whether the display is correct.

Question 3 asked how you would test whether the display for every font is correct. You can't do that with human inspection.

I don't know how many typefaces are in common use (that is, some people use them and everyone can easily get them) but I know the answer is greater than 20,000. In addition, people create their own typefaces. http://www.yourfonts.com/ is a example of a consumer product for making a handwriting font. There are also professional-grade tools. If you're curious, there are a lot of links here: http://desktoppub.about.com/od/makefonts/How_to_Make_Fonts_Tutorials_to_Create_Fonts.htm. I've worked with Fontographer and know graphic artists who use Fontlab Studio. In principle, then, there are more typefaces than you can ever test -- even if you test them all today, tomorrow there will be more.

Therefore, you are going to have to test only a sample of them and that leaves a risk of some errors remaining in the typefaces you did not test.

Every typeface comes in (or scales to) a variety of sizes and comes with a variety of shapes (in a well-made typeface, italics characters are different from regular ones, not just slanted). In addition, the typeface might define special glyphs for letter pairs (two specific letters in a specific order). The type designer might also change the shapes of the letters when the font is very small or very large.

Within a typeface, there are scrillions of different characters. Well, maybe not scrillions, but lots. See http://en.wikipedia.org/wiki/List_of_Unicode_characters.

It really is the case that a program might misdisplay only some characters. For example, a bug that I used to have to deal with was that the program might display W correctly at one size but not at another. Some old editors cut off the right serif of large italicized capital W's, or miscalculated their size and ran them into the next letter. The program might display some accented characters correctly but not others. The program might also display letters correctly but not numbers or get the spacing wrong between some pairs of characters.

Therefore, the following ideas are impractical:

- Create a test plan that specifies the typefaces to check and the reference glyphs. First, this is going to get you only to a tiny subset of the typefaces and probably only to a small subset of the sizes and glyphs (think of the glyph as the graphic image of the character). Second, it doesn't say how to do the comparison.

- Print the typefaces in different sizes and styles and measure the printed images. First, you run out of paper. Second, even if it prints correctly on the page, that doesn't mean it displays correctly. Third, how do you decide what to measure? One suggestion is to print with two programs and see if the two printouts are identical. This is the most practical variation (but see the first two problems).

- Measure the height of the characters (onscreen or on paper) to see if they are correct. Try printing a paragraph in each of the different typefaces on your computer. Leave the font size the same, just vary the typeface. Notice how the letters are way bigger in some typefaces and ittybitty in others? Unfortunately, there is no rule for always-correctly defining the height of a 12-point font.

The eyeball test is particularly impractical

The *eyeball test* is another way of saying *human oracle*.

In the typical test of this kind, you display the font with the program under test. Display it also with some other program that you trust more. Then have some person look at the two displays and decide whether they are the same.

Visually comparing a few letters in one typeface to a display of the same typeface in another program is a start, but:

- Do you have time to do this for every letter in every font?

- Will you be able to maintain concentration, to be able to notice mismatches if they are there? Most (or all) people will miss many errors under these conditions.

- It's hard to recognize the differences between many of the typefaces. To most people, Century Schoolbook, Bookman, Cambria, Goudy Old Style, Lucida Bright, Minion Pro, Times Roman, and Times New Roman are pretty similar. They are all serif fonts. How would you tell, by eye, whether the program is displaying the right typeface?

- Students who suggest this rarely ask how to know whether the font is displayed correctly in the other program

- Finally, really, do you have time to do this for every letter in every font (every typeface in every style in every size)?

Test against specifications?

Students in some classes think that there is a comprehensive specification somewhere that will perfectly describe all the typefaces. Maybe there is, but I've worked on the development of a lot of word processors, desktop publishers and printers and I've never seen such a specification. I have worked with books of typefaces that show samples of text printed in each face, for hundreds or thousands of faces. They show you what it looks like, but they don't tell you exactly what to look for in order to recognize the typeface. So if you want to work from a specification, you will have to translate this information, somehow, into something you can compare your program against.

Partial oracles that might be useful

A common approach is to try partial oracles rather than complete methods. For example, when they offer an answer like this, students often suggest looking at some specific characteristics of the letters, such as whether they are serif or sans serif and relative size of different parts of the letter. These are definitely partial oracles. There are thousands of sans serif fonts so if your font is supposed to be sans serif and the one on the screen is sans serif, that doesn't say that you've got the right one. But if the font displayed was not sans serif, it would have been obvious that the program had made an error. This is an example of a constraint oracle (see slide 129).

Automation? The simplest algorithmic answers don't work

Some students suggest that you might be able to capture the pixels on the screen when one program displays a character and compare these when the other program displays the same character. This can let us compare the typefaces, but probably not the sizes. The problem is that we can zoom both programs' displays. Even though we can adjust the zoom levels of the two programs until their letter sizes are about the same, what does this tell you?

Comparing pixel by pixel can be more uncertain than you might think. Unless the two programs are using the same library, one program's display of a letter might be insignificantly different from another. What if the letters differ by one pixel? Is that close enough to be called a match? If not, I think you'll miss a lot of reasonable matches. But if you accept one pixel difference, what about two? Three? How similar is similar enough?

Sometimes, someone comes up with an algorithm that makes a lot of sense.

Students sometimes suggest is that you could use a pattern-matching program that is designed to accept two things as matching if they are similar enough. There are plenty of algorithmic variations on this theme, but any of them can help you recognize that the text displayed by one program is (or is not) very similar to the text displayed by the other. Of course, you still have to choose the reference program wisely. And even if you do, a match might mean that both programs are wrong in the same way, and a failure-to-match might mean that the other program is wrong, not yours. I think this is a great idea, but it can sometimes give misleading results:

- If the algorithm's comparator is too strict, it will fail the program because the display in Program 1 is not identical to Program 2, even though a human, looking carefully at the output from both programs might recognize the typefaces as the same.

- If the comparator is not strict enough, it will accept fonts as matching even when they are not. Two typefaces that are almost the same would be classified as the same, even though they are different.

Students sometimes suggest that two programs might display fonts by using the same libraries. In this way, you might be able to confirm (by inspecting the code) that one program will display characters the same way as another (by checking that they make the same library calls). This is an excellent approach and it will catch bugs. But it is still possible that you will miss some problems.

Some students have taken this type of idea further, suggesting automated tests on Windows environments that look (glass-box) at the calls made by software under test to the Microsoft library functions that manage access to (display, manipulation, etc.) fonts. If the call made by the software under test is properly structured, if the selection of typeface is determined by a simple variable (e.g. a string), and if you run several tests and in each case, the function returns the appropriate font, it is reasonable to assume that any errors would be individual cases (somehow the wrong string is passed by the program) rather than the result of a systematic error. This doesn't tell you that the software is correct for all typefaces, but it gives you reason to think that it is probably correct whenever the typeface is correctly named. That might be good enough.

Sometimes a student comments that these ideas won't work if the font file is corrupted. They are right and wrong. If the font file is corrupted, it is not a bug in the program when the program reads the file and displays whatever stupid thing the file says is the right thing to display. The program can be correctly displaying what it has been given, even if that is not what you intend.

These oracles are all heuristic

No matter what oracle you choose for this assignment, it is a heuristic oracle. That is, if you choose it well, it will be right most of the time, but it can sometimes lead you to make incorrect decisions.

If you came out of the lab understanding that the font-matching problem is challenging and that the decision rules you adopt will be heuristics (useful but not always right), you learned everything you needed to learn from the lab.

Orientation: Testing An Integer Square Root Function

Imagine testing a program that includes an Integer Square Root function. This type of function reads a 32-bit word that is stored in memory, interprets the contents as an unsigned integer and then computes the square root of the integer. It returns the result as a floating-point number. For example, it might calculate the square root of the integer, 3, and return the floating-point number 1.732050808.

1. What values can you input to this function?

2. Can you imagine any invalid inputs to this function, inputs that should cause the function to return an error message?

3. If you were to test *all* of the inputs to this function, how many tests would there be?

4. How long do you think it would take you to run all these tests?

5. How would you test this function? Describe your thinking about your possible test strategies.

6. Would you add more tests if this function was in a life-critical program and you wanted to be sure it had no bugs? How many more tests? Which ones? Why these?

7. If the program computed the square root of 4 and reported 1.9999999999999999, would that be a passing result or a failure? How close would the answer have to be to 2.0 for the result to be a pass? Why?

Our Notes

The main objective of this exercise is to get you thinking about how many tests it would take to fully test a fairly simple function. Too many people think that it's possible to fully test a program. This exercise shows that the task is huge just to fully test a single function. The lecture follows this up with Hoffman's MASPAR example (which involved complete testing of a 32-bit integer square root function). Several students write this exercise with the belief that a relatively small sample of tests can fully test a simple function like this. Hoffman's paper provides a real-life example in which the test group really needed to run all 4,294,967,296 tests to find the two failures this function would yield.

As I have evolved this exercise, over about a 15-year period, I noticed several common mistakes and misunderstandings. The question set evolved, first to clarify the question and then to probe the things that seemed to be giving several students trouble.

- Some mistakes seem to reflect sloppy reading. People read assumptions or facts into the question that aren't there. This leads them to answer a question (or questions) that was never asked.

- Some mistakes seem to reflect a lack of knowledge about very basic storage in a computer. You need to know this stuff. There is just no getting around it. If you're going to test any kind of application, you need to know a little bit about how data are stored in memory and how functions read data from memory.

- Some mistakes seem to reflect a lack of knowledge of machine arithmetic. Again, you need to know this stuff or you will file bug reports that announce your cluelessness. You probably don't need to understand floating point arithmetic so well that you can do it or even well enough to know how to estimate probable and maximum extent of rounding error after a computation or even well enough to know how to thoroughly test a sequence of floating point calculations (like 0.2*4.67891234*1602.555+2.7659). Maybe you do need to know that, but that's beyond this course. As a very basic, very fundamental matter, though, you should at least know that all floating point operations are carried out to finite precision, and that leads to rounding errors, and that the higher the precision of calculations, the smaller the rounding errors.

Sloppy Reading

The most common mistake in addressing this question is the assumption that there is a user interface, probably a GUI. *Where does the question even hint that there is such a thing?* The question says,

> *The function reads a 32-bit word that is stored in memory,*

The number it reads is *already stored in memory.* How do you know that? The question says so.

How did the number in memory get there? Who knows? That's for a different question.

What we're trying to do now is to test the square root function, which operates on the number that is in memory, not that other function that puts the data in memory.

Too many testers hide from testing the underlying functionality of the program by spending all their time on the user interface. Some do this intentionally, others do it because it is what they were trained to do (by other testers who spend most of their time hiding from the program's functionality), others do it naturally without realizing what they are missing. This question insists that you address the function and not its user interface.

Reading Assumptions into the Question

The next mistake is to assume that the function might do something other than what the question says it does. The question says that the function reads a 32-bit word. It doesn't say the function might stop at the deli for supper one day and then read only 31 bits because it's feeling a bit full. Or that it might wolf down a 33rd bit when there's a full moon. It reads 32 bits. No exceptions.

I know there is a temptation to read statements of fact (a statement of fact is an assertion that can be proved true or false) as if they were suspect. That's a good idea for testing products against specifications, but a bad idea for answering exam questions. If the question says "X is true" then for that question, treat X as truly true. The function reads exactly 32 contiguous (stored all together, one after the other) bits. And it reads those 32 bits as an unsigned integer, each and every time.

In terms of real life, yes, testing error handling is important. But at some point, you have to ask whether the function itself works with all of the non-error data that it is supposed to accept. In asking exactly that, this question is setting a realistic task for you.

1. What values can you input to this function?

A 32-bit word has 32 binary digits. Each one can be 0 or 1. So, its value looks like 0101100001011000010 1100001011000. If the computer interprets those 32 bits as an unsigned integer, it reads that number as 1482184792. The computer could instead interpret this word as a string. Using the ASCII representation of characters, 01011000 is read as X (http://www.asciitable.com), so the full word is XXXX--if you read it as a series of alpha characters. There are lots of other ways to interpret the same bit pattern, but the question tells you how this function interprets it--as an unsigned integer. (http://en.wikipedia.org/wiki/Integer_(computer_science))

You can give this function any value between 00000000000000000000000000000000 and 11111111111111111 11111111111111. These are interpreted as unsigned integers, ranging from 0 to 4,294,967,295.

By the way, a 32-bit word is referring to a computer word (group of bits), not a word from the English language. Check out Wikipedia for more on that if you're interested.

2. Can you imagine any invalid inputs to this function, inputs that should cause the function to return an error message?

I can't control what you can *imagine* but any wild fantasies of invalid inputs to this function should be put back to bed.

- Can you give the function an input smaller or larger than 32 bits? *No.*

- Can you give it letters? *No.*

  You could think you gave it letters, like XXXX, but it will read the bit pattern as a number, because that's what it does: it "interprets the contents as an unsigned integer." You can have some fun with a little online converter that shows hows this works: http://www.evilgenius. net/asciibin.html)

- Similarly, you can't give it negative numbers. Consider giving it -1, for example. The binary representation of -1 (in a 32-bit word that you read as a *signed* integer) is 11111111111111111111 1111111111. But this function won't read 11111111111111111111111111111111 as -1. It will read it as 4,294,967,295.

So, the answer to this question should be short and simple: *No.*

3. If you were to test ALL of the inputs to this function, how many tests would there be?

The lecture gives a simple rule for calculating a total number of alternatives that applies here as well as applying to each of the calculation questions in the study guide (hint, hint). Here's a reminder of that rule:

If variable A has NA possible values and variable B has NB possible values, then the number of possible tests of A and B together is NA * NB.

Suppose A is the value of the first binary digit. It can have two values, 0 and 1. Suppose B is the value of the second binary digit. It can have two values, 0 and 1. So if we think of A and B together, we get NA (2) times NB (2) = 4 possible values. Here they are: 00, 01, 10, 11.

Now imagine A, B, C, with two possible values each. You have 2 x 2 x 2 possible values of the three taken together: 000, 001, 010, 011, 100, 101, 110, 111.

Now, imaginng 32 binary variables -- we get 2 x 2 x 2 x 2 x2 x 2 x 2 x 2 x2 x 2 x 2 x 2 x2 x 2 x 2 x 2 x2 x 2 x 2 x 2 x2 x 2 x 2 x 2 x2 x 2 x 2 x 2 = 2^{32} = 4,294,967,296 possible values.

4. How long do you think it would take you to run all these tests?

It might actually take less time than you think. Hoffman reports that on the MASPAR system, it took six minutes. On a slower computer, it would take longer. We did some tests recently on a consumer-grade Lenovo laptop. Depending on how we wrote the code, what language or test tool, times varied from about eight minutes to a much longer time (we stopped the computer but based on the amount achieved in the time we let it run, times ran as high as a few years).

If it takes T units of time to run one test, it takes $T*2^{32}$ to run all of them.

Imagine testing a just-slightly-more complex function, the square root of a 64 bit number. Now there are 2^64 possible tests instead of 2^32, and it would take the MASPAR computer about (2^32) times six minutes (25769803776 minutes--about 49000 years) to test all of these.

5. How would you test this function? Describe your thinking about your possible test strategies.

Common strategies include:

- a small random sample of values

- exhaustive testing

- stratified sampling that uses some type of rule for deciding which values will be considered representative of the full set. One common approach would include:

  - all bits 0 (00000000000000000000000000000000)

  - all bits set (11111111111111111111111111111111)

  - all numbers with only 1 bit set (00000000000000000000000000000001, 000000000000000000000000 0000000010, etc.)

  - all numbers with only 1 bit zero (11111111111111111111111111111110, 1111111111111111111111111111 11101, etc.)

  There's nothing magically good about this group but you might ask, if it passed these 66 tests, what others you might feel you need to add (unless you feel like you need to include all 2^32 tests).

To answer this question well, you should state at least two *strategies* (the question asks for thinking about possible test *strategies*, not test *strategy*) and for each, state what you think about it.

6. Would you add more tests if this function was in a life-critical program and you wanted to be sure it had no bugs? How many more tests? Which ones? Why these?

Hoffman's answer was, test all 2^{32} cases. If you're going to do less than that, how do you decide how much less?

Several students said they would do a lot of extra testing for life-critical software. What about business software? Have you ever had an error in your bank statement or a credit card bill? How much more time are you planning to invest for the life-critical software? What is the cost / benefit of investing that time for commercial software?

7. If the program computed the square root of 4 and reported 1.9999999999999999, would that be a passing result or a failure? How close would the answer have to be to 2.0 for the result to be a pass? Why?

Double-precision floating point calculations in Java are 15-digit precision. Thus, 1.9999999999999999 is 17 digits long. If we rounded to 15 digits, it would be 2.000000000000000. Excel and Open Office Calc are 15 digits too, if I recall correctly. Rounding errors are unavoidable in standard floating point calculations. For more explanation, see http://blogs.msdn.com/excel/archive/2008/04/10/understanding-floating-point-precision-aka-why-does-excel-give-me-seemingly-wrong-answers.aspx.

Here's a different way of considering an error this small. The square root of 3 is (approximately) 1.73205080756887729. Would you be as upset by a mistake like this: *1.73205080756887728 instead of*

1.73205080756887729 as you might be by *1.99999999999999999 instead of 2.0*? It's the same size mistake in both cases, right?

According to my calculator, the square root of 3 is 1.7320508075688772935274463415059, not 1.73205080756887729, so even this "right" number is wrong.

- If the program reports 1.73205080756887729, is that a bug?

- 1.73205080756887729 * 1.73205080756887729 is (almost exactly) 2.9999999999999999987780567431077 7, do you still think reporting 1.73205080756887729 is not a bug?

- Suppose you think that the program must report the exact square root. What should we do with Square-root(3), which is an "irrational number" (http://en.wikipedia.org/wiki/Irrational_ number) which means that the sequence of numbers after the decimal point is infinitely long.

Bug reports that complain about an *expected* rounding error are commonplace. Unfortunately, these aren't really reports of bugs in the software--they are taken by the programmers and project managers as reports about the bugs in the education of the tester. They make the tester look uneducated and foolish.

There are *unreasonable* rounding errors. If that intrigues you, grab a book on numerical analysis.

Orientation: What Makes A Measurement?

Kaner and Bond define measurement as follows: "Measurement is the empirical, objective assignment of numbers to attributes of objects or events (according to a rule derived from a model or theory) with the intent of describing them."

Consider this case:

A professor decides to base the grades in her class on the height of her students. The taller the student, the higher the grade. Grades will be assigned on a 1-100 scale. The tallest student earns 100, all other students are given a score that matches the ratio (expressed as a percentage) of their height to the tallest student's height.

    a. Is this a measurement under this definition?

    b. Justify your answer to (a)

    c. Briefly describe three advantages or problems with this proposed measure.

    d. On balance, do the advantages outweigh the problems for using this as a measure?

Our notes

a. Is this a measurement under this definition?

No, this is not a measurement under this definition.

b. Justify your answer to (a)

Many students convince themselves that height is a measure for this question because it is "an empirical, objective assignment of numbers." The critical missing component is the model or theory that ties height to class performance.

Think carefully about the attribute being measured:

- The attribute is not the height of the student. The professor is trying to calculate a grade. Academic grades are supposed to reflect knowledge (or effort, or skill, or something like that).

- The attribute is not the grade of the student. A grade is a measurement. It's a quantity (whether expressed as a letter or a number) that is assigned to reflect the student's underlying academic achievement (knowledge, effort, skill, etc..)

If you don't know what you are trying to measure, you won't be able to evaluate a proposed measure of it.

Without demonstrating a relationship between height and class performance, this professor's decision fails under the Kaner and Bond definition of measurement.

c. Briefly describe three advantages or problems with this proposed measure.

The primary advantage is that the measure is objective. Two people who take the same measurement will get the same result (or results close to each other).

- Suppose you wanted to measure the distance from New York to Mumbai. To do this, pull out a piece of paper money from your wallet and measure how wide it is. That's the distance from New York to Mumbai.

- No? You don't think so? But surely it is a good measure because it objective and repeatable.

The overwhelming problem is that there is no way that a measurement of height describes how well a person knows the content or skills that were taught in the course.

> *A **different way of saying** THIS is not a measurement of THAT **is to say** This is an invalid measure of THAT **or** This measure of that has NO CONSTRUCT VALIDITY.*

The reason we present this exercise is that so many software engineering metrics are like it.

- They are cheap, easy to collect, objective, and devoid of construct validity.

- Using them causes dysfunction because people will change what they do in order to get better numbers.

- But even if they seem obviously wrong, many people will accept them as measurements because they don't understand how to say that a measure that has no construct validity is not a measure.

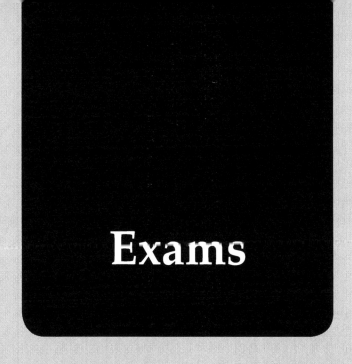

Exams

WRITING ESSAY EXAMS

A Sample Exam Question

When we teach instructor-led versions of BBST, we give students a list of questions at the start of the class and tell them that the questions on the exam will all come from the questions in this list.

We expect the students to prepare answers to the questions with some care. The exam is closed book (students can't refer to their notes when they write the exam.) However, good preparation leads to good answers on the exam.

When we grade the exam, we expect to see well-organized answers. We expect you to understand the question. If you have doubts about what the question means, you can ask about that before the exam. Not during the exam.

When you are preparing your answer, we expect you to look up information in the slides, in this workbook, and if you need to, in other reference sources (such as searching the web).

Here's an example of the type of question we ask:

> *Given that complete testing is impossible, what are some*
> *potential stopping rules (rules for deciding when to stop*

testing)? Describe the rules you propose, and for each, explain the tradeoffs involved in using it (what's good about it, what's bad about it, what risks does it introduce, etc.).

We recommend that you try to answer this yourself before you look at our notes on it:

- Start by creating an outline of your answer. What are all the sections and subsections of your answer?

- Then answer the question. Use the outline to organize your answer. Make sure that every topic in the outline is in your answer.

- Consider using headings and bulleted lists to make the structure of your answer as obvious as you can.

We are supplying notes on this question. You'll find them when you turn over the next page. Don't flip the page until you have tried the question yourself.

This page intentionally left blank.

Our Notes on the Answer

The goals for this task are to help you:

- identify the call of the question

- develop a structure for your answer that addresses each part of the call of the question

- write an answer that applies the structure

Some thoughts on the content of the answer

Students suggest many different types of stopping rules. Here are some of the themes we often see, with a couple of examples within each theme. For the exam, we expect three rules, each quite different from the others--for example each from a different theme.

- Resources exhausted

  - Out of time (the release date has arrived)

  - Out of money

- Contractual

  - The contract specifies stopping criteria and you have met them.

  - You have tested all the items identified in the contract and they meet the expected acceptance criteria

  - The contract specified a set of acceptance tests and the program passes them

- Statistical

  - The bug counts this week are less than N

  - The bug count curve shows a declining trend and there were fewer than N bugs (or fewer than N serious bugs) this week (or over the past K weeks)

  - There are no unfixed bugs of severity worse than S

  - The project has survived H hours of duration testing with no significant failures

  - The cost of finding new bugs has been greater than the perceived benefit of fixing the bugs found

- Qualitative

  - An important person (customer representatives / marketing manager / etc.) has evaluated the software and pronounced it worthy

  - The testers feel comfortable with the quality of the software (and the other key stakeholders are not uncomfortable with it)

  - The test group have tried a variety of test techniques and have run out of good ideas for finding new bugs

- Code coverage

  - You have tested all statements

  - You have tested all subpaths of length N

- Test coverage

- You have defined a series of tests that you consider a sufficient set and the program passes all of them
- You have tested all the specification (/ requirements) items with at least one test
- You have tested all the specification (/ requirements) items extensively enough that you are satisfied with your testing of them and with the program's responses
- You have listed a set of benefits of the program and run powerful-enough scenarios against all of them
- You have tested every feature of the program
■ Project management
    - The project is canceled
    - The customer insists on taking delivery
    - The Vice-President in charge of saying "Ship It" has spoken
■ Crisis management
    - The product is obviously better than the one it is replacing, and replacement is urgently needed
■ Information objective achieved
    - The goal of the project was to find specific information and you have found what was needed. (Example: you were retained by a law firm to find evidence that certain defects were present in the software and you found them).

Some thoughts on the tradeoffs

The question asked you to evaluate each rule by considering its tradeoffs. Examples of tradeoffs are:

- benefits versus costs
- what's good about it versus what's bad about it
- advantages versus disadvantages
- benefits versus risks

How many of each of these should you provide?

We normally answer the "how many" question with the heuristic of three. That is, if an essay question asks you for more than one idea or example, give three.

The heuristic of three doesn't apply well to this question. You'd have to write too much. We'd normally be glad with two examples of positives (benefits / advantages) and two examples of negatives (costs / risks / disadvantages) for each rule.

Some thoughts on the structure of the answer:

Students often skip the outlining task or provide an outline that is so generic that it doesn't help them organize their thinking. *Unfortunately, the students who do this are often the ones who need the outline the most.*

- Your outline should tie your answer to the question.
    - Every part of the question that was asked should have a distinct, clearly identified section in the outline.

- If a question is broken into several sub-questions, the outline should also show several sub-questions

■ Your outline should provide just barely enough information about the content of the answer to remind you of what you're going to write when write the actual essay.

- The outline should provide enough detail that you can recognize redundancy in the answers. *This can be harder to notice in a fully-detailed answer.*

- Another reason you want the detail is that it's amazing how quickly you can forget details under pressure or when you are anxious.

Students who skip the outline often provide answers that are nonresponsive, redundant, incomplete, or difficult for the reader to follow.

A few editorial notes on the choices of answers

There are many different possible stopping rules.Why did you choose the set that you did?

■ Some testers choose deterministic rules that don't depend on the quality of testing or the opinions of the testers. For example, someone might choose (a) out of time/money; (b) all planned test cases complete; (c) all bugs rated serious or fatal have been closed.

■ Contrast this with the tester who chooses rules that depend heavily on the quality of testing or the opinions of the testers. For example, (a) the testers rate the product acceptable; (b) the cost of finding new bugs is higher than the value of the bugs being found; (c) you have tested all the benefits with powerful scenarios and are satisfied with the results.

Your choice of stopping rules might be a window into your sense of how much influence testers have (or should have) over the decisions to keep testing and over what tests to run next. Look back at your choices from that perspective--are these consistent with your view of the role that testers should play?

Exams

ADVICE FOR ANSWERING ESSAY QUESTIONS

Overview

This section describes my expectations and grading standards for examinations in most of my courses. The same standards will be applied by graders (including other instructors) who work with me on these courses.

Some students who should pass on the basis of their knowledge fail because of their weak essay-answering skills. We expect students to be able to parse an essay-style question and write an organized answer. That expectation is not going to change.

In this course, your exam will be based on the list of questions in the Study Guide.

- My typical midterm university exam includes 100 points worth of questions, with 20 points each for long answer questions and 10 points each for short answers. For example, the exam might have 2 long answers and 6 shorts, or 3 long answers and 4 shorts. (These exams run 75 minutes.)

- My typical final exam includes 140 points (such as 4 long answers and 6 shorts). (These exams run 120 minutes.)

■ The typical professional development course final exam includes three long answer questions and three short answer questions. (The time limit for these depends on the format of the course.)

Having the pool of questions in advance gives you the opportunity to prepare well for the exam. Unfortunately, not everyone prepares effectively. There are common problems in these types of exams. Students often:

■ *Miss the point of the question,* wasting space and time on irrelevant material.

■ *Answer the question the student wished was asked,* instead of the question that was actually asked. If the student is lucky, s/he gets a few points for parts of the answer that were relevant to the question. It is not uncommon for faculty to realize the student is not answering the question and award a zero without digging through the question to try to find something that is accidentally relevant.

■ *Miss a section (or two) of a multiple-issue question,* losing critical points simply because they don't answer that section (even though the student probably knew the answer).

■ *Are so disorganized that it takes significant work to find relevant material* in the mass of irrelevancy.

■ *Contain obvious errors that demonstrate that the student doesn't understand the answer.* This is most common when students study together and one student memorizes an answer written by the other students.

Here are some tips for avoiding these problems and writing great exams.

Preparing for the Exam

1. Put together a list of source materials for the exam.

   This includes the relevant chapters of the course textbook and all required readings. Also note any references that were listed as "optional" but recommended. These often provide additional insights that will help you understand the material (including an exam question on the material).

2. Get copies of all of the source materials (including recommended readings)

3. Create a list of all the key words used in the class. Prepare definitions for each one.

   An exam might not have any questions that specifically ask for definitions, but you will often find it useful to define a term as part of your answer to an essay question.

4. Now answer the Study Guide questions.

   No one would prepare to run a race primarily by talking about races with friends, or watching a race on television, or reading about races in books.

   ● To prepare to run a race, you have to practice running.

   ● To prepare to write an exam, you have to practice outlining and answering questions of the kind you will face in the exam.

   Your first attempt for each question should be open book with no time limit. Check your lecture notes AND any other readings.

5. *After* you have tried your own answers, compare notes with friends.

   ● The best way to prepare for these tests is to attempt each question on your own. *After* you have tried your own answers, compare notes with your friends. I recommend that you study with one or more partners. 3-5 people is a good sized group. Eight is too many.

- Working with others will help you discover and work through ambiguities before you take the test. If a question is unclear, send your instructor a note before the test. If you tell the instructor early enough, s/he can fix it. If you wait until the exam to complain, I will not modify or explain the question. By the time of the exam, it is your responsibility to understand every question.

- If you find during your preparation session that a question takes too long to answer, ask for advice about that (before the exam) too.

Starting the Exam

Before starting to write the answers for individual questions, take a minute to see what is in the exam and to plan your response to it:

Skim the questions

- Get a fast overview of the structure and coverage of the exam.

- The study guide will point out some exam questions that are designed to allow variation. For example, you might have to analyze a program that can loop up to N times, but the size of N might vary from one exam to another. Does the exam include one of these? If so, you might have to budget extra time to analyze and answer this.

Develop a budget for your time

- All exams are time-limited, but some exams are intended to be easy to finish in the time available; others will be high-pressure.

- If this is a time-pressured exam, quickly build a time budget for it. For example, if the exam is 100 points long, and you have 60 minutes for the exam, then you must earn 1.67 points per minute. A 20-point essay is worth 12.5 minutes. If you spend more than your budget on one question, you will be short on another one. *The ideal time budget should allow at least 10 minutes at the end of the exam for review.*

Choose the order of your answers

In almost every exam, you can answer the questions in any order that you choose.

- If you are nervous, start by answering the question you find easiest. Then the second-easiest, and so on. By the time you have reached the harder questions, you will probably have relaxed enough to remember the relevant material.

- If you are not so nervous, answer questions in any order that seems sensible. For example, some students tend to spend too long on short answer questions. They should answer long essays first and cram in their short answers at the end, when time pressure is more obvious.

Answering the Questions

Make sure that you understand the question before you answer it, and then organize the answer to highlight your understanding.

Look for the call of the question

Every well written exam question asks specifically for some information. Your task is to provide the information that the question is calling for, and to *not* provide information that the question does not call for.

- Don't answer what has not been asked. For example, if the exam asks you to define one thing, don't define that and then give the definition of something related to it. If you do, (a) your instructor won't give you extra credit, (b) your instructor will probably think you don't know the difference between the two things, and (c) if you make a mistake, your instructor will take off points.

- Give the number of items requested. For example, if your instructor asks for two scenario tests, don't give one or three. If you give one, you miss points. If you give three, I will either grade the first two and ignore the third (this is my normal approach) or grade the first two that I happen to read (whatever their order on the page) and ignore the third. I will never read the full list and grade what I think are the best two out of three.

The call of the question is usually identified with a question mark or a directive.

Consider this example:

> SoftCo publishes software. Their president hates Easter Eggs and has instructed the test group to find every one (if there are any) in the product it is testing. As lead tester, it is your task to figure out how to test for Easter Eggs and when to declare the job done. How will you decide when you have finished this task? Present your ideas, their strengths and weaknesses.

This question includes the following background information:

> SoftCo publishes software. Their president hates Easter Eggs and has instructed the test group to find every one (if there are any) in the product it is testing. As lead tester, it is your task to figure out how to test for Easter Eggs and when to declare the job done.

Some people think this question requires you to describe how to test for Easter Eggs, but where does the question actually ask for that?

What the question asks for is this:

> How will you decide when you have finished this task? Present your ideas, their strengths and weaknesses.

The first sentence ends with a question mark. (Answer the question, please.) The second gives you a specific task that you are supposed to do right now. (So do that task.)

A typical question does *not* require you to provide definitions of X or Y, but providing these definitions will often help you write a clearer and more concise answer. If an exam question is worth 20 points (a long answer question, in my grading structure), I will allow 21 or 22 points, giving the extra points to definitions. You can get a full 20 points without the definitions but (to encourage you to write this way), I make a high score easier if you include the definitions.

Be aware of the meaning of the question's words and answer appropriately.

For example, these are typical meanings of some frequently used exam words:

- *Compare:* When you compare two things, point out (and perhaps explain or describe) similarities between them.

- *Contrast:* When you contrast two things, point out (and perhaps explain or describe) differences between them.

- *Compare & Contrast X and Y:* These questions require you to describe what is similar between X and Y (compare X and Y) and what is different (contrast X and Y).

  - In a long answer question, I expect three points of comparison and three points of contrast.

  - In a short answer question, I expect a total of three points including at least one comparison and at least one contrast.

- *List:* When you provide a list of items, write briefly, using only one or a few words per item. No explanation of the items is needed.

- *Identify:* Same as list.

- *Describe:* A description of something attempts to give the reader a picture of it. A description of a process is often chronological, explaining the steps of the process in order. A description of an abstract concept includes details (perhaps examples) that make it easier for the reader to understand or imagine.

  - If you are asked to describe the relationship among things, you might find it easiest to work from a chart or a picture. You are probably not required to use a diagram or chart, but many professors will welcome it if it helps you get across your answer.

  - If the question asks you to describe or define something that is primarily visual (such as a table or a graph), your answer will probably be easier to write and understand if you draw an example of what you are defining or describing.

- *Define:* Provide the meaning of a word or phrase. Some teachers expect formal definitions. I just want you to describe the concept behind the word. Use examples if they help you clarify the definition.

- *Analyze:* Normally means, to break a concept or process or set down into component parts and discuss the relationships among the components. Sometimes you are asked to analyze in a specific way, such as "analyze the impact of X on Y." In this example, you might explain the effects of X (and the components of X) on Y.

- *Explain:* Help the reader understand something. Explanations often focus on "why" or "how".

- *Evaluate:* Discuss something in a way that allows you to reach a judgment (a conclusion) about it. In your answer, explain the rationale behind your conclusion. In a mathematically or formally oriented question, "evaluate" might mean to work through the formal material in order to reach the result. (Think of evaluating an expression.)

- *Argue:* Pick a position in a debate or controversy, state it, and provide a series of arguments that support your position.

- *Discuss:* This is a vague word. It is often intended as an open question, inviting you to choose the best way to address the question. For example, "Discuss the effect of X on Y" might be best addressed as "Describe and explain the effect of X on Y". If the relationship between X and Y is controversial, then "discuss" invites you to present multiple viewpoints and the data that support them.

If I ask you to analyze something according to the method described in a particular paper or by a particular person, I expect you to do it their way. If I ask you to *describe* their way, do so. If I ask you to *apply* their way, you don't have to describe it in detail, but you must do the things they would do in the order they would do them, and to use their vocabulary to describe what you are doing.

If the question asks you for the result of a calculation, such as the number of paths through a loop, show your calculations or explain them. Let your instructor understand how you arrived at the answer.

Outline your answer

Unless your answer will be trivially simple, develop a structure for the information that you will provide.

- Often, the best outline explicitly connects to the question, using the key words in the question.

- The outline should explicitly cover every issue raised in the question.

- If the question contains multiple parts, make a separate section for each part.

An example:

> Define the characteristics of a "good test" and a "bad test." Explain the differences, why good is good and why bad is bad. Provide and justify a definition of a good tester.

In analyzing a question like this, it is essential to look for the *call of the question* -- the specific issues you are being asked to address:

- *DEFINE* the characteristics of a good test

- *DEFINE* the characteristics of a bad test

- *EXPLAIN THE DIFFERENCES:* why good is good and why bad is bad

- *PROVIDE and JUSTIFY a definition of a good tester.*

Many answers fail because they simply omit some parts of this question. For example, answers fail to contract good versus bad tests or fail to *justify* the definition of a good tester.

Structure your answer according to the outline. Emphasize the structure

The general rule (based on research of graders in several fields) is that a paper that is easy to read and obviously well organized will often be seen as more credible and will get more points than one with equally good content but poorer presentation. Often, the increase in grade goes beyond the instructor's intended allowance for "style". Make this work for you, instead of against you.

- Make your organization of the answer easily visible to the grader. For example, use the structure of the outline as headings.

- If the question contains multiple parts, make a separate section for each part. Provide a heading for each section, or use bulleted lists, to emphasize your structure.

Example:

> What is the difference between black box and white box testing? Describe the advantages and disadvantages of each.

You could organize this with five headings:

- Difference between black and white

- Advantages of black box

- Disadvantages of black box

- Advantages of white box

- Disadvantages of white box

Example:

> Compare and contrast two lifecycle models. What advantages or disadvantages does each model have over the other?

Some students circle or underline keys words in a question like this, and use arrows to highlight relationships. They check off circles and arrows as they answer that part of the questions. A marked-up version of this question might look like:

> [Compare and contrast] <u>**two**</u> [lifecycle models.] What <u>**advantages**</u> or <u>**disadvantages**</u> does [each model] have [over the other]?

This works well for some people. I sometimes find it too concise so I might create a list of the elements of a multi-part question:

1. Compare two lifecycle models

2. Contrast two lifecycle models

3. What advantages does each model have *over the other*?

4. What disadvantages does each model have *over the other*?

This list (4 points) defines the call of the question. It specifies what information is requested (called for).

- Notice that you have *not* been asked to define a lifecycle model (or a model in general)

- Notice that you have *not* been asked for empirical research results

- Notice that you have *not* been asked for a longer list of models -- just two, please.

- Notice that when you describe an advantage of one model, it should be an advantage *over the other* For example, suppose you contrast spiral and evolution. Both of these have a common advantage over the waterfall model--they both expect requirements to change over time and have sensible ways to deal with change, whereas the waterfall does not. *However*, even though the ability to cope with changing requirements is an advantage for any incremental process over waterfall, it is not clear that spiral has this as an advantage over evolution (or that evolution has this as an advantage over spiral). You have to explain what makes spiral better than evolution and what makes evolution better than spiral.

- Provide appropriate amounts of information or detail.

- If a question asks about "some", that means at least two. I normally expect three items in response to a "some". Similarly if the question asks for a list, I expect a list of at least three.

- If I ask you for the result of a calculation, such as the number of paths through a loop, show your calculations or explain them. Let me understand how you arrived at the answer.

Ground Rules

- You may not use any reference materials during the exam.

  You may not consult your notes, web sites, any materials on the course web site, or any other source of information.

- Beware of simply memorizing.

  Beware of memorizing someone else's answer or points off a slide. If I think you are giving a memorized list without understanding what you are writing, I will ruthlessly mark you down for memorization errors. In general, if you are repeating a set of bullet points, write enough detail that I can tell that you understand them.

- Deal with confusion and ambiguity before the exam starts.

  - One of the advantages of circulating the questions in advance is that the students can challenge them before the exam. Surprisingly, a question might be perfectly clear to the students in one semester but ambiguous to the students in the next semester.

  - I encourage students to draw ambiguities to my attention. I resolve the ambiguities by sending an electronic mail message to the course (rather than giving an answer only to one student). I may exclude the question from the exam if the correction came too late or the answer to the corrected question is too complex.

  - I will not answer questions about the meaning of an exam question during the exam. By the time you come to the exam, you should have studied the questions already and cleared up your confusions.

A Closer Look At Some Common Problems

Structure

Consider the following question as an example:

> Define a scenario test and describe the characteristics of a good scenario test. Imagine developing a set of scenario tests for the Outlining feature of the word processing module of Open Office. What research would you do in order to develop a series of scenario tests for Outlining? Describe two scenario tests that you would use and explain why each is a good test. Explain how these tests would relate to your research.

This has several components:

- Define a scenario test
- Describe the characteristics of a good scenario test
- What research would you do in order to develop a series of scenario tests for Outlining?
- Describe two scenario tests you would use.
- Explain why each of the two scenario tests is a good test
- Explain how these two scenario tests would relate to your research

A well organized answer to this question will have at least six sections, one for each of the bulleted components. You might have two additional sections, by splitting

- Describe two scenario tests you would use and
- Explain why each of the two scenario tests is a good test

into two sections, one for each test.

Without structure, it is easy to miss a section and thereby to lose points.

Shotgun answers

A student using a shotgun strategy responds with a core dump of everything that seems relevant to the general topic. Much of this information might be correct, but if it is non-responsive to the call of the question, it is irrelevant and I will ignore it. However, to the extent that irrelevant information is incorrect, if I notice an error, I will deduct points for it.

This is a common strategy for dealing with shotgun answers--ignore irrelevant material unless it is wrong. If it is wrong, deduct points for the errors.

Here's an example of a question that appeared several times in the Florida Tech software engineering comprehensive exam:

> What is the most expensive phase in software engineering? Justify your answer

Parse the question:

- What is *the most expensive phase* in software engineering?
- *Justify* your answer.

It should be obvious that you are being asked to talk about **one** phase.

It should also be obvious that most of the points for the answer to this question will be in the justification of your choice.

In Florida Tech's software engineering graduate comprehensive exams, several failing answers wrote about several phases instead of the one the student considered consider the most expensive. In these cases, we assigned grades based on the first phase mentioned by the student and ignored anything said about any of the other phases.

Some of the answers got so muddled up in outlining costs across the lifecycle that the student never drew the conclusion as to which is the most expensive phase. Without that, nothing in the answer "justified" the answer that was never provided. These answers earned low grades, sometimes as low as zero. Here's another example, from Florida Tech's CSE3415 (Software Testing 1):

> Imagine that you are an external test lab, and Sun comes to you with Open Office. They want you to test the product. When you ask them what test documentation they want, they say that they want something appropriate but they are relying on your expertise. To decide what test documentation to give them, what questions would you ask (up to 7 questions) and for each answer, how would the answer to that question guide you?

This question asks what *test documentation* you will give them.

- Where does this question ask how you will *test* the product?
- Where does this question ask about software that controls medical devices and how to document the testing of that software? Or games? Or databases?
- Where does this question ask about the relationship between Sun and Oracle, or about Sun's computers or about the platforms on which Open Office runs, or about the consumer documentation that you can buy for Open Office? Perhaps these could be relevant to the question, but only if you tie them carefully to this exam question's actual focusing task (describe up to 7 questions that will help you decide what test documentation you will provide and explain how the answers to these questions would help you make those decisions).

People often provide irrelevant information because they don't have a good answer to the question that was asked and so they are answering the question they know the answer to. This might work in some courses but it is a failing strategy in my courses. Similarly, at work as a technical worker (such as programmer or tester), if you try to avoid direct questions by giving irrelevant answers, your reputation is likely to suffer.

Weak group preparation

The best way to prepare for these tests is for each student to attempt each question on his own. The first attempt should be open book with no time limit. After each student has his own answers, he should compare notes with other students. The diversity of approaches will highlight ambiguities in the question, hidden assumptions on the part of the student, and muddled, disorganized thinking about the structure and call of the question. Independent preparation by several students is essential.

Unfortunately, many students form study groups in which they either:

■ Divide up the questions. One or two students attempt to answer each question and then report back to the group. The rest of the students then attempt to memorize the answers.

■ Or, attempt to develop the answers in-group, four or more students arguing and together.

Neither of these approaches works well. There are so many questions in the study list that few (or no) students can effectively memorize all the answers. As a result, I often see answer fragments, relevant material mixed with irrelevant (something memorized for a different question), or answers that have been distorted (such as forgotten words, points made so far out of sequence that they don't make sense, etc.)

Participating in a group-writing meeting works better than simply memorizing answers, but often produces weak answers. The group tends to latch onto the first answer that appears to make sense. Or it latches onto the answer advocated by the loudest or most persuasive or most persistent student in the group.

It is much more effective to start from a diverse group of prepared answers, with the people who understand and can explain why they prepared the answers in the way they did.

I tell students this every term, and every term a significant group of students tries the divide-and-(oops)-don't-conquer strategy and the work-only-during-group-study sessions. Most learn their lesson the hard way when they write an unsatisfactory mid-term exam.

Weak answers propagate through the group

Sometimes, the entire class answers a question in a way that is obviously (to me) mistaken or otherwise sub-optimal. I've seen several class-specific exam answers like this. By class-specific, I mean that a different class, on encountering the same question, has handled it much better.

Failure to consult required readings

Surprisingly often, students consult the course's lecture slides but ignore the videos and/or required readings. Some questions in the study guide rely on the required readings and not on the lecture slides. Students who don't consult the readings give poor answers.

A more subtle problem arises when a question can be answered to a mediocre degree from the lecture notes, and much better from the required readings. In that case, the large majority of the class often gives the mediocre answer.

Resources

There are plenty of online resources for students who are learning how to write essay exams, such as:

- University of Wisconsin-La Crosse (Department of Biology), "Answering Essay and Short Answer Exam Questions", http://www.uwlax.edu/biology/communication/AnsweringEssayQuestions.htm

- Purdue Online Writing Lab (OWL), "Writing Essays for Exams", http://owl.english.purdue.edu/owl/resource/737/01/

- Joe Landsberger, "Terms or Directives for Essays, Reports, & Answering Questions", Study Guides and Strategies, http://www.studygs.net/essayterms.htm

- Writing@CSU, "Writing Guide: Answering Exam Questions," http://writing.colostate.edu/references/processes/exams

- Student Academic Resource Center, University of Central Florida, "Answering Essay Questions Made Easier", http://sarc.sdes.ucf.edu/ss50.pdf

- Martha Peters, "Exam Preparation," University of Iowa College of Law Academic Achievement Program, http://www.uiowa.edu/~aap001/ExamPreparation.htm

I created a video with a detailed example of the grading style presented in this memo, grading four very different answers to one question:

- How we grade essay exams (Part 1), http://www.testingeducation.org/BBST/videos/BBSTGradingFirstSet.wmv

- How we grade essay exams (Part 2: comparative grading of four exam answers), http://www.testingeducation.org/BBST/videos/BBSTGradingSecondSet.wmv

- How we grade essay exams [Slides], http://www.testingeducation.org/BBST/slides/Grading%20Essay%20Exams.pdf

It is a good idea to create an outline of your answer before writing out the complete answer. This will help you clarify and focus your thinking.

- Purdue University's Online Writing Lab's useful tutorial on writing a research paper includes excellent information on the how and why of outlines.

- For more information on outlines, please visit the web page on outlines from Indiana University at http://www.indiana.edu/%7Ewts/pamphlets/outlines.shtml.

Index

G

games 20, 48, 88
glass-box testing 15, 22, 198
Goldberg, D. 106
government contracts. *See* contract-based development
grading standards 25, 27
Gregory, G. 17
grey-box testing 15

H

hand-crafted oracle 83
hard problems 187
Hendrickson, E. 5, 32
Hetzel, B. 35
heuristics 54, 64, 92, 198
   guidelines, not rules 65
heuristics (for teaching) 98
hexadecimal numbers 123
Hoffman, D. 5, 53, 60, 73, 93, 100, 103, 141, 166, 181,
      199
Howden, W.E. 19, 53
human oracle 83, 196

I

Iberle, K. 5
IEEE Standard 610 (define testing) 35
IEEE Standard 829 (test specs) 60
IEEE Standard 1008 (unit testing) 17
ignorance-based testing 16
implementation-level testing 18
impossibility of complete testing. *See* complete testing
independent testing 21
independent test labs 21, 24, 46
Indiana University 223
infinite number of tests 40, 138
information 36
information objectives 37, 49
instructional heuristics 98
instructor-led courses 27, 195
integer square root (example) 107, 138, 143, 199
integration testing 18
interaction models (oracles) 81, 96
interrupts (control structure) 129, 131, 142
interval scale 174
invalid inputs 146, 201
inverse oracles 82, 96
investigation (testing as) 6, 35, 36
IT departments 45

J

Jacoby, L.L. 103
Jha, A. 5
Johnson, B. 5
Johnson, K. 5
Jorgensen, P. 130

Jorgenson, A. 5
jUnit 18

K

Kabbani, N. 166
Kahan, W. 107
Kaner, C. iii, 4, 32, 106, 133, 138, 166
Kattamuri, K. 5
Kelly, M. 54, 68, 138, 141
Koen, B. 54, 64, 102
Kohl, J. 32

L

Landsberger, J. 223
Lawrence, B. 5
lawyers (as testers) 43
learning objectives x, 7
lectures 8
Leme, F. 17
Leveson, N. 59
library functions 198
life-critical systems 202
lists (data type) 126
long-sequence bugs 162
loop (control structure) 128, 154
Los Altos Workshop on Software Testing 104

M

machine arithmetic. *See* arithmetic
maintainability 19
mantissa 116
Marick, B. 5, 106, 107, 132, 134
MASPAR 137, 143
Massol, V. 17
mathematical model (oracle) 82
MaxInt 122
McConda, J. 5
McGee, P. 5
measurement 165, 170
   always based on a model 173, 181
   attribute 177, 204
   bad underlying data 188
   construct validity 165, 176, 205
   dysfunction 166, 177, 183, 188
   errors 171
   essential for management 187
   instruments 171
   interval scale 174
   nominal scale 175
   ordinal scale 175
   precision 172
   ratio scale 174
   reading from the instrument 176
   scale 173
   scope 173
   software engineering metrics 175, 187, 205

Printed in Great Britain
by Amazon.co.uk, Ltd.,
Marston Gate.